The Ultimate Tower 2-Basket Air Fryer Cookbook

1600 Days Crispy and Healthy Tower 2-Basket Air Fryer Recipes for Beginners with Tips & Tricks to Fry, Grill, and Bake

Rosa Coleman

Copyright © 2023 by   All rights reserved.

The content contained within this book may not be reproduced, duplicated, or transmitted without direct written permission from the author or the publisher. Under no circumstances will any blame or legal responsibility be held against the publisher, or author, for any damages, reparation, or monetary loss due to the information contained within this book, either directly or indirectly.

Legal Notice: This book is copyright protected. It is only for personal use. You cannot amend, distribute, sell, use, quote or paraphrase any part, or the content within this book, without the consent of the author or publisher.

Disclaimer Notice: Please note the information contained within this document is for educational and entertainment purposes only. All effort has been executed to present accurate, up to date, reliable, complete information. No warranties of any kind are declared or implied. Readers acknowledge that the author is not engaged in the rendering of legal, financial, medical, or professional advice. The content within this book has been derived from various sources. Please consult a licensed professional before attempting any techniques outlined in this book. By reading this document, the reader agrees that under no circumstances is the author responsible for any losses, direct or indirect, that are incurred as a result of the use of the information contained within this document, including, but not limited to, errors, omissions, or inaccuracies.

Table of Contents

Table of Contents 3
Chapter 1: Introduction 7
History of the Air Fryer 7
Benefits of the Tower Dual Basket Air Fryer 7
Features of the Tower Dual Basket Air Fryer 7
Tips for Using the Tower Dual Basket Air Fryer 8
Cleaning and Maintenance of the Tower Dual Basket Air Fryer 8

Chapter 2: Measurement Conversions 9
BASIC KITCHEN CONVERSIONS & EQUIVALENTS 9

Chapter 3: Appetizers And Snacks 10
Mozzarella Arancini 11
Enticing Jalapeno Poppers 11
Roasted Peppers 11
Indian Cauliflower Tikka Bites 11
Roasted Red Pepper Dip 11
Crispy Deviled Eggs 12
Amazing Blooming Onion 12
Sweet-and-salty Pretzels 12
Curried Veggie Samosas 12
Buffalo Bites 13
Parmesan Cabbage Chips 13
Spiced Parsnip Chips 13
Salsa And Cheese Stuffed Mushrooms 13
Air Fried Pork With Fennel 13
Sugar-glazed Walnuts 13
Pita Chips 14
Roasted Grape Dip 14
Egg Roll Pizza Sticks 14
Curly's Cauliflower 14
Spicy Chickpeas 15
Hearty Greens Chips With Curried Yogurt Sauce 15
Curried Pickle Chips 15
Fried Bacon Slices 15
Za'atar Garbanzo Beans 15
Potato Skins 15
Granola Three Ways 16
Deviled Eggs With Ricotta 16
Garlic Parmesan Kale Chips 16
Mustard Greens Chips With Curried Sauce 17
Glazed Chicken Wings 17
Taquito Quesadillas 17
Crabby Fries 17
Beef Steak Sliders 17
Spinach And Crab Meat Cups 18
Cherry Chipotle Bbq Chicken Wings 18
Fried Olives 18
Chicken Bites With Coconut 19
Jalapeño Cheese Balls 19
Fried Brie With Cherry Tomatoes 19
Veggie Cheese Bites 19
Spicy Kale Chips 20
Spicy Turkey Meatballs 20
Black Bean Corn Dip 20
Veggie Shrimp Toast 20
Fried Dill Pickle Chips 20

Chapter 4: Bread And Breakfast Recipes 21
Tomatoes Hash With Cheddar Cheese 22
Baked Cauliflower With Paprika 22
Shakshuka-style Pepper Cups 22
Green Beans Bowls 22
Pumpkin Empanadas 22
Chocolate-hazelnut Bear Claws 23
Simple Tomato Cheese Sandwich 23
Egg White Cups 23
Oat And Chia Porridge 23
Orange-glazed Cinnamon Rolls 23
Effortless Toffee Zucchini Bread 24
Seedy Bagels 24
Cinnamon Pear Oat Muffins 24
Breakfast Scramble Casserole 24
Vanilla French Toast Sticks 24
Pretzels 25
Lorraine Egg Cups 25
Scrambled Eggs With Mushrooms 25
Mediterranean Granola 25
Egg Soufflé With Mushroom And Broccoli 26
Goat Cheese, Beet, And Kale Frittata 26
Simple Scotch Eggs 26
Cheesy Egg Bites 26
Chicken Scotch Eggs 26
Bacon And Broccoli Bread Pudding 27
Bacon Eggs 27
Dried Fruit Beignets 27
Feta Stuffed Peppers With Broccoli 27
Blueberry Scones 28
Strawberry Streusel Muffins 28
Tasty Hash Browns With Radish 28
Herbed Omelet 28
Egg Muffins 29
Coconut & Peanut Rice Cereal 29
Fruity Blueberry Muffin Cups 29
Classic Cinnamon Rolls 29
English Scones 29
Canadian Bacon & Cheese Sandwich 30
Spinach Frittata With Mozzarella 30
Lime Muffins 30

Mushroom & Cavolo Nero Egg Muffins 30
Buttery Scallops 30
Three-berry Dutch Pancake 31
Nutty Whole Wheat Muffins 31
Roasted Tomato And Cheddar Rolls 31

Cheddar-ham-corn Muffins 32
Baked Potato Breakfast Boats 32
Breakfast Potatoes 32
Baked Eggs With Bacon-tomato Sauce 32
Creamy Baked Sausage 33

Chapter 5: Vegetarians Recipes 34

Roasted Cauliflower 35
Sweet And Sour Brussel Sprouts 35
Spinach And Feta Pinwheels 35
Ricotta Veggie Potpie 35
Easy Baked Root Veggies 35
Powerful Jackfruit Fritters 36
Chili Tofu & Quinoa Bowls 36
Pinto Taquitos 36
Caprese-style Sandwiches 36
Cauliflower Steaks Gratin 36
Arancini With Marinara 37
Fennel Tofu Bites 37
Tofu & Spinach Lasagna 37
Roasted Vegetable Pita Pizza 38
Corn On The Cob 38
Cottage And Mayonnaise Stuffed Peppers 38
Crispy Avocados With Pico De Gallo 38
Mushroom Bolognese Casserole 38

Almond Flour Battered Wings 39
Garlicky Brussel Sprouts With Saffron Aioli 39
Vegan Buddha Bowls(2) 39
Smoked Paprika Sweet Potato Fries 39
Bell Peppers Cups 39
Cheesy Brussel Sprouts 40
Garden Fresh Green Beans 40
Lemony Green Beans 40
Easy Glazed Carrots 40
Vegetarian Stuffed Bell Peppers 40
Vegetarian Eggplant "pizzas" 40
Spinach And Cheese Calzone 41
Tex-mex Stuffed Sweet Potatoes 41
Fried Potatoes With Bell Peppers 41
Roasted Vegetable Lasagna 41
Cheddar Stuffed Portobellos With Salsa 42
Fried Rice With Curried Tofu 42

Chapter 6: Beef, pork & Lamb Recipes 43

Chili-lime Pork Loin 44
Pork Tenderloins 44
Cheese Beef Roll 44
Lollipop Lamb Chops 44
Glazed Tender Pork Chops 44
Provençal Grilled Rib-eye 45
Spiced Pork Chops 45
Bacon With Shallot And Greens 45
Sage Pork With Potatoes 45
Stuffed Pork Chops 45
Juicy Spiced Rib-eye Steaks 45
Rice And Meatball Stuffed Bell Peppers 46
Beef And Broccoli Stir Fry 46
Beefy Quesadillas 46
Baby Back Ribs 47
Rib Eye Steak Seasoned With Italian Herb 47
Paprika Pork Chops 47
Cheese-stuffed Steak Burgers 47
Italian-style Honey Pork 47
Panko-breaded Pork Chops 48
Thai Burgers 48
Roasted Garlic Ribeye With Mayo 48
Quick & Easy Meatballs 48
Spice Meatloaf 48
Chipotle Pork Meatballs 49

Italian Lamb Chops With Avocado Mayo 49
Buttery Pork Chops 49
Mozzarella-stuffed Meatloaf 49
Sriracha Pork Strips With Rice 49
Lamb Burgers 50
Garlic Fillets 50
Garlic Beef With Egg And Bell Pepper 50
Ritzy Skirt Steak Fajitas 50
Homemade Ham Cheese Sandwiches 51
Meatloaf 51
Homemade Toad In The Hole 51
Marinated Beef And Vegetable Stir Fry 51
Pesto Coated Rack Of Lamb 51
Tacos Norteños 52
Pork Burgers With Cheddar Cheese 52
Tender Steak With Salsa Verde 52
Beef & Sauerkraut Spring Rolls 52
Carne Asada Tacos 53
Vietnamese Beef Lettuce Wraps 53
Pork Kabobs With Pineapple 53
Tasty Pork Chops 53
Greek Lamb Rack 54
Rib Eye Cheesesteaks With Fried Onions 54
Italian-style Cheeseburgers With Cheese Slices 54
Delicious Cheeseburgers 54

Chapter 7: Fish And Seafood Recipes 55

Parmesan Tilapia With Parsley 56
Crispy Parmesan Lobster Tails 56
Sesame-glazed Salmon 56
Spiced Shrimp With Zucchini 56
Spicy Orange Shrimp 56
Fish Piccata With Crispy Potatoes 57

Classic Crab Cakes 57
Shrimp Teriyaki 57
Feta & Shrimp Pita 57
Mahi-mahi "burrito" Fillets 58
Shrimp "scampi" 58
Ginger Salmon Fillet 58

Lemon-roasted Salmon Fillets 58	Catfish Fillets With Tortilla Chips 62
Honey-glazed Salmon 59	Teriyaki Salmon 62
Hearty Lemon Salmon 59	Sweet And Sour Glazed Cod 63
Lemon-basil On Cod Filet 59	Tuna-stuffed Tomatoes 63
Tuna And Fruit Kebabs 59	Pecan-crusted Tilapia 63
Fish Sticks With Tartar Sauce 59	Salmon 63
Cod Nuggets 60	Crusty Catfish With Parmesan Cheese 64
Baltimore Crab Cakes 60	Garlic-lemon Steamer Clams 64
Asparagus & Salmon Spring Rolls 60	Spicy Salmon And Fennel Salad 64
Grouper With Miso-honey Sauce 60	Cajun Salmon 64
Lemon Shrimp And Zucchinis 61	Shrimp Sliders With Avocado 64
Pancetta-wrapped Scallops With Pancetta Slices 61	Snow Crab Legs 65
Easy Marinated Salmon Fillets 61	Nutty Shrimp With Amaretto Glaze 65
Spanish Garlic Shrimp 61	Bacon-wrapped Scallops 65
Salty German-style Shrimp Pancakes 61	Basil Mushroom & Shrimp Spaghetti 65
Scallops And Spring Veggies 62	Fish Sticks 66
Spicy Prawns 62	Glazed Salmon With Soy Sauce 66
Parmesan Fish Bites 62	Garlic-lemon Scallops 66
Restaurant-style Flounder Cutlets 62	Salmon Croquettes 66

Chapter 8: Poultry Recipes *67*

Piri-piri Chicken Thighs 68	Air Fryer Naked Chicken Tenders 73
Chicken Burgers With Blue Cheese Sauce 68	Cranberry Turkey Quesadillas 73
Basic Chicken Breasts. 68	Healthy Chicken With Veggies 74
Chicken With 20 Cloves Of Garlic 68	Chicken Tenders With Basil-strawberry Glaze 74
Crispy Italian Chicken Thighs 68	Yogurt-marinated Chicken Legs 74
Fajita Chicken Strips 69	Garlic Turkey With Tomato Mix 74
Za'atar Chicken Thighs 69	Indian Chicken Tandoori 74
Nutty Chicken Tenders 69	Thai Turkey And Zucchini Meatballs 75
Celery Chicken 69	Turkey Sausage With Veggies 75
Southwest Gluten-free Turkey Meatloaf 69	Yummy Stuffed Chicken Breast 75
Cornflake Chicken Nuggets 70	Sage & Paprika Turkey Cutlets 75
Party Buffalo Chicken Drumettes 70	Barbecued Chicken Thighs 75
Grilled Cajun Chicken 70	Dill Chicken Strips 76
Chicken Pigs In Blankets 70	Herb Seasoned Turkey Breast 76
Teriyaki Chicken Bites 70	Jerk Chicken Wings 76
Roasted Chicken And Vegetable Salad 71	Honey Rosemary Chicken 76
Pecan-crusted Turkey Cutlets 71	Cheese Turkey Meatloaf 76
Basil Turkey With Chili Mayo 71	Crispy Parmesan Chicken Breasts 77
Garlic Parmesan Drumsticks 71	Buttered Chicken Thighs 77
Hoisin Turkey Burgers 72	The Ultimate Chicken Bulgogi 77
Parmesan Chicken Tenderloins 72	Turkey Scotch Eggs 77
Chicken Skewers 72	Air Fried Chicken Tenderloin 78
Herb-buttermilk Chicken Breast 72	Yummy Shredded Chicken 78
Cheesy Chicken Tenders 73	Turkey Burgers 78
Gruyère Asparagus & Chicken Quiche 73	Goat Cheese Stuffed Turkey Roulade 78

Chapter 9: Vegetable Side Dishes Recipes *79*

Mashed Potato Tots 80	Dauphinoise (potatoes Au Gratin) 82
Cheddar Tomatillos With Lettuce 80	Curried Fruit 82
Tuna Platter 80	Grits Again 82
Garlicky Brussels Sprouts 80	Burger Bun For One 83
Corn Muffins 81	Turmeric Tofu Cubes 83
Lemony Cabbage Slaw 81	Ajillo Mushrooms 83
Sesame Taj Tofu 81	Radishes And Green Onions Mix 83
Mushroom Mozzarella Risotto 81	Breadcrumb Crusted Agnolotti 83
Cheesy Zucchini Tots 81	Spicy Fries 83
Garlic Kale Mash 81	Sweet And Sour Tofu 84
Open-faced Sandwich 82	Fried Cauliflowerwith Parmesan Lemon Dressing 84
Potato And Broccoli With Tofu Scramble 82	Blistered Tomatoes 84

Sweet Potatoes With Zucchini 84	Turmeric Cauliflower With Cilantro 87
Creamy Cauliflower Puree 85	Simple Baked Potatoes With Dill Yogurt 87
Yellow Squash And Zucchinis Dish 85	Tasty Cauliflower Croquettes 87
Spiced Okra 85	Cayenne Chicken Wing Dip 87
Rosemary New Potatoes 85	Roasted Brown Butter Carrots 87
Tasty Brussels Sprouts With Guanciale 85	Potatoes With Zucchinis 88
Parmesan Zucchini Gratin 85	Mashed Sweet Potato Tots 88
Cheesy Loaded Broccoli 86	Portobello Pizzas 88
Broccoli Tots 86	Broccoli Au Gratin 88
Asparagus With Garlic 86	Garlicky Mushrooms With Parsley 89
Yukon Gold Potato Purée 86	Awesome Chicken Taquitos 89
Roasted Lemony Broccoli 86	Creole Seasoned Okra 89
Perfect Broccolini 87	Spicy Bean Stuffed Potatoes 89

Chapter 10: Desserts And Sweets Recipes *90*

Banana Slices With Cardamom 91	Apple Chips With Cinnamon 97
One-bowl Chocolate Buttermilk Cake 91	Oreo-coated Peanut Butter Cups 97
Brownies With White Chocolate 91	Fried Pineapple Chunks 97
Vanilla Cupcakes With Chocolate Chips 91	Honey-roasted Pears With Ricotta 98
Fried Oreos 92	Moist Cinnamon Muffins 98
Lemon Nut Bars 92	Pineapple And Chocolate Cake 98
Vanilla Bars With Sesame Seeds 92	Oatmeal Raisin Bars 98
Banana And Rice Pudding 92	Ricotta Lemon Cake 99
Apple Turnovers 92	Lemon Cookies 99
Vanilla Muffins With Pecans 93	Lemon Creamy Muffins 99
Peanut Butter Cup Doughnut Holes 93	Chocolate Donuts 99
Vanilla Berry Cobbler 93	Nutty Fudge Muffins 99
Struffoli 94	Simple Donuts 100
Brownies 94	Simple Almond Muffins With Blueberries 100
Vanilla-strawberry Muffins 94	Ricotta Lemon Poppy Seed Cake 100
Orange Marmalade 94	Plum Apple Crumble With Cranberries 100
Cinnamon Tortilla Crisps 95	Berry Streusel Cake 101
German Streusel-stuffed Baked Apples 95	Baked Apple 101
Caramel Apple Crumble 95	Yummy Berry Cheesecake 101
Rich Chocolate Cookie 95	Cheese Muffins With Cinnamon 101
Apple-blueberry Hand Pies 95	Grilled Spiced Fruit 101
Graham Cracker Cheesecake 96	Banana Bread Cake 102
Enticing Chocolate Cake 96	Apple Crisp 102
Strawberry Muffins With Cinnamon 96	Coffee Cookies 102
Chocolate Macaroons 97	Honey Donuts 103

Recipes Index *104*

Chapter 1: Introduction

History of the Air Fryer

The concept of air frying has revolutionized the way we cook our favorite foods. With the increasing emphasis on healthier eating habits, the quest for tasty yet guilt-free food has become more important than ever before. The air fryer, a kitchen appliance that uses hot air circulation to cook food, has emerged as a popular solution to this dilemma.

The origins of the air fryer can be traced back to the early 2000s when Philips introduced the concept of using hot air to fry food, reducing the need for excessive oil. This innovation opened up a whole new world of possibilities, allowing people to enjoy crispy and delicious fried food with significantly reduced fat content. Over time, air fryers have gained immense popularity and become an essential kitchen appliance for health-conscious individuals worldwide.

Benefits of the Tower Dual Basket Air Fryer

The Tower Dual Basket Air Fryer is a cutting-edge kitchen appliance designed to provide you with a healthier alternative to traditional deep frying. This air fryer offers a wide range of benefits that make it a must-have addition to your kitchen.

1. Healthier Cooking - The Tower Dual Basket Air Fryer requires little to no oil to cook your favorite foods. By using hot air circulation technology, it creates a crispy exterior while retaining the moisture inside, resulting in delicious dishes with up to 75% less fat than traditional frying methods.
2. Versatile Cooking - With its dual basket design, the Tower Dual Basket Air Fryer allows you to cook two different dishes simultaneously, saving you time and effort in the kitchen. Whether you're craving fried chicken, crispy fries, or even a batch of homemade snacks, this air fryer can handle it all.
3. Time-Saving Convenience - The Tower Dual Basket Air Fryer not only cooks food quickly, but it also eliminates the need for preheating. It features a powerful heating element and high-speed air circulation, reducing cooking times by up to 30%. This means you can have a delicious meal on the table in no time, making it ideal for busy individuals and families.
4. Easy to Use - Operating the Tower Dual Basket Air Fryer is a breeze, thanks to its intuitive digital control panel. With pre-set cooking programs and adjustable temperature and time settings, you can easily achieve your desired results with the touch of a button. Additionally, the fryer's large capacity and wide temperature range make it suitable for a variety of cooking techniques beyond frying, such as baking, grilling, and roasting.

Features of the Tower Dual Basket Air Fryer

The Tower Dual Basket Air Fryer boasts a range of features that elevate its performance and functionality. These features ensure that you get the most out of this innovative kitchen appliance.

1. Dual Basket Design - The Tower Dual Basket Air Fryer comes with two separate frying baskets, allowing you to cook different dishes simultaneously without mixing flavors. Each basket has a generous capacity, ensuring you can easily cook meals for the whole family.
2. Rapid Air Circulation Technology - With its powerful 360° hot air circulation system, the Tower Dual Basket Air Fryer ensures even and quick cooking. The technology ensures that the food is cooked to perfection, resulting in crispy exteriors and tender interiors every time.
3. Digital Touch Control Panel - The intuitive digital control panel makes it effortless to operate the Tower Dual Basket Air Fryer. With just a few touches, you can adjust temperature and time settings, select pre-set cooking programs, and monitor the cooking progress on the built-in LED display.
4. Adjustable Temperature and Time - The Tower Dual Basket Air Fryer allows you to customize the cooking temperature and time according to your preferences. The adjustable temperature range (100°F-400°F) and customizable timer (up to 60 minutes) provide flexibility and precision in achieving your desired

The Ultimate Tower 2-Basket Air Fryer Cookbook

cooking results.

5. Easy-Clean Design - Cleaning up after cooking is hassle-free with the Tower Dual Basket Air Fryer. The cooking baskets are non-stick, allowing for easy food release and cleaning. Additionally, the fryer features a removable oil tray to collect any excess oil or grease, making maintenance a breeze.

Tips for Using the Tower Dual Basket Air Fryer

To optimize your cooking experience with the Tower Dual Basket Air Fryer, here are some helpful tips:

1. Preheat the Fryer - While the Tower Dual Basket Air Fryer doesn't require preheating, it is recommended to preheat the appliance for a few minutes before adding the food. This helps to ensure even cooking and a crispy texture.
2. Use the Right Amount of Oil - Despite the air fryer's ability to cook with minimal oil, using a little oil can enhance the flavor and texture of certain dishes. However, it's essential to use oil sparingly to avoid unnecessary fat consumption.
3. Don't Overcrowd the Baskets - For the best results, it's essential not to overcrowd the cooking baskets. Overcrowding can hinder proper air circulation, leading to uneven cooking. Instead, cook in multiple batches if necessary, ensuring each piece of food has enough space for the hot air to circulate around it.
4. Shake or Flip the Food - To ensure even cooking and a crispy exterior, it's advisable to shake or flip the food items halfway through the cooking time. This helps to promote consistent browning and crispiness on all sides.
5. Experiment with Cooking Times and Temperatures - While the Tower Dual Basket Air Fryer provides pre-set cooking programs, don't be afraid to experiment with different time and temperature settings to achieve your preferred level of doneness. Keep a note of the settings that work best for your favorite dishes for future reference.

Cleaning and Maintenance of the Tower Dual Basket Air Fryer

Proper cleaning and maintenance are essential to keep your Tower Dual Basket Air Fryer in optimal condition. These steps will help you maintain hygiene and extend the appliance's lifespan:

1. Allow the Fryer to Cool Down - Before cleaning, ensure that the fryer has cooled down completely. The heating element and cooking baskets can get very hot during operation, so it's crucial to exercise caution.
2. Remove and Clean the Baskets - Gently remove the cooking baskets from the fryer and wash them with warm soapy water. The non-stick coating makes it easy to remove any food residue. Alternatively, you can place them in the dishwasher if they are dishwasher safe.
3. Wipe Down the Exterior - Use a damp cloth or sponge to wipe down the exterior of the fryer. Avoid using abrasive cleaners or scouring pads, as they can damage the surface.
4. Clean the Oil Tray - Remove the oil tray and discard any collected oil or grease. Wash it with warm soapy water or place it in the dishwasher if it's dishwasher safe.
5. Regular Maintenance - Regularly check the air fryer for any signs of wear or damage. Ensure that the heating element and fan are clean and free from debris. Refer to the user manual for any specific maintenance instructions provided by the manufacturer.

Conclusion

The Tower Dual Basket Air Fryer brings the benefits of healthier cooking, versatility, time-saving convenience, and ease of use to your kitchen. With its dual basket design, rapid air circulation technology, and intuitive controls, it allows you to enjoy delicious, crispy food with reduced fat content. By following the tips for using the air fryer and practicing proper cleaning and maintenance, you can ensure optimal performance and longevity. Upgrade your cooking experience with the Tower Dual Basket Air Fryer and indulge in guilt-free, flavorful meals.

Chapter 2: Measurement Conversions

BASIC KITCHEN CONVERSIONS & EQUIVALENTS

DRY MEASUREMENTS CONVERSION CHART

3 TEASPOONS = 1 TABLESPOON = 1/16 CUP
6 TEASPOONS = 2 TABLESPOONS = 1/8 CUP
12 TEASPOONS = 4 TABLESPOONS = 1/4 CUP
24 TEASPOONS = 8 TABLESPOONS = 1/2 CUP
36 TEASPOONS = 12 TABLESPOONS = 3/4 CUP
48 TEASPOONS = 16 TABLESPOONS = 1 CUP

METRIC TO US COOKING CONVERSIONS
OVEN TEMPERATURES

120 °C = 250 °F
160 °C = 320 °F
180° C = 360 °F
205 °C = 400 °F
220 °C = 425 °F

LIQUID MEASUREMENTS CONVERSION CHART

8 FLUID OUNCES = 1 CUP = 1/2 PINT = 1/4 QUART
16 FLUID OUNCES = 2 CUPS = 1 PINT = 1/2 QUART
32 FLUID OUNCES = 4 CUPS = 2 PINTS = 1 QUART = 1/4 GALLON
128 FLUID OUNCES = 16 CUPS = 8 PINTS = 4 QUARTS = 1 GALLON

BAKING IN GRAMS

1 CUP FLOUR = 140 GRAMS
1 CUP SUGAR = 150 GRAMS
1 CUP POWDERED SUGAR = 160 GRAMS
1 CUP HEAVY CREAM = 235 GRAMS

VOLUME

1 MILLILITER = 1/5 TEASPOON
5 ML = 1 TEASPOON
15 ML = 1 TABLESPOON
240 ML = 1 CUP OR 8 FLUID OUNCES
1 LITER = 34 FL. OUNCES

WEIGHT

1 GRAM = .035 OUNCES
100 GRAMS = 3.5 OUNCES
500 GRAMS = 1.1 POUNDS
1 KILOGRAM = 35 OUNCES

US TO METRIC COOKING CONVERSIONS

1/5 TSP = 1 ML
1 TSP = 5 ML
1 TBSP = 15 ML
1 FL OUNCE = 30 ML
1 CUP = 237 ML
1 PINT (2 CUPS) = 473 ML
1 QUART (4 CUPS) = .95 LITER
1 GALLON (16 CUPS) = 3.8 LITERS
1 OZ = 28 GRAMS
1 POUND = 454 GRAMS

BUTTER

1 CUP BUTTER = 2 STICKS = 8 OUNCES = 230 GRAMS = 8 TABLESPOONS

WHAT DOES 1 CUP EQUAL

1 CUP = 8 FLUID OUNCES
1 CUP = 16 TABLESPOONS
1 CUP = 48 TEASPOONS
1 CUP = 1/2 PINT
1 CUP = 1/4 QUART
1 CUP = 1/16 GALLON
1 CUP = 240 ML

BAKING PAN CONVERSIONS

1 CUP ALL-PURPOSE FLOUR = 4.5 OZ
1 CUP ROLLED OATS = 3 OZ 1 LARGE EGG = 1.7 OZ
1 CUP BUTTER = 8 OZ 1 CUP MILK = 8 OZ
1 CUP HEAVY CREAM = 8.4 OZ
1 CUP GRANULATED SUGAR = 7.1 OZ
1 CUP PACKED BROWN SUGAR = 7.75 OZ
1 CUP VEGETABLE OIL = 7.7 OZ
1 CUP UNSIFTED POWDERED SUGAR = 4.4 OZ

BAKING PAN CONVERSIONS

9-INCH ROUND CAKE PAN = 12 CUPS
10-INCH TUBE PAN =16 CUPS
11-INCH BUNDT PAN = 12 CUPS
9-INCH SPRINGFORM PAN = 10 CUPS
9 X 5 INCH LOAF PAN = 8 CUPS
9-INCH SQUARE PAN = 8 CUPS

Chapter 3: Appetizers And Snacks

Mozzarella Arancini

Servings: 16
Cooking Time: 8 To 11 Minutes
Ingredients:
- 2 cups cooked rice, cooled
- 2 eggs, beaten
- 1½ cups panko bread crumbs, divided
- ½ cup grated Parmesan cheese
- 2 tablespoons minced fresh basil
- 16 ¾-inch cubes Mozzarella cheese
- 2 tablespoons olive oil

Directions:
1. Preheat the air fryer to 400°F (204°C).
2. In a medium bowl, combine the rice, eggs, ½ cup of the bread crumbs, Parmesan cheese, and basil. Form this mixture into 16 1½-inch balls.
3. Poke a hole in each of the balls with your finger and insert a Mozzarella cube. Form the rice mixture firmly around the cheese.
4. On a shallow plate, combine the remaining 1 cup of the bread crumbs with the olive oil and mix well. Roll the rice balls in the bread crumbs to coat.
5. Air fry the arancini in batches for 8 to 11 minutes or until golden brown.
6. Serve hot.

Enticing Jalapeno Poppers

Servings: 5
Cooking Time: 13 Minutes
Ingredients:
- 5 jalapeno peppers, slice in ½ and deseeded
- 2 tablespoons salsa
- 4 ounces goat cheese, crumbled
- ¼ teaspoon chili powder
- ½ teaspoon garlic, minced
- Black pepper
- Salt

Directions:
1. In a suitable bowl, mix together cheese, salsa, chili powder, garlic, black pepper, and salt.
2. Spoon cheese mixture into each jalapeno halves and place in air fryer basket.
3. Cook jalapeno poppers at 350 degrees F/ 175 degrees C for 13 minutes.
4. Serve and enjoy.

Roasted Peppers

Servings: 4
Cooking Time: 40 Minutes
Ingredients:
- 12 medium bell peppers
- 1 sweet onion, small
- 1 tbsp. Maggi sauce
- 1 tbsp. extra virgin olive oil

Directions:
1. Warm up the olive oil and Maggi sauce in Air Fryer at 320°F.
2. Peel the onion, slice it into 1-inch pieces, and add it to the Air Fryer.
3. Wash and de-stem the peppers. Slice them into 1-inch pieces and remove all the seeds, with water if necessary.
4. Place the peppers in the Air Fryer.
5. Cook for about 25 minutes, or longer if desired. Serve hot.

Indian Cauliflower Tikka Bites

Servings: 6
Cooking Time: 20 Minutes
Ingredients:
- 1 cup plain Greek yogurt
- 1 teaspoon fresh ginger
- 1 teaspoon minced garlic
- 1 teaspoon vindaloo
- ½ teaspoon cardamom
- ½ teaspoon paprika
- ½ teaspoon turmeric powder
- ½ teaspoon cumin powder
- 1 large head of cauliflower, washed and cut into medium-size florets
- ½ cup panko breadcrumbs
- 1 lemon, quartered

Directions:
1. Preheat the air fryer to 350°F.
2. In a large bowl, mix the yogurt, ginger, garlic, vindaloo, cardamom, paprika, turmeric, and cumin. Add the cauliflower florets to the bowl, and coat them with the yogurt.
3. Remove the cauliflower florets from the bowl and place them on a baking sheet. Sprinkle the panko breadcrumbs over the top. Place the cauliflower bites into the air fryer basket, leaving space between the florets. Depending on the size of your air fryer, you may need to make more than one batch.
4. Cook the cauliflower for 10 minutes, shake the basket, and continue cooking another 10 minutes (or until the florets are lightly browned).
5. Remove from the air fryer and keep warm. Continue to cook until all the florets are done.
6. Before serving, lightly squeeze lemon over the top. Serve warm.

Roasted Red Pepper Dip

Servings: 2
Cooking Time: 15 Minutes
Ingredients:
- 2 Medium-size red bell pepper(s)
- 1¾ cups Canned white beans, drained and rinsed
- 1 tablespoon Fresh oregano leaves, packed
- 3 tablespoons Olive oil
- 1 tablespoon Lemon juice
- ½ teaspoon Table salt
- ½ teaspoon Ground black pepper

Directions:
1. Preheat the air fryer to 400°F.
2. Set the pepper(s) in the basket and air-fry undisturbed for 15 minutes, until blistered and even blackened.

3. Use kitchen tongs to transfer the pepper(s) to a zip-closed plastic bag or small bowl. Seal the bag or cover the bowl with plastic wrap. Set aside for 20 minutes.
4. Peel each pepper, then stem it, cut it in half, and remove all its seeds and their white membranes.
5. Set the pieces of the pepper in a food processor. Add the beans, oregano, olive oil, lemon juice, salt, and pepper. Cover and process until smooth, stopping the machine at least once to scrape down the inside of the canister. Scrape the dip into a bowl and serve warm, or cover and refrigerate for up to 3 days.

Crispy Deviled Eggs

Servings: 12
Cooking Time: 25 Minutes
Ingredients:
- 7 large eggs, divided
- 1 ounce plain pork rinds, finely crushed
- 2 tablespoons mayonnaise
- ¼ teaspoon salt
- ¼ teaspoon ground black pepper

Directions:
1. Place 6 whole eggs into ungreased air fryer basket. Adjust the temperature to 220°F and set the timer for 20 minutes. When done, place eggs into a bowl of ice water to cool 5 minutes.
2. Peel cool eggs, then cut in half lengthwise. Remove yolks and place aside in a medium bowl.
3. In a separate small bowl, whisk remaining raw egg. Place pork rinds in a separate medium bowl. Dip each egg white into whisked egg, then gently coat with pork rinds. Spritz with cooking spray and place into ungreased air fryer basket. Adjust the temperature to 400°F and set the timer for 5 minutes, turning eggs halfway through cooking. Eggs will be golden when done.
4. Mash yolks in bowl with mayonnaise until smooth. Sprinkle with salt and pepper and mix.
5. Spoon 2 tablespoons yolk mixture into each fried egg white. Serve warm.

Amazing Blooming Onion

Servings: 4
Cooking Time: 40 Minutes
Ingredients:
- 4 medium/small onions
- 1 tbsp. olive oil
- 4 dollops of butter

Directions:
1. Peel the onion. Cut off the top and bottom.
2. To make it bloom, cut as deeply as possible without slicing through it completely. 4 cuts should do it.
3. Place the onions in a bowl of salted water and allow to absorb for 4 hours to help eliminate the sharp taste and induce the blooming process.
4. Pre-heat your Air Fryer to 355°F.
5. Transfer the onions to the Air Fryer. Pour over a light drizzle of olive oil and place a dollop of butter on top of each onion.
6. Cook or roast for 30 minutes. Remove the outer layer before serving if it is too brown.

Sweet-and-salty Pretzels

Servings: 4
Cooking Time: 5 Minutes
Ingredients:
- 2 cups Plain pretzel nuggets
- 1 tablespoon Worcestershire sauce
- 2 teaspoons Granulated white sugar
- 1 teaspoon Mild smoked paprika
- ½ teaspoon Garlic or onion powder

Directions:
1. Preheat the air fryer to 350°F.
2. Put the pretzel nuggets, Worcestershire sauce, sugar, smoked paprika, and garlic or onion powder in a large bowl. Toss gently until the nuggets are well coated.
3. When the machine is at temperature, pour the nuggets into the basket, spreading them into as close to a single layer as possible. Air-fry, shaking the basket three or four times to rearrange the nuggets, for 5 minutes, or until the nuggets are toasted and aromatic. Although the coating will darken, don't let it burn, especially if the machine's temperature is 360°F.
4. Pour the nuggets onto a wire rack and gently spread them into one layer. Cool for 5 minutes before serving.

Curried Veggie Samosas

Servings: 4
Cooking Time: 30 Minutes
Ingredients:
- 4 cooked potatoes, mashed
- ¼ cup peas
- 2 tsp coconut oil
- 3 garlic cloves, minced
- 1 ½ tbsp lemon juice
- 1 ½ tsp cumin powder
- 1 tsp onion powder
- 1 tsp ground coriander
- Salt to taste
- ½ tsp curry powder
- ¼ tsp cayenne powder
- 10 rice paper wrappers
- 1 cup cilantro chutney

Directions:
1. Preheat air fryer to 390°F. In a bowl, place the mashed potatoes, peas, oil, garlic, lemon juice, cumin, onion powder, coriander, salt, curry powder, and cayenne. Stir.
2. Fill a bowl with water. Soak a rice paper wrapper in the water for a few seconds. Lay it on a flat surface. Place ¼ cup of the potato filling in the center of the wrapper and roll like a burrito or spring roll. Repeat the process until you run out of ingredients. Place the "samosas" inside in the greased frying basket, separating them. Air Fry for 8-10 minutes or until hot and crispy around the edges. Let cool for a few minutes. Enjoy with the cilantro chutney.

Buffalo Bites

Servings: 16
Cooking Time: 12 Minutes
Ingredients:
- 1 pound ground chicken
- 8 tablespoons buffalo wing sauce
- 2 ounces Gruyère cheese, cut into 16 cubes
- 1 tablespoon maple syrup

Directions:
1. Mix 4 tablespoons buffalo wing sauce into all the ground chicken.
2. Shape chicken into a log and divide into 16 equal portions.
3. With slightly damp hands, mold each chicken portion around a cube of cheese and shape into a firm ball. When you have shaped 8 meatballs, place them in air fryer basket.
4. Cook at 390°F for approximately 5minutes. Shake basket, reduce temperature to 360°F, and cook for 5 minutes longer.
5. While the first batch is cooking, shape remaining chicken and cheese into 8 more meatballs.
6. Repeat step 4 to cook second batch of meatballs.
7. In a medium bowl, mix the remaining 4 tablespoons of buffalo wing sauce with the maple syrup. Add all the cooked meatballs and toss to coat.
8. Place meatballs back into air fryer basket and cook at 390°F for 2 minutes to set the glaze. Skewer each with a toothpick and serve.

Parmesan Cabbage Chips

Servings: 6
Cooking Time: 30 Minutes
Ingredients:
- 1 large cabbage head, tear cabbage leaves into pieces
- 2 tablespoons olive oil
- ¼ cup parmesan cheese, grated
- Black pepper
- Salt

Directions:
1. At 250 degrees F/ 120 degrees C, preheat your air fryer.
2. Add all the recipe ingredients into the suitable mixing bowl and toss well.
3. Grease its air fryer basket with cooking spray.
4. Divide cabbage in batches.
5. Add 1 cabbage chips batch in air fryer basket and cook for 25-30 minutes at 250 degrees F/ 120 degrees C or until chips are crispy and lightly golden brown.
6. Serve and enjoy.

Spiced Parsnip Chips

Servings: 2
Cooking Time: 35 Minutes
Ingredients:
- ½ tsp smoked paprika
- ¼ tsp chili powder
- ¼ tsp garlic powder
- ⅛ tsp onion powder
- ⅛ tsp cayenne pepper
- ⅛ tsp granulated sugar
- 1 tsp salt
- 1 parsnip, cut into chips
- 2 tsp olive oil

Directions:
1. Preheat air fryer to 400ºF. Mix all spices in a bowl and reserve. In another bowl, combine parsnip chips, olive oil, and salt. Place parsnip chips in the lightly greased frying basket and Air Fry for 12 minutes, shaking once. Transfer the chips to a bowl, toss in seasoning mix, and let sit for 15 minutes before serving.

Salsa And Cheese Stuffed Mushrooms

Servings: 5
Cooking Time: 10 Minutes
Ingredients:
- 8 ounces large portobello mushrooms
- ⅓ cup salsa
- ½ cup shredded Cheddar cheese
- Cooking oil

Directions:
1. Cut the stem out of the mushrooms: First, chop off the end of the stem, and then make a circular cut around the area where the stem was. Continue to cut until you have removed the rest of the stem.
2. Stuff the mushrooms with the salsa. Sprinkle the shredded cheese on top.
3. Place the mushrooms in the air fryer. Cook for 8 minutes.
4. Cool before serving.

Air Fried Pork With Fennel

Servings: 6
Cooking Time: 25 Minutes
Ingredients:
- 2 pounds pork belly, cut into strips
- 2 tablespoons olive oil
- 2 teaspoons fennel seeds
- A pinch of salt and black pepper
- A pinch of basil, dried

Directions:
1. Mix all the ingredients in a clean bowl.
2. Toss well and arrange the marinated pork strips to the basket of your air fryer.
3. Cook for 25 minutes at 425 degrees F/ 220 degrees C.
4. Before serving as a snack, divide into bowls.

Sugar-glazed Walnuts

Servings: 6
Cooking Time: 5 Minutes
Ingredients:
- 1 Large egg white(s)
- 2 tablespoons Granulated white sugar
- ⅛ teaspoon Table salt
- 2 cups Walnut halves

Directions:
1. Preheat the air fryer to 400°F.

The Ultimate Tower 2-Basket Air Fryer Cookbook

2. Use a whisk to beat the egg white(s) in a large bowl until quite foamy, more so than just well combined but certainly not yet a meringue.
3. If you're working with the quantities for a small batch, remove half of the foamy egg white.
4. If you're working with the quantities for a large batch, remove a quarter of it. It's fine to eyeball the amounts.
5. You can store the removed egg white in a sealed container to save for another use.
6. Stir in the sugar and salt. Add the walnut halves and toss to coat evenly and well, including the nuts' crevasses.
7. When the machine is at temperature, use a slotted spoon to transfer the walnut halves to the basket, taking care not to dislodge any coating. Gently spread the nuts into as close to one layer as you can. Air-fry undisturbed for 2 minutes.
8. Break up any clumps, toss the walnuts gently but well, and air-fry for 3 minutes more, tossing after 1 minute, then every 30 seconds thereafter, until the nuts are browned in spots and very aromatic. Watch carefully so they don't burn.
9. Gently dump the nuts onto a lipped baking sheet and spread them into one layer. Cool for at least 10 minutes before serving, separating any that stick together. The walnuts can be stored in a sealed container at room temperature for up to 5 days.

Pita Chips

Servings: 4
Cooking Time: 10 Minutes
Ingredients:
- 2 rounds Pocketless pita bread
- Olive oil spray or any flavor spray you prefer, even coconut oil spray
- Up to 1 teaspoon Fine sea salt, garlic salt, onion salt, or other flavored salt

Directions:
1. Preheat the air fryer to 400°F.
2. Lightly coat the pita round(s) on both sides with olive oil spray, then lightly sprinkle each side with salt.
3. Cut each coated pita round into 8 even wedges. Lay these in the basket in as close to a single even layer as possible. Many will overlap or even be on top of each other, depending on the exact size of your machine.
4. Air-fry for 6 minutes, shaking the basket and rearranging the wedges at the 4-minute marks, until the wedges are crisp and brown. Turn them out onto a wire rack to cool a few minutes or to room temperature before digging in.

Roasted Grape Dip

Servings: 6
Cooking Time: 8 To 12 Minutes
Ingredients:
- 2 cups seedless red grapes, rinsed and patted dry (see Tip)
- 1 tablespoon apple cider vinegar
- 1 tablespoon honey
- 1 cup low-fat Greek yogurt
- 2 tablespoons 2 percent milk
- 2 tablespoons minced fresh basil

Directions:

1. In the air fryer basket, sprinkle the grapes with the cider vinegar and drizzle with the honey. Toss to coat. Roast the grapes for 8 to 12 minutes, or until shriveled but still soft. Remove from the air fryer.
2. In a medium bowl, stir together the yogurt and milk.
3. Gently blend in the grapes and basil. Serve immediately, or cover and chill for 1 to 2 hours.

Egg Roll Pizza Sticks

Servings: 4
Cooking Time: 5 Minutes
Ingredients:
- Olive oil
- 8 pieces reduced-fat string cheese
- 8 egg roll wrappers
- 24 slices turkey pepperoni
- Marinara sauce, for dipping (optional)

Directions:
1. Spray a fryer basket lightly with olive oil. Fill a small bowl with water.
2. Place each egg roll wrapper diagonally on a work surface. It should look like a diamond.
3. Place 3 slices of turkey pepperoni in a vertical line down the center of the wrapper.
4. Place 1 mozzarella cheese stick on top of the turkey pepperoni.
5. Fold the top and bottom corners of the egg roll wrapper over the cheese stick.
6. Fold the left corner over the cheese stick and roll the cheese stick up to resemble a spring roll. Dip a finger in the water and seal the edge of the roll
7. Repeat with the rest of the pizza sticks.
8. Place them in the fryer basket in a single layer, making sure to leave a little space between each one. Lightly spray the pizza sticks with oil. You may need to cook these in batches.
9. Air fry until the pizza sticks are lightly browned and crispy, about 5 minutes.
10. These are best served hot while the cheese is melted. Accompany with a small bowl of marinara sauce, if desired.

Curly's Cauliflower

Servings: 4
Cooking Time: 30 Minutes
Ingredients:
- 4 cups bite-sized cauliflower florets
- 1 cup friendly bread crumbs, mixed with 1 tsp. salt
- ¼ cup melted butter [vegan/other]
- ¼ cup buffalo sauce [vegan/other]
- Mayo [vegan/other] or creamy dressing for dipping

Directions:
1. In a bowl, combine the butter and buffalo sauce to create a creamy paste.
2. Completely cover each floret with the sauce.
3. Coat the florets with the bread crumb mixture. Cook the florets in the Air Fryer for approximately 15 minutes at 350°F, shaking the basket occasionally.
4. Serve with a raw vegetable salad, mayo or creamy dressing.

Spicy Chickpeas

Servings: 4
Cooking Time: 20 Minutes
Ingredients:
- Olive oil
- ½ teaspoon ground cumin
- ½ teaspoon chili powder
- ¼ teaspoon cayenne pepper
- ¼ teaspoon salt
- 1 (19-ounce) can chickpeas, drained and rinsed

Directions:
1. Spray a fryer basket lightly with olive oil.
2. In a small bowl, combine the cumin, chili powder, cayenne pepper, and salt.
3. In a medium bowl, add the chickpeas and lightly spray them with olive oil. Add the spice mixture and toss until coated evenly.
4. Transfer the chickpeas to the fryer basket. Air fry until the chickpeas reach your desired level of crunchiness, 15 to 20 minutes, making sure to shake the basket every 5 minutes.

Hearty Greens Chips With Curried Yogurt Sauce

Servings: 4
Cooking Time: 5 To 6 Minutes
Ingredients:
- 1 cup low-fat Greek yogurt
- 1 tablespoon freshly squeezed lemon juice
- 1 tablespoon curry powder
- ½ bunch curly kale, stemmed, ribs removed and discarded, leaves cut into 2- to 3-inch pieces
- ½ bunch chard, stemmed, ribs removed and discarded, leaves cut into 2- to 3-inch pieces
- 1½ teaspoons olive oil

Directions:
1. In a small bowl, stir together the yogurt, lemon juice, and curry powder. Set aside.
2. In a large bowl, toss the kale and chard with the olive oil, working the oil into the leaves with your hands. This helps break up the fibers in the leaves so the chips are tender.
3. Air-fry the greens in batches for 5 to 6 minutes, until crisp, shaking the basket once during cooking. Serve with the yogurt sauce.

Curried Pickle Chips

Servings: 4
Cooking Time: 25 Minutes
Ingredients:
- 2 dill pickles, sliced
- 1 cup breadcrumbs
- 2 eggs, beaten
- A pinch of white pepper
- 1 tsp curry powder
- ½ tsp mustard powder

Directions:
1. Preheat air fryer to 350°F. Combine the breadcrumbs, curry, mustard powder, and white pepper in a mixing bowl. Coat the pickle slices with the crumb mixture; then dip into the eggs, then dip again into the dry ingredients. Arrange the coated pickle pieces on the greased frying basket in an even layer. Air Fry for 15 minutes, shaking the basket several times during cooking until crispy, golden brown and perfect. Serve warm.

Fried Bacon Slices

Servings: 11
Cooking Time: 10 Minutes
Ingredients:
- 11 bacon slices

Directions:
1. Place ½ bacon slices in air fryer basket.
2. Cook at almost 400 degrees F/ 205 degrees C for almost 10 minutes.
3. Cook remaining ½ bacon slices using same steps.
4. Serve and enjoy.

Za'atar Garbanzo Beans

Servings: 6
Cooking Time: 12 Minutes
Ingredients:
- One 14.5-ounce can garbanzo beans, drained and rinsed
- 1 tablespoon extra-virgin olive oil
- 6 teaspoons za'atar seasoning mix
- 2 tablespoons chopped parsley
- Salt and pepper, to taste

Directions:
1. Preheat the air fryer to 390°F.
2. In a medium bowl, toss the garbanzo beans with olive oil and za'atar seasoning.
3. Pour the beans into the air fryer basket and cook for 12 minutes, or until toasted as you like. Stir every 3 minutes while roasting.
4. Remove the beans from the air fryer basket into a serving bowl, top with fresh chopped parsley, and season with salt and pepper.

Potato Skins

Servings: 4
Cooking Time: 35 Minutes Per Batch
Ingredients:
- 4 large russet potatoes
- ½ cup shredded sharp Cheddar cheese
- 1 teaspoon salt
- ½ teaspoon ground black pepper
- ½ cup sour cream
- 1 medium green onion, sliced

Directions:
1. Preheat the air fryer to 400°F.
2. Using a fork, poke several holes in potatoes. Place potatoes in the air fryer basket and cook 30 minutes until fork tender.
3. Once potatoes are cool enough to handle, slice them in half lengthwise and scoop out the insides, being careful to maintain the structural integrity of the potato skins. Reserve potato flesh for another use.

4. Sprinkle insides of potato skins with Cheddar, salt, and pepper. Working in batches if needed, place back in the air fryer basket and cook 5 minutes until cheese is melted and bubbling.
5. Let cool 5 minutes, then top with sour cream and green onion. Serve.

Granola Three Ways

Servings: 4
Cooking Time: 10 Minutes
Ingredients:
- Nantucket Granola
- ¼ cup maple syrup
- ¼ cup dark brown sugar
- 1 tablespoon butter
- 1 teaspoon vanilla extract
- 1 cup rolled oats
- ½ cup dried cranberries
- ½ cup walnuts, chopped
- ¼ cup pumpkin seeds
- ¼ cup shredded coconut
- Blueberry Delight
- ¼ cup honey
- ¼ cup light brown sugar
- 1 tablespoon butter
- 1 teaspoon lemon extract
- 1 cup rolled oats
- ½ cup sliced almonds
- ½ cup dried blueberries
- ¼ cup pumpkin seeds
- ¼ cup sunflower seeds
- Cherry Black Forest Mix
- ¼ cup honey
- ¼ cup light brown sugar
- 1 tablespoon butter
- 1 teaspoon almond extract
- 1 cup rolled oats
- ½ cup sliced almonds
- ½ cup dried cherries
- ¼ cup shredded coconut
- ¼ cup dark chocolate chips
- oil for misting or cooking spray

Directions:
1. Combine the syrup or honey, brown sugar, and butter in a small saucepan or microwave-safe bowl. Heat and stir just until butter melts and sugar dissolves. Stir in the extract.
2. Place all other dry ingredients in a large bowl. (For the Cherry Black Forest Mix, don't add the chocolate chips yet.)
3. Pour melted butter mixture over dry ingredients and stir until oat mixture is well coated.
4. Lightly spray a baking pan with oil or cooking spray.
5. Pour granola into pan and cook at 390°F for 5minutes. Stir. Continue cooking for 5minutes, stirring every minute or two, until golden brown. Watch closely. Once the mixture begins to brown, it will cook quickly.
6. Remove granola from pan and spread on wax paper. It will become crispier as it cools.
7. For the Cherry Black Forest Mix, stir in chocolate chips after granola has cooled completely.
8. Store in an airtight container.

Deviled Eggs With Ricotta

Servings: 4
Cooking Time: 17 Minutes
Ingredients:
- 2 eggs
- ½ teaspoon harissa
- ½ teaspoon chili flakes
- ¼ teaspoon chili powder
- 1 teaspoon ricotta cheese
- ½ teaspoon dried thyme

Directions:
1. At 250 degrees F/ 120 degrees C, preheat your air fryer.
2. Place 2 eggs in the air fryer basket and cook them for almost 17 minutes.
3. Then cool and peel the eggs. Cut the peeled eggs into halves and remove the egg yolks.
4. Stir the egg yolks with the help of the fork until they are smooth.
5. After this, add chili flakes, harissa, chili powder, ricotta cheese, and dried thyme.
6. Stir the mass until smooth. Fill the egg whites with hot egg yolk mixture.
7. Serve.

Garlic Parmesan Kale Chips

Servings: 2
Cooking Time: 6 Minutes
Ingredients:
- 16 large kale leaves, washed and thick stems removed
- 1 tablespoon avocado oil
- ½ teaspoon garlic powder
- 1 teaspoon soy sauce or tamari
- ¼ cup grated Parmesan cheese

Directions:
1. Preheat the air fryer to 370°F.
2. Make a stack of kale leaves and cut them into 4 pieces.
3. Place the kale pieces into a large bowl. Drizzle the avocado oil onto the kale and rub to coat. Add the garlic powder, soy sauce or tamari, and cheese, tossing to coat.
4. Pour the chips into the air fryer basket and cook for 3 minutes, shake the basket, and cook another 3 minutes, checking for crispness every minute. When done cooking, pour the kale chips onto paper towels and cool at least 5 minutes before serving.

Mustard Greens Chips With Curried Sauce

Servings: 4
Cooking Time: 20 Minutes
Ingredients:
- 1 cup plain yogurt
- 1 tbsp lemon juice
- 1 tbsp curry powder
- 1 bunch of mustard greens
- 2 tsp olive oil
- Sea salt to taste

Directions:
1. Preheat air fryer to 390°F. Using a sharp knife, remove and discard the ribs from the mustard greens. Slice the leaves into 2-3-inch pieces. Transfer them to a large bowl, then pour in olive oil and toss to coat. Air Fry for 5-6 minutes. Shake at least once. The chips should be crispy when finished. Sprinkle with a little bit of sea salt. Mix the yogurt, lemon juice, salt, and curry in a small bowl. Serve the greens with the sauce.

Glazed Chicken Wings

Servings: 4
Cooking Time: 25 Minutes
Ingredients:
- 8 chicken wings
- 3 tablespoons honey
- 1 tablespoons lemon juice
- 1 tablespoon low sodium chicken stock
- 2 cloves garlic, minced
- ¼ cup thinly sliced green onion
- ¾ cup low sodium barbecue sauce
- 4 stalks celery, cut into pieces

Directions:
1. Pat the chicken wings dry. Cut off the small end piece and discard or freeze it to make chicken stock later.
2. Put the wings into the air fryer basket. Air fry for 20 minutes, shaking the basket twice while cooking.
3. Meanwhile, combine the honey, lemon juice, chicken stock, and garlic, and whisk until combined.
4. Remove the wings from the air fryer and put into a 6″ x 2″ pan. Pour the sauce over the wings and toss gently to coat.
5. Return the pan to the air fryer and air fry for another 4 to 5 minutes or until the wings are glazed and a food thermometer registers 165°F. Sprinkle with the green onion and serve the wings with the barbecue sauce and celery.

Taquito Quesadillas

Servings: 4
Cooking Time: 35 Minutes
Ingredients:
- 8 tbsp Mexican blend shredded cheese
- 8 soft corn tortillas
- 2 tsp olive oil
- ¼ cup chopped cilantro

Directions:
1. Preheat air fryer at 350ºF. Spread cheese and coriander over 4 tortillas; top each with the remaining tortillas and brush the tops lightly with oil. Place quesadillas in the frying basket and Air Fry for 6 minutes. Serve warm.

Crabby Fries

Servings: 2
Cooking Time: 30 Minutes
Ingredients:
- 2 to 3 large russet potatoes, peeled and cut into ½-inch sticks
- 2 tablespoons vegetable oil
- 2 tablespoons butter
- 2 tablespoons flour
- 1 to 1½ cups milk
- ½ cup grated white Cheddar cheese
- pinch of nutmeg
- ½ teaspoon salt
- freshly ground black pepper
- 1 tablespoon Old Bay® Seasoning

Directions:
1. Bring a large saucepan of salted water to a boil on the stovetop while you peel and cut the potatoes. Blanch the potatoes in the boiling salted water for 4 minutes while you Preheat the air fryer to 400°F. Strain the potatoes and rinse them with cold water. Dry them well with a clean kitchen towel.
2. Toss the dried potato sticks gently with the oil and place them in the air fryer basket. Air-fry for 25 minutes, shaking the basket a few times while the fries cook to help them brown evenly.
3. While the fries are cooking, melt the butter in a medium saucepan. Whisk in the flour and cook for one minute. Slowly add 1 cup of milk, whisking constantly. Bring the mixture to a simmer and continue to whisk until it thickens. Remove the pan from the heat and stir in the Cheddar cheese. Add a pinch of nutmeg and season with salt and freshly ground black pepper. Transfer the warm cheese sauce to a serving dish. Thin with more milk if you want the sauce a little thinner.
4. As soon as the French fries have finished air-frying transfer them to a large bowl and season them with the Old Bay® Seasoning. Return the fries to the air fryer basket and air-fry for an additional 3 to 5 minutes. Serve immediately with the warm white Cheddar cheese sauce.

Beef Steak Sliders

Servings: 8
Cooking Time: 22 Minutes
Ingredients:
- 1 pound top sirloin steaks, about ¾-inch thick
- salt and pepper
- 2 large onions, thinly sliced
- 1 tablespoon extra-light olive oil
- 8 slider buns
- Horseradish Mayonnaise
- 1 cup light mayonnaise
- 4 teaspoons prepared horseradish

- 2 teaspoons Worcestershire sauce
- 1 teaspoon coarse brown mustard

Directions:
1. Place steak in air fryer basket and cook at 390°F for 6minutes. Turn and cook 6 more minutes for medium rare. If you prefer your steak medium, continue cooking for 3 minutes.
2. While the steak is cooking, prepare the Horseradish Mayonnaise by mixing all ingredients together.
3. When steak is cooked, remove from air fryer, sprinkle with salt and pepper to taste, and set aside to rest.
4. Toss the onion slices with the oil and place in air fryer basket. Cook at 390°F for 7 minutes, until onion rings are soft and browned.
5. Slice steak into very thin slices.
6. Spread slider buns with the horseradish mayo and pile on the meat and onions. Serve with remaining horseradish dressing for dipping.

Spinach And Crab Meat Cups

Servings:30
Cooking Time: 10 Minutes
Ingredients:
- 1 (6-ounce / 170-g) can crab meat, drained to yield ⅓ cup meat
- ¼ cup frozen spinach, thawed, drained, and chopped
- 1 clove garlic, minced
- ½ cup grated Parmesan cheese
- 3 tablespoons plain yogurt
- ¼ teaspoon lemon juice
- ½ teaspoon Worcestershire sauce
- 30 mini frozen phyllo shells, thawed
- Cooking spray

Directions:
1. Preheat the air fryer to 390ºF (199ºC).
2. Remove any bits of shell that might remain in the crab meat.
3. Mix the crab meat, spinach, garlic, and cheese together.
4. Stir in the yogurt, lemon juice, and Worcestershire sauce and mix well.
5. Spoon a teaspoon of filling into each phyllo shell.
6. Spray the air fryer basket with cooking spray and arrange half the shells in the basket. Air fry for 5 minutes. Repeat with the remaining shells.
7. Serve immediately.

Cherry Chipotle Bbq Chicken Wings

Servings: 2
Cooking Time: 12 Minutes
Ingredients:
- 1 teaspoon smoked paprika
- ½ teaspoon dry mustard powder
- 1 teaspoon dried oregano
- 1 teaspoon dried thyme
- ½ teaspoon chili powder
- 1 teaspoon salt
- 2 pounds chicken wings
- vegetable oil or spray
- salt and freshly ground black pepper
- 1 to 2 tablespoons chopped chipotle peppers in adobo sauce
- ⅓ cup cherry preserves ¼ cup tomato ketchup

Directions:
1. Combine the first six ingredients in a large bowl. Prepare the chicken wings by cutting off the wing tips and discarding (or freezing for chicken stock). Divide the drumettes from the win-gettes by cutting through the joint. Place the chicken wing pieces in the bowl with the spice mix. Toss or shake well to coat.
2. Preheat the air fryer to 400°F.
3. Spray the wings lightly with the vegetable oil and air-fry the wings in two batches for 10 minutes per batch, shaking the basket halfway through the cooking process. When both batches are done, toss all the wings back into the basket for another 2 minutes to heat through and finish cooking.
4. While the wings are air-frying, combine the chopped chipotle peppers, cherry preserves and ketchup in a bowl.
5. Remove the wings from the air fryer, toss them in the cherry chipotle BBQ sauce and serve with napkins!

Fried Olives

Servings: 5
Cooking Time: 10 Minutes
Ingredients:
- ⅓ cup All-purpose flour or tapioca flour
- 1 Large egg white(s)
- 1 tablespoon Brine from the olive jar
- ⅔ cup Plain dried bread crumbs (gluten-free, if a concern)
- 15 Large pimiento-stuffed green olives
- Olive oil spray

Directions:
1. Preheat the air fryer to 400°F.
2. Pour the flour in a medium-size zip-closed plastic bag. Whisk the egg white and pickle brine in a medium bowl until foamy. Spread out the bread crumbs on a dinner plate.
3. Pour all the olives into the bag with the flour, seal, and shake to coat the olives. Remove a couple of olives, shake off any excess flour, and drop them into the egg white mixture. Toss gently but well to coat. Pick them up one at a time and roll each in the bread crumbs until well coated on all sides, even the ends. Set them aside on a cutting board as you finish the rest. When done, coat the olives with olive oil spray on all sides.
4. Place the olives in the basket in one layer. Air-fry for 8 minutes, gently shaking the basket once halfway through the cooking process to rearrange the olives, until lightly browned.
5. Gently pour the olives onto a wire rack and cool for at least 10 minutes before serving. Once cooled, the olives may be stored in a sealed container in the fridge for up to 2 days. To rewarm them, set them in the basket of a heated 400°F air fryer undisturbed for 2 minutes.

Chicken Bites With Coconut

Servings: 4
Cooking Time: 20 Minutes
Ingredients:
- 2 teaspoons garlic powder
- 2 eggs
- Salt and black pepper to the taste
- ¾ cup coconut flakes
- Cooking spray
- 1 pound chicken breasts, skinless, boneless, and cubed

Directions:
1. In a bowl, put the coconut in and mix the eggs with garlic powder, salt and pepper in a second one.
2. Dredge the chicken cubes in eggs and then in coconut.
3. Arrange all the prepared chicken cubes to the basket.
4. Grease with cooking spray and cook them at 370 degrees F/ 185 degrees C for 20 minutes.
5. When cooked, place the chicken bites on a platter and serve as an appetizer.

Jalapeño Cheese Balls

Servings: 12
Cooking Time: 15 Minutes
Ingredients:
- 4 ounces cream cheese
- ⅓ cup shredded mozzarella cheese
- ⅓ cup shredded Cheddar cheese
- 2 jalapeños, finely chopped
- ½ cup bread crumbs
- 2 eggs
- ½ cup all-purpose flour
- Salt
- Pepper
- Cooking oil

Directions:
1. In a medium bowl, combine the cream cheese, mozzarella, Cheddar, and jalapeños. Mix well.
2. Form the cheese mixture into balls about an inch thick. Using a small ice cream scoop works well.
3. Arrange the cheese balls on a sheet pan and place in the freezer for 15 minutes. This will help the cheese balls maintain their shape while frying.
4. Spray the air fryer basket with cooking oil.
5. Place the bread crumbs in a small bowl. In another small bowl, beat the eggs. In a third small bowl, combine the flour with salt and pepper to taste, and mix well.
6. Remove the cheese balls from the freezer. Dip the cheese balls in the flour, then the eggs, and then the bread crumbs.
7. Place the cheese balls in the air fryer. (It is okay to stack them.) Spray with cooking oil. Cook for 8 minutes.
8. Open the air fryer and flip the cheese balls. I recommend flipping them instead of shaking so the balls maintain their form. Cook an additional 4 minutes.
9. Cool before serving.

Fried Brie With Cherry Tomatoes

Servings: 8
Cooking Time: 15 Minutes
Ingredients:
- 1 baguette*
- 2 pints red and yellow cherry tomatoes
- 1 tablespoon olive oil
- salt and freshly ground black pepper
- 1 teaspoon balsamic vinegar
- 1 tablespoon chopped fresh parsley
- 1 (8-ounce) wheel of Brie cheese
- olive oil
- ½ teaspoon Italian seasoning (optional)
- 1 tablespoon chopped fresh basil

Directions:
1. Preheat the air fryer to 350°F.
2. Start by making the crostini. Slice the baguette diagonally into ½-inch slices and brush the slices with olive oil on both sides. Air-fry the baguette slices at 350°F in batches for 6 minutes or until lightly browned on all sides. Set the bread aside on your serving platter.
3. Toss the cherry tomatoes in a bowl with the olive oil, salt and pepper. Air-fry the cherry tomatoes for 3 to 5 minutes, shaking the basket a few times during the cooking process. The tomatoes should be soft and some of them will burst open. Toss the warm tomatoes with the balsamic vinegar and fresh parsley and set aside.
4. Cut a circle of parchment paper the same size as your wheel of Brie cheese. Brush both sides of the Brie wheel with olive oil and sprinkle with Italian seasoning, if using. Place the circle of parchment paper on one side of the Brie and transfer the Brie to the air fryer basket, parchment side down. Air-fry at 350°F for 8 to 10 minutes, or until the Brie is slightly puffed and soft to the touch.
5. Watch carefully and remove the Brie before the rind cracks and the cheese starts to leak out. Transfer the wheel to your serving platter and top with the roasted tomatoes. Sprinkle with basil and serve with the toasted bread slices.

Veggie Cheese Bites

Servings: 4
Cooking Time: 8 Minutes
Ingredients:
- 2 cups riced vegetables (see the Note below)
- ½ cup shredded zucchini
- ½ teaspoon garlic powder
- ¼ teaspoon black pepper
- ¼ teaspoon salt
- 1 large egg
- ¾ cup shredded cheddar cheese
- ⅓ cup whole-wheat flour

Directions:
1. Preheat the air fryer to 350°F.
2. In a large bowl, mix together the riced vegetables, zucchini, garlic powder, pepper, and salt. Mix in the egg. Stir in the shredded cheese and whole-wheat flour until a thick, doughlike consistency forms. If you need to, add 1 teaspoon of flour at a time so you can mold the batter into balls.
3. Using a 1-inch scoop, portion the batter out into about 12 balls.
4. Liberally spray the air fryer basket with olive oil spray. Then place the veggie bites inside. Leave enough room between each bite so the air can flow around them.

5. Cook for 8 minutes, or until the outside is slightly browned. Depending on the size of your air fryer, you may need to cook these in batches.
6. Remove and let cool slightly before serving.

Spicy Kale Chips

Servings: 4
Cooking Time: 8 To 12 Minutes
Ingredients:
- 5 cups kale, large stems removed and chopped
- 2 teaspoons canola oil
- ¼ teaspoon smoked paprika
- ¼ teaspoon kosher salt
- Cooking spray

Directions:
1. Preheat the air fryer to 390ºF (199ºC).
2. In a large bowl, toss the kale, canola oil, smoked paprika, and kosher salt.
3. Spray the air fryer basket with cooking spray, then place half the kale in the basket and air fry for 2 to 3 minutes.
4. Shake the basket and air fry for 2 to 3 more minutes, or until crispy. Repeat this process with the remaining kale.
5. Remove the kale and allow to cool on a wire rack for 3 to 5 minutes before serving.

Spicy Turkey Meatballs

Servings: 18
Cooking Time: 15 Minutes
Ingredients:
- 1 pound 85/15 ground turkey
- 1 large egg, whisked
- ¼ cup sriracha hot chili sauce
- ½ teaspoon salt
- ½ teaspoon paprika
- ¼ teaspoon ground black pepper

Directions:
1. Combine all ingredients in a large bowl. Roll mixture into eighteen meatballs, about 3 tablespoons each.
2. Place meatballs into ungreased air fryer basket. Adjust the temperature to 375°F and set the timer for 15 minutes, shaking the basket three times during cooking. Meatballs will be done when browned and internal temperature is at least 165°F. Serve warm.

Black Bean Corn Dip

Servings: 4
Cooking Time: 10 Minutes
Ingredients:
- ½ (15-ounce) can black beans, drained and rinsed
- ½ (15-ounce) can corn, drained and rinsed
- ¼ cup chunky salsa
- 2 ounces reduced-fat cream cheese, softened
- ¼ cup shredded reduced-fat Cheddar cheese
- ½ teaspoon ground cumin
- ½ teaspoon paprika
- Salt
- Freshly ground black pepper

Directions:
1. In a medium bowl, mix together the black beans, corn, salsa, cream cheese, Cheddar cheese, cumin, and paprika. Season with salt and pepper and stir until well combined.
2. Spoon the mixture into an air fryer–safe baking dish.
3. Place baking dish in the fryer basket and air fry until heated through, about 10 minutes.
4. Serve hot.

Veggie Shrimp Toast

Servings: 4
Cooking Time: 3 To 6 Minutes
Ingredients:
- 8 large raw shrimp, peeled and finely chopped
- 1 egg white
- 2 garlic cloves, minced
- 3 tablespoons minced red bell pepper
- 1 medium celery stalk, minced
- 2 tablespoons cornstarch
- ¼ teaspoon Chinese five-spice powder
- 3 slices firm thin-sliced no-sodium whole-wheat bread

Directions:
1. Preheat the air fryer to 350ºF (177ºC).
2. In a small bowl, stir together the shrimp, egg white, garlic, red bell pepper, celery, cornstarch, and five-spice powder. Top each slice of bread with one-third of the shrimp mixture, spreading it evenly to the edges. With a sharp knife, cut each slice of bread into 4 strips.
3. Place the shrimp toasts in the air fryer basket in a single layer. You may need to cook them in batches. Air fry for 3 to 6 minutes, until crisp and golden brown.
4. Serve hot.

Fried Dill Pickle Chips

Servings: 4
Cooking Time: 12 Minutes
Ingredients:
- 1 cup All-purpose flour or tapioca flour
- 1 Large egg white(s)
- 1 tablespoon Brine from a jar of dill pickles
- 1 cup Seasoned Italian-style dried bread crumbs (gluten-free, if a concern)
- 2 Large dill pickle(s), cut into ½-inch-thick rounds
- Vegetable oil spray

Directions:
1. Preheat the air fryer to 400°F.
2. Set up and fill three shallow soup plates or small pie plates on your counter: one for the flour, one for the egg white(s) whisked with the pickle brine, and one for the bread crumbs.
3. Set a pickle round in the flour and turn it to coat all sides, even the edge. Gently shake off the excess flour, then dip the round into the egg-white mixture and turn to coat both sides and the edge. Let any excess egg white mixture slip back into the rest, then set the round in the bread crumbs and turn it to coat both sides as well as the edge. Set aside on a cutting board and soldier on, dipping and coating the remaining rounds. Lightly coat the coated rounds on both sides with vegetable oil spray.
4. Set the pickle rounds in the basket in one layer. Air-fry undisturbed for 7 minutes, or until golden brown and crunchy. Cool in the basket for a few minutes before using kitchen tongs to transfer the rounds to a serving platter.

Chapter 4: Bread And Breakfast Recipes

Tomatoes Hash With Cheddar Cheese
Servings: 4
Cooking Time: 25 Minutes
Ingredients:
- 2 tablespoons olive oil
- 1-pound tomatoes, chopped
- ½ pound cheddar, shredded
- 1½ tablespoons chives, chopped
- Salt and black pepper to the taste
- 6 eggs, whisked

Directions:
1. Gently grease a baking pan that fits in your air fryer with oil.
2. Before cooking, heat your air fryer with the baking pan to 350 degrees F/ 175 degrees C.
3. Add the whisked eggs, salt, chopped tomatoes, and pepper in the baking pan and whisk to combine well.
4. Top the mixture with the shredded cheddar cheese.
5. Sprinkle over with the chopped chives.
6. Cook in the preheated air fryer at 350 degrees F/ 175 degrees C for 25 minutes.
7. When cooked, remove from the air fryer.
8. Serve on plates and enjoy your breakfast.

Baked Cauliflower With Paprika
Servings: 4
Cooking Time: 20 Minutes
Ingredients:
- 2 cups cauliflower florets, separated
- 4 eggs, whisked
- 1 teaspoon sweet paprika
- 2 tablespoons butter, melted
- A pinch of salt and black pepper

Directions:
1. Before cooking, heat your air fryer to 320 degrees F/ 160 degrees C.
2. Gently grease a baking pan that fits in your air fryer with butter.
3. Place cauliflower florets on the pan and add the whisked eggs, salt, pepper, and paprika. Toss well to combine.
4. Cook in your air fryer for 20 minutes.
5. When the cooking time is up, remove from the air fryer and serve on plates.
6. Enjoy your breakfast.

Shakshuka-style Pepper Cups
Servings: 4
Cooking Time: 35 Minutes
Ingredients:
- 2 tbsp ricotta cheese crumbles
- 1 tbsp olive oil
- ½ yellow onion, diced
- 2 cloves garlic, minced
- ¼ tsp turmeric
- 1 can diced tomatoes
- 1 tbsp tomato paste
- ½ tsp smoked paprika
- ½ tsp salt
- ½ tsp granular sugar
- ¼ tsp ground cumin
- ¼ tsp ground coriander
- ⅛ tsp cayenne pepper
- 4 bell peppers
- 4 eggs
- 2 tbsp chopped basil

Directions:
1. Warm the olive oil in a saucepan over medium heat. Stir-fry the onion for 10 minutes or until softened. Stir in the garlic and turmeric for another 1 minute. Add diced tomatoes, tomato paste, paprika, salt, sugar, cumin, coriander, and cayenne. Remove from heat and stir.
2. Preheat air fryer to 350°F. Slice the tops off the peppers, and carefully remove the core and seeds. Put the bell peppers in the frying basket. Divide the tomato mixture among bell peppers. Crack 1 egg into tomato mixture in each pepper. Bake for 8-10 minutes. Sprinkle with ricotta cheese and cook for 1 more minute. Let rest 5 minutes. Garnish with fresh basil and serve immediately.

Green Beans Bowls
Servings: 2
Cooking Time: 20 Minutes
Ingredients:
- 1 cup green beans, halved
- 2 spring onions, chopped
- 4 eggs, whisked
- Salt and black pepper to the taste
- ¼ teaspoon cumin, ground

Directions:
1. Preheat the air fryer at 360°F, add all the ingredients, toss, cover, cook for 20 minutes, divide into bowls and serve for breakfast.

Pumpkin Empanadas
Servings: 4
Cooking Time: 30 Minutes
Ingredients:
- 1 can pumpkin purée
- ¼ cup white sugar
- 2 tsp cinnamon
- 1 tbsp brown sugar
- ½ tbsp cornstarch
- ¼ tsp vanilla extract
- 2 tbsp butter
- 4 empanada dough shells

Directions:
1. Place the puree in a pot and top with white and brown sugar, cinnamon, cornstarch, vanilla extract, 1 tbsp of water and butter and stir thoroughly. Bring to a boil over medium heat. Simmer for 4-5 minutes. Allow to cool.
2. Preheat air fryer to 360°F. Lay empanada shells flat on a clean counter. Spoon the pumpkin mixture into each of the shells. Fold the empanada shells over to cover completely. Seal the edges with water and press down with a fork to secure. Place the empanadas on the greased frying basket and Bake for 15 minutes, flipping once halfway through until golden. Serve hot.

Chocolate-hazelnut Bear Claws

Servings: 4
Cooking Time: 10 Minutes
Ingredients:
- 1 sheet frozen puff pastry dough, thawed
- 1 large egg, beaten
- ½ cup chocolate-hazelnut spread
- 1 tablespoon confectioners' sugar
- 1 tablespoon sliced almonds

Directions:
1. Preheat the air fryer to 320°F.
2. Unfold puff pastry and cut into four equal squares.
3. Brush egg evenly over puff pastry.
4. To make each bear claw, spread 2 tablespoons chocolate-hazelnut spread over a pastry square. Fold square horizontally to form a triangle and cut four evenly spaced slits about halfway through the top of folded square. Repeat with remaining spread and pastry squares.
5. Sprinkle confectioners' sugar and almonds over bear claws and place directly in the air fryer basket. Cook 10 minutes until puffy and golden brown. Serve warm.

Simple Tomato Cheese Sandwich

Servings: 2
Cooking Time: 6 Minutes
Ingredients:
- 8 tomato slices
- 4 bread slices
- 2 Swiss cheese slices
- Black pepper and salt as needed
- 4 teaspoons margarine

Directions:
1. On a flat kitchen surface, plug your air fryer and turn it on.
2. Preheat your air fryer for about 4-5 minutes to 355 degrees F/ 180 degrees C.
3. Gently coat an air frying basket with cooking oil or spray.
4. In the basket, place one cheese slice over one bread slice.
5. Then add 2 tomato slices on top. Sprinkle with salt and pepper. Top with another bread slice.
6. Insert the basket inside the air fryer. Let it cook for about 5 minutes.
7. Remove the basket; spread 2 teaspoons of margarine on both sides of each sandwich. Cook for about one more minute.
8. Serve warm!

Egg White Cups

Servings: 4
Cooking Time: 15 Minutes
Ingredients:
- 2 cups 100% liquid egg whites
- 3 tablespoons salted butter, melted
- ¼ teaspoon salt
- ¼ teaspoon onion powder
- ½ medium Roma tomato, cored and diced
- ½ cup chopped fresh spinach leaves

Directions:
1. In a large bowl, whisk egg whites with butter, salt, and onion powder. Stir in tomato and spinach, then pour evenly into four 4" ramekins greased with cooking spray.
2. Place ramekins into air fryer basket. Adjust the temperature to 300°F and set the timer for 15 minutes. Eggs will be fully cooked and firm in the center when done. Serve warm.

Oat And Chia Porridge

Servings: 4
Cooking Time: 5 Minutes
Ingredients:
- 2 tablespoons peanut butter
- 4 tablespoons honey
- 1 tablespoon butter, melted
- 4 cups milk
- 2 cups oats
- 1 cup chia seeds

Directions:
1. Preheat the air fryer to 390°F (199°C).
2. Put the peanut butter, honey, butter, and milk in a bowl and stir to mix. Add the oats and chia seeds and stir.
3. Transfer the mixture to a bowl and bake in the air fryer for 5 minutes. Give another stir before serving.

Orange-glazed Cinnamon Rolls

Servings:
Cooking Time: 30 Minutes
Ingredients:
- ½ cup + 1 tbsp evaporated cane sugar
- 1 cup Greek yogurt
- 2 cups flour
- 2 tsp baking powder
- ½ tsp salt
- 4 tbsp butter, softened
- 2 tsp ground cinnamon
- 4 oz cream cheese
- ¼ cup orange juice
- 1 tbsp orange zest
- 1 tbsp lemon juice

Directions:
1. Preheat air fryer to 350°F. Grease a baking dish. Combine yogurt, 1 ¾ cups flour, baking powder, salt, and ¼ cup sugar in a large bowl until dough forms. Dust the rest of the flour onto a flat work surface. Transfer the dough on the flour and roll into a ¼-inch thick rectangle. If the dough continues to stick to the rolling pin, add 1 tablespoon of flour and continue to roll.
2. Mix the butter, cinnamon, orange zest and 1 tbsp of sugar in a bowl. Spread the butter mixture evenly over the dough. Roll the dough into a log, starting with the long side. Tuck in the end. Cut the log into 6 equal pieces. Place in the baking dish swirl-side up. The rolls can touch each other. Bake in the air fryer for 10-12 minutes until the rolls are cooked through, and the tops are golden. Let cool for 10 minutes. While the rolls are cooling, combine cream cheese, the rest of the sugar, lemon juice, and orange juice in a small bowl. When the rolls are cool enough, top with glaze and serve.

Effortless Toffee Zucchini Bread
Servings: 6
Cooking Time: 30 Minutes
Ingredients:
- 1 cup flour
- ½ tsp baking soda
- ½ cup granulated sugar
- ¼ tsp ground cinnamon
- ¼ tsp nutmeg
- ¼ tsp salt
- 1/3 cup grated zucchini
- 1 egg
- 1 tbsp olive oil
- 1 tsp vanilla extract
- 2 tbsp English toffee bits
- 2 tbsp mini chocolate chips
- 1/2 cup chopped walnuts

Directions:
1. Preheat air fryer at 375°F. Combine the flour, baking soda, toffee bits, sugar, cinnamon, nutmeg, salt, zucchini, egg, olive oil, vanilla and chocolate chips in a bowl. Add the walnuts to the batter and mix until evenly distributed.
2. Pour the mixture into a greased cake pan. Place the pan in the fryer and Bake for 20 minutes. Let sit for 10 minutes until slightly cooled before slicing. Serve immediately.

Seedy Bagels
Servings: 4
Cooking Time: 25 Minutes
Ingredients:
- 1 ¼ cups flour
- 2 tsp baking powder
- ½ tsp salt
- 1 cup plain Greek yogurt
- 1 egg
- 1 tsp water
- 1 tsp poppy seeds
- ½ tsp white sesame seeds
- ½ tsp black sesame seeds
- ½ tsp coriander seeds
- 1 tsp cumin powder
- ½ tsp dried minced onion
- 1 tsp coarse salt

Directions:
1. Preheat air fryer to 300°F. Mix 1 cup flour, baking powder, salt, and cumin in a bowl. Stir in yogurt until a sticky dough forms. Separate the dough into 4 equal portions. Dust a flat work surface with ¼ cup flour. Roll out each portion of dough into a 6-inch log. Pull the two ends around to meet and press the ends together to seal.
2. Whisk egg and water in a small bowl. Prepare the topping in another small bowl by combining poppy seeds, white sesame seeds, black sesame seeds, coriander seeds, minced onion, and salt. Brush the egg wash on the bagel tops and sprinkle with the topping. Transfer to the frying basket and bake for 12 to 15 minutes until the tops are golden. Serve and enjoy.

Cinnamon Pear Oat Muffins
Servings: 6
Cooking Time: 30 Minutes + Cooling Time
Ingredients:
- ½ cup apple sauce
- 1 large egg
- 1/3 cup brown sugar
- 2 tbsp butter, melted
- ½ cup milk
- 11/3 cups rolled oats
- 1 tsp ground cinnamon
- ½ tsp baking powder
- Pinch of salt
- ½ cup diced peeled pears

Directions:
1. Preheat the air fryer to 350°F. Place the apple sauce, egg, brown sugar, melted butter, and milk into a bowl and mix to combine. Stir in the oats, cinnamon, baking powder, and salt and mix well, then fold in the pears.
2. Grease 6 silicone muffin cups with baking spray, then spoon the batter in equal portions into the cups. Put the muffin cups in the frying basket and Bake for 13-18 minutes or until set. Leave to cool for 15 minutes. Serve.

Breakfast Scramble Casserole
Servings: 4
Cooking Time: 10 Minutes
Ingredients:
- 6 slices bacon
- 6 eggs
- Salt
- Pepper
- Cooking oil
- ½ cup chopped red bell pepper
- ½ cup chopped green bell pepper
- ½ cup chopped onion
- ¾ cup shredded Cheddar cheese

Directions:
1. In a skillet over medium-high heat, cook the bacon, 5 to 7 minutes, flipping to evenly crisp. Drain on paper towels, crumble, and set aside.
2. In a medium bowl, whisk the eggs. Add salt and pepper to taste.
3. Spray a barrel pan with cooking oil. Make sure to cover the bottom and sides of the pan.
4. Add the beaten eggs, crumbled bacon, red bell pepper, green bell pepper, and onion to the pan. Place the pan in the air fryer. Cook for 6 minutes.
5. Open the air fryer and sprinkle the cheese over the casserole. Cook for an additional 2 minutes.
6. Cool before serving.

Vanilla French Toast Sticks
Servings: 6
Cooking Time: 10 Minutes
Ingredients:
- 4 slices Texas toast
- 1 tablespoon butter
- 1 egg

- 1 teaspoon stevia
- 1 teaspoon ground cinnamon
- ¼ cup milk
- 1 teaspoon vanilla extract
- Cooking oil

Directions:
1. Cut the bread into sticks and keep them aside.
2. Beat the rest of the recipe ingredients in a suitable wide bowl.
3. At 400 degrees F/ 205 degrees C, preheat your air fryer.
4. Dip the bread sticks in the prepared egg mixture and place in the air fryer.
5. Air fry the bread sticks for 10 minutes.
6. Serve.

Pretzels

Servings: 24
Cooking Time: 6 Minutes
Ingredients:
- 2 teaspoons yeast
- 1 cup water, warm
- 1 teaspoon sugar
- 1 teaspoon salt
- 2½ cups all-purpose flour
- 2 tablespoons butter, melted, plus more as needed
- 1 cup boiling water
- 1 tablespoon baking soda
- Coarse sea salt, to taste

Directions:
1. Combine the yeast and water in a small bowl. Combine the sugar, salt and flour in the bowl of a stand mixer. With the mixer running and using the dough hook, drizzle in the yeast mixture and melted butter and knead dough until smooth and elastic, about 10 minutes. Shape into a ball and let the dough rise for 1 hour.
2. Punch the dough down to release any air and divide the dough into 24 portions.
3. Roll each portion into a skinny rope using both hands on the counter and rolling from the center to the ends of the rope. Spin the rope into a pretzel shape (or tie the rope into a knot) and place the tied pretzels on a parchment lined baking sheet.
4. Preheat the air fryer to 350ºF (177ºC).
5. Combine the boiling water and baking soda in a shallow bowl and whisk to dissolve. Let the water cool so you can put the hands in it. Working in batches, dip the pretzels (top side down) into the baking soda mixture and let them soak for 30 seconds to a minute. Then remove the pretzels carefully and return them (top side up) to the baking sheet. Sprinkle the coarse salt on the top.
6. Air fry in batches for 3 minutes per side. When the pretzels are finished, brush them generously with the melted butter and enjoy them warm.

Lorraine Egg Cups

Servings: 6
Cooking Time: 30 Minutes
Ingredients:
- 3 eggs
- 2 tbsp half-and-half
- Garlic salt and pepper to taste
- 2 tbsp diced white onion
- 1 tbs dried parsley
- 3 oz cooked bacon, crumbled
- ¼ cup grated Swiss cheese
- 1 tomato, sliced

Directions:
1. Preheat air fryer at 350ºF. Whisk the egg, half-and-half, garlic sea salt, parsley and black pepper in a bowl. Divide onion, bacon, and cheese between 6 lightly greased silicone cupcakes. Spread the egg mixture between cupcakes evenly. Top each cup with 1 tomato slice. Place them in the frying basket and Bake for 8-10 minutes. Serve immediately.

Scrambled Eggs With Mushrooms

Servings: 4
Cooking Time: 11 Minutes
Ingredients:
- 4 eggs
- 4 strips of bacon
- 2 mushrooms
- black pepper, to taste
- salt, to taste

Directions:
1. Slice the mushrooms, season with salt, black pepper and sprinkle with oil.
2. Fry in an air fryer at about 360 degrees F/ 180 degrees C, shaking halfway.
3. Fry the bacon strips for 5-6 minutes, shaking halfway.
4. Now we are preparing the scramble. Beat the eggs, mix well, add black pepper and salt to taste. Sprinkle the bottom of the air fryer or a cooking dish with olive oil.
5. Cook the scramble at 360 degrees F/ 180 degrees C for 5 minutes, stirring every minute.
6. Serve and enjoy.

Mediterranean Granola

Servings: 6
Cooking Time: 40 Minutes
Ingredients:
- 1 cup rolled oats
- ¼ cup dried cherries, diced
- ¼ cup almond slivers
- ¼ cup hazelnuts, chopped
- ¼ cup pepitas
- ¼ cup hemp hearts
- 3 tbsp honey
- 1 tbsp olive oil
- 1 tsp ground cinnamon
- ¼ tsp ground nutmeg
- ¼ tsp salt
- 2 tbsp dark chocolate chips
- 3 cups Greek yogurt

Directions:
1. Preheat air fryer to 260ºF. Stir the oats, cherries, almonds, hazelnuts, pepitas, hemp hearts, 2 tbsp of honey,

olive oil, cinnamon, nutmeg, and salt in a bowl, mixing well. Pour the mixture onto the parchment-lined frying basket and spread it into a single layer. Bake for 25-30 minutes, shaking twice. Let the granola cool completely. Stir in the chocolate chips. Divide between 6 cups. Top with Greek yogurt and remaining honey to serve.

Egg Soufflé With Mushroom And Broccoli

Servings: 4
Cooking Time: 20 Minutes
Ingredients:
- 4 large eggs
- 1 teaspoon onion powder
- 1 teaspoon garlic powder
- 1 teaspoon red pepper, crushed
- ½ cup broccoli florets, chopped
- ½ cup mushrooms, chopped

Directions:
1. Sprinkle 4 ramekins with cooking spray and set aside.
2. In a suitable bowl, whisk eggs with onion powder, garlic powder, and red pepper.
3. Add mushrooms and broccoli and stir well.
4. Pour egg mixture into the prepared ramekins and place ramekins into the air fryer basket.
5. Cook at almost 350 degrees F/ 175 degrees C for almost 15 minutes. Make sure soufflé is cooked if soufflé is not cooked then cook for 5 minutes more.
6. Serve and enjoy.

Goat Cheese, Beet, And Kale Frittata

Servings: 6
Cooking Time: 20 Minutes
Ingredients:
- 6 large eggs
- ½ teaspoon garlic powder
- ¼ teaspoon black pepper
- ¼ teaspoon salt
- 1 cup chopped kale
- 1 cup cooked and chopped red beets
- ⅓ cup crumbled goat cheese

Directions:
1. Preheat the air fryer to 320°F.
2. In a medium bowl, whisk the eggs with the garlic powder, pepper, and salt. Mix in the kale, beets, and goat cheese.
3. Spray an oven-safe 7-inch springform pan with cooking spray. Pour the egg mixture into the pan and place it in the air fryer basket.
4. Cook for 20 minutes, or until the internal temperature reaches 145°F.
5. When the frittata is cooked, let it set for 5 minutes before removing from the pan.
6. Slice and serve immediately.

Simple Scotch Eggs

Servings:4
Cooking Time: 25 Minutes
Ingredients:
- 4 large hard boiled eggs
- 1 (12-ounce / 340-g) package pork sausage
- 8 slices thick-cut bacon
- Special Equipment:
- 4 wooden toothpicks, soaked in water for at least 30 minutes

Directions:
1. Slice the sausage into four parts and place each part into a large circle.
2. Put an egg into each circle and wrap it in the sausage. Put in the refrigerator for 1 hour.
3. Preheat the air fryer to 450°F (235°C).
4. Make a cross with two pieces of thick-cut bacon. Put a wrapped egg in the center, fold the bacon over top of the egg, and secure with a toothpick.
5. Air fry in the preheated air fryer for 25 minutes.
6. Serve immediately.

Cheesy Egg Bites

Servings: 6
Cooking Time: 35 Minutes
Ingredients:
- ½ cup shredded Muenster cheese
- 5 eggs, beaten
- 3 tbsp sour cream
- ½ tsp dried oregano
- Salt and pepper to taste
- 1/3 cup minced bell pepper
- 3 tbsp minced scallions

Directions:
1. Preheat the air fryer to 325°F. Make a foil sling: Fold an 18-inch-long piece of heavy-duty aluminum foil lengthwise into thirds. Combine the eggs, sour cream, oregano, salt, and pepper in a bowl. Add the bell peppers, scallions, and cheese and stir. Add the mixture to 6 egg bite cups, making sure to get some of the solids in each cup.
2. Put the egg bite pan on the sling you made and lower it into the fryer. Leave the foil in but bend down the edges so they fit. Bake the bites for 10-15 minutes or until a toothpick inserted into the center comes out clean. Remove the egg bite pan using the foil sling. Cool for 5 minutes, then turn the pan upside down over a plate to remove the egg bites. Serve warm.

Chicken Scotch Eggs

Servings:4
Cooking Time: 25 Minutes
Ingredients:
- 1 lb ground chicken
- 2 tsp Dijon mustard
- 2 tsp grated yellow onion
- 1 tbsp chopped chives
- 1 tbsp chopped parsley
- ⅛ tsp ground nutmeg
- 1 lemon, zested
- Salt and pepper to taste
- 4 hard-boiled eggs, peeled
- 1 egg, beaten
- 1 cup bread crumbs

- 2 tsp olive oil

Directions:
1. Preheat air fryer to 350ºF. In a bowl, mix the ground chicken, mustard, onion, chives, parsley, nutmeg, salt, lemon zest and pepper. Shape into 4 oval balls and form the balls evenly around the boiled eggs. Submerge them in the beaten egg and dip in the crumbs. Brush with olive oil. Place the scotch eggs in the frying basket and Air Fry for 14 minutes, flipping once. Serve hot.

Bacon And Broccoli Bread Pudding
Servings:4
Cooking Time: 48 Minutes
Ingredients:
- ½ pound (227 g) thick cut bacon, cut into ¼-inch pieces
- 3 cups brioche bread, cut into ½-inch cubes
- 2 tablespoons butter, melted
- 3 eggs
- 1 cup milk
- ½ teaspoon salt
- Freshly ground black pepper, to taste
- 1 cup frozen broccoli florets, thawed and chopped
- 1½ cups grated Swiss cheese

Directions:
1. Preheat the air fryer to 400ºF (204ºC).
2. Air fry the bacon for 8 minutes until crispy, shaking the basket a few times to help it air fry evenly. Remove the bacon and set it aside on a paper towel.
3. Air fry the brioche bread cubes for 2 minutes to dry and toast lightly.
4. Butter a cake pan. Combine all the ingredients in a large bowl and toss well. Transfer the mixture to the buttered cake pan, cover with aluminum foil and refrigerate the bread pudding overnight, or for at least 8 hours.
5. Remove the cake pan from the refrigerator an hour before you plan to bake and let it sit on the countertop to come to room temperature.
6. Preheat the air fryer to 330ºF (166ºC). Transfer the covered cake pan to the basket of the air fryer, lowering the pan into the basket. Fold the ends of the aluminum foil over the top of the pan before returning the basket to the air fryer.
7. Air fry for 20 minutes. Remove the foil and air fry for an additional 20 minutes. If the top browns a little too much before the custard has set, simply return the foil to the pan. The bread pudding has cooked through when a skewer inserted into the center comes out clean.
8. Serve warm.

Bacon Eggs
Servings: 2
Cooking Time: 5 Minutes
Ingredients:
- 2 eggs, hard-boiled, peeled
- 4 bacon slices
- ½ teaspoon avocado oil
- 1 teaspoon mustard

Directions:
1. Preheat the air fryer to 400°F. Then sprinkle the air fryer basket with avocado oil and place the bacon slices inside. Flatten them in one layer and cook for 2 minutes from each side. After this, cool the bacon to the room temperature. Wrap every egg into 2 bacon slices. Secure the eggs with toothpicks and place them in the air fryer. Cook the wrapped eggs for 1 minute at 400°F.

Dried Fruit Beignets
Servings:16
Cooking Time:5 To 8 Minutes
Ingredients:
- 1 teaspoon active quick-rising dry yeast
- ⅓ cup buttermilk
- 3 tablespoons packed brown sugar
- 1 egg
- 1½ cups whole-wheat pastry flour
- 3 tablespoons chopped dried cherries
- 3 tablespoons chopped golden raisins
- 2 tablespoons unsalted butter, melted
- Powdered sugar, for dusting (optional)

Directions:
1. In a medium bowl, mix the yeast with 3 tablespoons of water. Let it stand for 5 minutes, or until it bubbles.
2. Stir in the buttermilk, brown sugar, and egg until well mixed.
3. Stir in the pastry flour until combined.
4. With your hands, work the cherries and raisins into the dough. Let the mixture stand for 15 minutes.
5. Pat the dough into an 8-by-8-inch square and cut into 16 pieces. Gently shape each piece into a ball.
6. Drizzle the balls with the melted butter. Place them in a single layer in the air fryer basket so they don't touch. You may have to cook these in batches. Air-fry for 5 to 8 minutes, or until puffy and golden brown.
7. Dust with powdered sugar before serving, if desired.

Feta Stuffed Peppers With Broccoli
Servings: 2
Cooking Time: 40 Minutes
Ingredients:
- 4 eggs
- ½ cup cheddar cheese, grated
- 2 bell peppers cut in ½ and remove seeds
- ½ teaspoon garlic powder
- 1 teaspoon dried thyme
- ¼ cup feta cheese, crumbled
- ½ cup broccoli, cooked
- ¼ teaspoon black pepper
- ½ teaspoon salt

Directions:
1. At 325 degrees F/ 160 degrees C, preheat your air fryer.
2. Stuff feta and broccoli into the bell peppers halved.
3. Beat egg in a suitable bowl with seasoning and pour egg mixture into the black pepper halved over feta and broccoli.
4. Place bell pepper halved into the air fryer basket and cook for 35-40 minutes.
5. Top with cheddar, grated cheese and cook until cheese melted.
6. Serve and enjoy.

Blueberry Scones

Servings: 8
Cooking Time: 15 Minutes
Ingredients:
- ½ cup cold salted butter, divided
- 2 cups all-purpose flour
- ½ cup granulated sugar
- 1 teaspoon baking powder
- 1 large egg
- ½ cup whole milk
- ½ cup fresh blueberries

Directions:
1. Chill 6 tablespoons butter in the freezer 10 minutes. In a small microwave-safe bowl, microwave remaining 2 tablespoons butter 30 seconds until melted.
2. Preheat the air fryer to 320°F. Cut parchment paper to fit the air fryer basket.
3. In a large bowl, mix flour, sugar, and baking powder.
4. Add egg and milk and stir until a sticky dough forms.
5. Remove butter from freezer and grate into bowl. Fold grated butter into dough until just combined.
6. Fold in blueberries. Turn dough onto a lightly floured surface. Sprinkle dough with flour and fold a couple of times, then gently form into a 6" round. Cut into eight triangles.
7. Place scones on parchment in the air fryer basket, leaving at least 2" of space between each, working in batches as necessary.
8. Brush each scone with melted butter and cook 15 minutes until scones are dark golden brown and crispy on the edges, and a toothpick inserted into the center comes out clean. Serve warm.

Strawberry Streusel Muffins

Servings: 12
Cooking Time: 14 Minutes
Ingredients:
- 1¾ cups all-purpose flour
- ½ cup granulated sugar
- 2 teaspoons baking powder
- ¼ teaspoon baking soda
- ½ teaspoon salt
- ½ cup plain yogurt
- ½ cup milk
- ¼ cup vegetable oil
- 2 large eggs
- 1 teaspoon vanilla extract
- ½ cup freeze-dried strawberries
- 2 tablespoons brown sugar
- ¼ cup oats
- 2 tablespoons butter

Directions:
1. Preheat the air fryer to 330°F.
2. In a large bowl, whisk together the flour, sugar, baking powder, baking soda, and salt; set aside.
3. In a separate bowl, whisk together the yogurt, milk, vegetable oil, eggs, and vanilla extract.
4. Make a well in the dry ingredients; then pour the wet ingredients into the well of the dry ingredients. Using a rubber spatula, mix the ingredients for 1 minute or until slightly lumpy. Fold in the strawberries.
5. In a small bowl, use your fingers to mix together the brown sugar, oats, and butter until coarse crumbles appear. Divide the mixture in half.
6. Using silicone muffin liners, fill 6 muffin liners two-thirds full.
7. Crumble half of the streusel topping onto the first batch of muffins.
8. Carefully place the muffin liners in the air fryer basket and bake for 14 minutes (or until the tops are browned and a toothpick inserted in the center comes out clean). Carefully remove the muffins from the basket and repeat with the remaining batter and topping.
9. Serve warm.

Tasty Hash Browns With Radish

Servings: 4
Cooking Time: 13 Minutes
Ingredients:
- 1-pound radishes, washed and cut off roots
- 1 tablespoon olive oil
- ½ teaspoon paprika
- ½ teaspoon onion powder
- ½ teaspoon garlic powder
- 1 medium onion
- ¼ teaspoon black pepper
- ¾ teaspoon salt

Directions:
1. Slice onion and radishes using a mandolin slicer.
2. Add sliced onion and radishes in a suitable mixing bowl and toss with olive oil.
3. Transfer onion and radish slices in air fryer basket and cook at almost 360 degrees F/ 180 degrees C for 8 minutes. Shake basket twice.
4. Return onion and radish slices in a suitable mixing bowl and toss with seasonings.
5. Again, cook onion and radish slices in air fryer basket for 5 minutes at 400 degrees F/ 205 degrees C. Shake the basket halfway through.
6. Serve and enjoy.

Herbed Omelet

Servings: 4
Cooking Time: 20 Minutes
Ingredients:
- 10 eggs, whisked
- ½ cup cheddar, shredded
- 2 tablespoons parsley, chopped
- 2 tablespoons chives, chopped
- 2 tablespoons basil, chopped
- Cooking spray
- Salt and black pepper to the taste

Directions:
1. Mix all ingredients except the cheese and the cooking spray together in a bowl until whisked well.
2. Before cooking, heat your air fryer to 350 degrees F/ 175 degrees C.
3. Grease the baking pan with cooking spray.
4. Pour the egg mixture inside the pan.
5. Cook in your air fryer for 20 minutes.
6. Serve on plates.

Egg Muffins

Servings: 4
Cooking Time: 11 Minutes
Ingredients:
- 4 eggs
- salt and pepper
- olive oil
- 4 English muffins, split
- 1 cup shredded Colby Jack cheese
- 4 slices ham or Canadian bacon

Directions:
1. Preheat air fryer to 390°F.
2. Beat together eggs and add salt and pepper to taste. Spray air fryer baking pan lightly with oil and add eggs. Cook for 2minutes, stir, and continue cooking for 4minutes, stirring every minute, until eggs are scrambled to your preference. Remove pan from air fryer.
3. Place bottom halves of English muffins in air fryer basket. Take half of the shredded cheese and divide it among the muffins. Top each with a slice of ham and one-quarter of the eggs. Sprinkle remaining cheese on top of the eggs. Use a fork to press the cheese into the egg a little so it doesn't slip off before it melts.
4. Cook at 360°F for 1 minute. Add English muffin tops and cook for 4minutes to heat through and toast the muffins.

Coconut & Peanut Rice Cereal

Servings: 4
Cooking Time: 15 Minutes
Ingredients:
- 4 cups rice cereal
- 1 cup coconut shreds
- 2 tbsp peanut butter
- 1 tsp vanilla extract
- ¼ cup honey
- 1 tbsp light brown sugar
- 2 tsp ground cinnamon
- ¼ cup hazelnut flour
- Salt to taste

Directions:
1. Preheat air fryer at 350ºF. Combine the rice cereal, coconut shreds, peanut butter, vanilla extract, honey, brown sugar, cinnamon, hazelnut flour, and salt in a bowl. Press mixture into a greased cake pan. Place cake pan in the frying basket and Air Fry for 5 minutes, stirring once. Let cool completely for 10 minutes before crumbling. Store it into an airtight container up to 5 days.

Fruity Blueberry Muffin Cups

Servings: 2
Cooking Time: 30 Minutes
Ingredients:
- ½ cup white sugar
- 1 ½ cups all-purpose flour
- 2 tsp baking powder
- ½ tsp salt
- 1/3 cup vegetable oil
- 1 egg
- ¼ cup unsweetened yogurt
- 2 tsp vanilla extract
- 1 cup blueberries
- 1 banana, mashed
- 1 tbsp brown sugar

Directions:
1. Preheat air fryer to 350°F. In a bowl, add 1 tbsp of flour and throw in the blueberries and bananas to coat. In another bowl, combine white sugar, baking powder, remaining flour and salt. Mix well. In a third bowl, add oil, egg, yogurt and vanilla. Beat until well combined.
2. Add the wet into the dry mixture and whisk with a fork. Put in the blueberries-banana mix and stir. Spoon the batter into muffin cups, 3/4th way up. Top with brown sugar and Bake for 10-12 minutes until a toothpick inserted comes out clean.

Classic Cinnamon Rolls

Servings: 4
Cooking Time: 6 Minutes
Ingredients:
- 1½ cups all-purpose flour
- 1 tablespoon granulated sugar
- 2 teaspoons baking powder
- ½ teaspoon salt
- 4 tablespoons butter, divided
- ½ cup buttermilk
- 2 tablespoons brown sugar
- 1 teaspoon cinnamon
- 1 cup powdered sugar
- 2 tablespoons milk

Directions:
1. Preheat the air fryer to 360°F.
2. In a large bowl, stir together the flour, sugar, baking powder, and salt. Cut in 3 tablespoons of the butter with a pastry blender or two knives until coarse crumbs remain. Stir in the buttermilk until a dough forms.
3. Place the dough onto a floured surface and roll out into a square shape about ½ inch thick.
4. Melt the remaining 1 tablespoon of butter in the microwave for 20 seconds. Using a pastry brush or your fingers, spread the melted butter onto the dough.
5. In a small bowl, mix together the brown sugar and cinnamon. Sprinkle the mixture across the surface of the dough. Roll the dough up, forming a long log. Using a pastry cutter or sharp knife, cut 10 cinnamon rolls.
6. Carefully place the cinnamon rolls into the air fryer basket. Then bake at 360°F for 6 minutes or until golden brown.
7. Meanwhile, in a small bowl, whisk together the powdered sugar and milk.
8. Plate the cinnamon rolls and drizzle the glaze over the surface before serving.

English Scones

Servings: 8
Cooking Time: 8 Minutes
Ingredients:
- 2 cups all-purpose flour

- 1 tablespoon baking powder
- ½ teaspoon salt
- 2 tablespoons sugar
- ¼ cup unsalted butter
- ⅔ cup plus 1 tablespoon whole milk, divided

Directions:
1. Preheat the air fryer to 380°F.
2. In a large bowl, whisk together the flour, baking powder, salt, and sugar. Using a pastry blender or your fingers, cut in the butter until pea-size crumbles appear. Make a well in the center and pour in ⅔ cup of the milk. Quickly mix the batter until a ball forms. Knead the dough 3 times.
3. Place the dough onto a floured surface and, using your hands or a rolling pin, flatten the dough until it's ¾ inch thick. Using a biscuit cutter or drinking glass, cut out 10 circles, reforming the dough and flattening as needed to use up the batter.
4. Brush the tops lightly with the remaining 1 tablespoon of milk.
5. Place the scones into the air fryer basket. Cook for 8 minutes or until golden brown and cooked in the center.

Canadian Bacon & Cheese Sandwich

Servings: 1
Cooking Time: 30 Minutes
Ingredients:
- 1 English muffin, halved
- 1 egg
- 1 Canadian bacon slice
- 1 slice provolone cheese

Directions:
1. Preheat air fryer to 350°F. Put the muffin, crusty side up, in the frying basket. Place a slice of bacon next to the muffins and Bake for 5 minutes. Flip the bacon and muffins, and lay a slice of provolone cheese on top of the muffins. Beat the egg in a small heatproof bowl.
2. Add the bowl in the frying basket next to the bacon and muffins and Bake for 15 minutes, or until the cheese melts, bacon is crispy and eggs set. Remove the muffin to a plate, layer a slice of bacon, then the egg and top with the second toasted muffin.

Spinach Frittata With Mozzarella

Servings: 1
Cooking Time: 8 Minutes
Ingredients:
- 3 eggs
- 1 cup spinach, chopped
- 1 small onion, minced
- 2 tablespoon mozzarella cheese, grated
- Black pepper
- Salt

Directions:
1. At 350 degrees F/ 175 degrees C, preheat your air fryer. Spray air fryer basket with cooking spray.
2. In a suitable bowl, whisk eggs with remaining ingredients until well combined.
3. Pour the prepared egg mixture into the pan and place pan in the preheated air fryer basket.
4. Cook frittata for 8 minutes or until set. Serve and enjoy.

Lime Muffins

Servings: 6
Cooking Time: 30 Minutes
Ingredients:
- 1 ½ tbsp butter, softened
- 6 tbsp sugar
- 1 egg
- 1 egg white
- 1 tsp vanilla extract
- 1 tsp lime juice
- 1 lime, zested
- 5 oz Greek yogurt
- ¾ cup + 2 tbsp flour
- ¾ cup raspberries

Directions:
1. Beat butter and sugar in a mixer for 2 minutes at medium speed. In a separate bowl, whisk together the egg, egg white and vanilla. Pour into the mixer bowl, add lime juice and zest. Beat until combined. At a low speed, add yogurt then flour. Fold in the raspberries. Divide the mixture into 6 greased muffin cups using an ice cream scoop. The cups should be filled about ¾ of the way.
2. Preheat air fryer to 300°F. Put the muffins into the air fryer and Bake for 15 minutes until the tops are golden and a toothpick in the center comes out clean. Allow to cool before serving.

Mushroom & Cavolo Nero Egg Muffins

Servings: 6
Cooking Time: 20 Minutes
Ingredients:
- 8 oz baby Bella mushrooms, sliced
- 6 eggs, beaten
- 1 garlic clove, minced
- Salt and pepper to taste
- ½ tsp chili powder
- 1 cup cavolo nero
- 2 scallions, diced

Directions:
1. Preheat air fryer to 320°F. Place the eggs, garlic, salt, pepper, and chili powder in a bowl and beat until well combined. Fold in the mushrooms, cavolo nero, and scallions. Divide the mixture between greased muffin cups. Place into the air fryer and Bake for 12-15 minutes, or until the eggs are set. Cool for 5 minutes. Enjoy!

Buttery Scallops

Servings: 2
Cooking Time: 8 Minutes
Ingredients:
- 1 lb jumbo scallops
- 1 tbsp fresh lemon juice
- 2 tbsp butter, melted

Directions:

1. Preheat the air fryer to 400°F.
2. In a small bowl, mix together lemon juice and butter.
3. Brush scallops with lemon juice and butter mixture and place into the air fryer basket.
4. Cook scallops for 4 minutes. Turn halfway through.
5. Again brush scallops with lemon butter mixture and cook for 4 minutes more. Turn halfway through.
6. Serve and enjoy.

Three-berry Dutch Pancake

Servings: 4
Cooking Time:12 To 16 Minutes
Ingredients:
- 2 egg whites
- 1 egg
- ½ cup whole-wheat pastry flour
- ½ cup 2 percent milk
- 1 teaspoon pure vanilla extract
- 1 tablespoon unsalted butter, melted
- 1 cup sliced fresh strawberries
- ½ cup fresh blueberries
- ½ cup fresh raspberries

Directions:
1. In a medium bowl, use an eggbeater or hand mixer to quickly mix the egg whites, egg, pastry flour, milk, and vanilla until well combined.
2. Use a pastry brush to grease the bottom of a 6-by-2-inch pan with the melted butter. Immediately pour in the batter and put the basket back in the fryer. Bake for 12 to 16 minutes, or until the pancake is puffed and golden brown.
3. Remove the pan from the air fryer; the pancake will fall. Top with the strawberries, blueberries, and raspberries. Serve immediately.

Nutty Whole Wheat Muffins

Servings: 8
Cooking Time: 11 Minutes
Ingredients:
- ½ cup whole-wheat flour, plus 2 tablespoons
- ¼ cup oat bran
- 2 tablespoons flaxseed meal
- ¼ cup brown sugar
- ½ teaspoon baking soda
- ½ teaspoon baking powder
- ¼ teaspoon salt
- ½ teaspoon cinnamon
- ½ cup buttermilk
- 2 tablespoons melted butter
- 1 egg
- ½ teaspoon pure vanilla extract
- ½ cup grated carrots
- ¼ cup chopped pecans
- ¼ cup chopped walnuts
- 1 tablespoon pumpkin seeds
- 1 tablespoon sunflower seeds
- 16 foil muffin cups, paper liners removed
- cooking spray

Directions:

1. Preheat air fryer to 330°F.
2. In a large bowl, stir together the flour, bran, flaxseed meal, sugar, baking soda, baking powder, salt, and cinnamon.
3. In a medium bowl, beat together the buttermilk, butter, egg, and vanilla. Pour into flour mixture and stir just until dry ingredients moisten. Do not beat.
4. Gently stir in carrots, nuts, and seeds.
5. Double up the foil cups so you have 8 total and spray with cooking spray.
6. Place 4 foil cups in air fryer basket and divide half the batter among them.
7. Cook at 330°F for 11minutes or until toothpick inserted in center comes out clean.
8. Repeat step 7 to cook remaining 4 muffins.

Roasted Tomato And Cheddar Rolls

Servings: 12
Cooking Time: 55 Minutes
Ingredients:
- 4 Roma tomatoes
- ½ clove garlic, minced
- 1 tablespoon olive oil
- ¼ teaspoon dried thyme
- salt and freshly ground black pepper
- 4 cups all-purpose flour
- 1 teaspoon active dry yeast
- 2 teaspoons sugar
- 2 teaspoons salt
- 1 tablespoon olive oil
- 1 cup grated Cheddar cheese, plus more for sprinkling at the end
- 1½ cups water

Directions:
1. Cut the Roma tomatoes in half, remove the seeds with your fingers and transfer to a bowl. Add the garlic, olive oil, dried thyme, salt and freshly ground black pepper and toss well.
2. Preheat the air fryer to 390°F.
3. Place the tomatoes, cut side up in the air fryer basket and air-fry for 10 minutes. The tomatoes should just start to brown. Shake the basket to redistribute the tomatoes, and air-fry for another 5 to 10 minutes at 330°F until the tomatoes are no longer juicy. Let the tomatoes cool and then rough chop them.
4. Combine the flour, yeast, sugar and salt in the bowl of a stand mixer. Add the olive oil, chopped roasted tomatoes and Cheddar cheese to the flour mixture and start to mix using the dough hook attachment. As you're mixing, add 1¼ cups of the water, mixing until the dough comes together. Continue to knead the dough with the dough hook for another 10 minutes, adding enough water to the dough to get it to the right consistency.
5. Transfer the dough to an oiled bowl, cover with a clean kitchen towel and let it rest and rise until it has doubled in volume – about 1 to 2 hours. Then, divide the dough into 12 equal portions. Roll each portion of dough into a ball. Lightly coat each dough ball with oil and let the dough balls rest and rise a second time, covered

lightly with plastic wrap for 45 minutes. (Alternately, you can place the rolls in the refrigerator overnight and take them out 2 hours before you bake them.)
6. Preheat the air fryer to 360°F.
7. Spray the dough balls and the air fryer basket with a little olive oil. Place three rolls at a time in the basket and bake for 10 minutes. Add a little grated Cheddar cheese on top of the rolls for the last 2 minutes of air frying for an attractive finish.

Cheddar-ham-corn Muffins

Servings: 8
Cooking Time: 8 Minutes
Ingredients:
- ¾ cup yellow cornmeal
- ¼ cup flour
- 1½ teaspoons baking powder
- ¼ teaspoon salt
- 1 egg, beaten
- 2 tablespoons canola oil
- ½ cup milk
- ½ cup shredded sharp Cheddar cheese
- ½ cup diced ham
- 8 foil muffin cups, liners removed and sprayed with cooking spray

Directions:
1. Preheat air fryer to 390°F.
2. In a medium bowl, stir together the cornmeal, flour, baking powder, and salt.
3. Add egg, oil, and milk to dry ingredients and mix well.
4. Stir in shredded cheese and diced ham.
5. Divide batter among the muffin cups.
6. Place 4 filled muffin cups in air fryer basket and bake for 5minutes.
7. Reduce temperature to 330°F and bake for 1 to 2minutes or until toothpick inserted in center of muffin comes out clean.
8. Repeat steps 6 and 7 to cook remaining muffins.

Baked Potato Breakfast Boats

Servings:4
Cooking Time: 20 Minutes
Ingredients:
- 2 large russet potatoes, scrubbed
- Olive oil
- Salt
- Freshly ground black pepper
- 4 eggs
- 2 tablespoons chopped, cooked bacon
- 1 cup shredded cheddar cheese

Directions:
1. Poke holes in the potatoes with a fork and microwave on full power for 5 minutes.
2. Turn potatoes over and cook an additional 3 to 5 minutes, or until the potatoes are fork tender.
3. Cut the potatoes in half lengthwise and use a spoon to scoop out the inside of the potato. Be careful to leave a layer of potato so that it makes a sturdy "boat."
4. Lightly spray the fryer basket with olive oil. Spray the skin side of the potatoes with oil and sprinkle with salt and pepper to taste.
5. Place the potato skins in the fryer basket skin side down. Crack one egg into each potato skin.
6. Sprinkle ½ tablespoon of bacon pieces and ¼ cup of shredded cheese on top of each egg. Sprinkle with salt and pepper to taste.
7. Air fry until the yolk is slightly runny, 5 to 6 minutes, or until the yolk is fully cooked, 7 to 10 minutes.

Breakfast Potatoes

Servings:6
Cooking Time: 20 Minutes
Ingredients:
- 1½ teaspoons olive oil, divided, plus more for misting
- 4 large potatoes, skins on, cut into cubes
- 2 teaspoons seasoned salt, divided
- 1 teaspoon minced garlic, divided
- 2 large green or red bell peppers, cut into 1-inch chunks
- ½ onion, diced

Directions:
1. Lightly mist the fryer basket with olive oil.
2. In a medium bowl, toss the potatoes with ½ teaspoon of olive oil. Sprinkle with 1 teaspoon of seasoned salt and ½ teaspoon of minced garlic. Stir to coat.
3. Place the seasoned potatoes in the fryer basket in a single layer.
4. Cook for 5 minutes. Shake the basket and cook for another 5 minutes.
5. Meanwhile, in a medium bowl, toss the bell peppers and onion with the remaining ½ teaspoon of olive oil.
6. Sprinkle the peppers and onions with the remaining 1 teaspoon of seasoned salt and ½ teaspoon of minced garlic. Stir to coat.
7. Add the seasoned peppers and onions to the fryer basket with the potatoes.
8. Cook for 5 minutes. Shake the basket and cook for an additional 5 minutes.

Baked Eggs With Bacon-tomato Sauce

Servings: 1
Cooking Time: 12 Minutes
Ingredients:
- 1 teaspoon olive oil
- 2 tablespoons finely chopped onion
- 1 teaspoon chopped fresh oregano
- pinch crushed red pepper flakes
- 1 (14-ounce) can crushed or diced tomatoes
- salt and freshly ground black pepper
- 2 slices of bacon, chopped
- 2 large eggs
- ¼ cup grated Cheddar cheese
- fresh parsley, chopped

Directions:
1. Start by making the tomato sauce. Preheat a medium saucepan over medium heat on the stovetop. Add the

olive oil and sauté the onion, oregano and pepper flakes for 5 minutes. Add the tomatoes and bring to a simmer. Season with salt and freshly ground black pepper and simmer for 10 minutes.

2. Meanwhile, Preheat the air fryer to 400°F and pour a little water into the bottom of the air fryer drawer. (This will help prevent the grease that drips into the bottom drawer from burning and smoking.) Place the bacon in the air fryer basket and air-fry at 400°F for 5 minutes, shaking the basket every once in a while.

3. When the bacon is almost crispy, remove it to a paper-towel lined plate and rinse out the air fryer drawer, draining away the bacon grease.

4. Transfer the tomato sauce to a shallow 7-inch pie dish. Crack the eggs on top of the sauce and scatter the cooked bacon back on top. Season with salt and freshly ground black pepper and transfer the pie dish into the air fryer basket. You can use an aluminum foil sling to help with this by taking a long piece of aluminum foil, folding it in half lengthwise twice until it is roughly 26-inches by 3-inches. Place this under the pie dish and hold the ends of the foil to move the pie dish in and out of the air fryer basket. Tuck the ends of the foil beside the pie dish while it cooks in the air fryer.

5. Air-fry at 400°F for 5 minutes, or until the eggs are almost cooked to your liking. Sprinkle cheese on top and air-fry for an additional 2 minutes. When the cheese has melted, remove the pie dish from the air fryer, sprinkle with a little chopped parsley and let the eggs cool for a few minutes – just enough time to toast some buttered bread in your air fryer!

Creamy Baked Sausage

Servings: 6
Cooking Time: 23 Minutes

Ingredients:
- 2 jalapeno peppers, sliced
- 7 ounces ground sausages
- 1 teaspoon dill seeds
- 3 ounces Colby Jack Cheese, shredded
- 4 eggs, beaten
- 1 tablespoon cream cheese
- ½ teaspoon salt
- 1 teaspoon butter, softened
- 1 teaspoon olive oil

Directions:
1. Before cooking, heat your skillet and then pour the olive oil inside the skillet.
2. Place salt and ground sausage in the skillet and cook for 5 to 8 minutes on medium heat.
3. During cooking, stir the mixture from time to time.
4. At the same time, heat your air fryer ahead of time to 400 degrees F/ 205 degrees C.
5. Using softened butter, grease your air fryer basket.
6. Transfer the cooked sausage inside the greased basket and flatten the mixture.
7. Sprinkle the sliced jalapeno pepper on the top of the mixture.
8. Then add shredded cheese.
9. In a second bowl, beat the eggs together and mix together with cream cheese.
10. Pour the egg-cheese mixture over the sausage mixture.
11. Sprinkle with dill seeds.
12. Cook the egg-cheese mixture in your air fryer at 400 degrees F/ 205 degrees C for 16 minutes.
13. If prefer a crunchy crust, cook for a few more minutes.

Chapter 5: Vegetarians Recipes

Roasted Cauliflower

Servings: 2
Cooking Time: 20 Minutes
Ingredients:
- medium head cauliflower
- 2 tbsp. salted butter, melted
- 1 medium lemon
- 1 tsp. dried parsley
- ½ tsp. garlic powder

Directions:
1. Having removed the leaves from the cauliflower head, brush it with the melted butter. Grate the rind of the lemon over it and then drizzle some juice. Finally add the parsley and garlic powder on top.
2. Transfer the cauliflower to the basket of the fryer.
3. Cook for fifteen minutes at 350°F, checking regularly to ensure it doesn't overcook. The cauliflower is ready when it is hot and fork tender.
4. Take care when removing it from the fryer, cut up and serve.

Sweet And Sour Brussel Sprouts

Servings:2
Cooking Time:10 Minutes
Ingredients:
- 2 cups Brussels sprouts, trimmed and halved lengthwise
- 1 tablespoon balsamic vinegar
- 1 tablespoon maple syrup
- Salt, as required

Directions:
1. Preheat the Air fryer to 400°F and grease an Air fryer basket.
2. Mix all the ingredients in a bowl and toss to coat well.
3. Arrange the Brussel sprouts in the Air fryer basket and cook for about 10 minutes, shaking once halfway through.
4. Dish out in a bowl and serve hot.

Spinach And Feta Pinwheels

Servings:4
Cooking Time: 15 Minutes
Ingredients:
- 1 sheet frozen puff pastry, thawed
- 3 ounces full-fat cream cheese, softened
- 1 bag frozen spinach, thawed and drained
- ¼ teaspoon salt
- ⅓ cup crumbled feta cheese
- 1 large egg, whisked

Directions:
1. Preheat the air fryer to 320°F. Unroll puff pastry into a flat rectangle.
2. In a medium bowl, mix cream cheese, spinach, and salt until well combined.
3. Spoon cream cheese mixture onto pastry in an even layer, leaving a ½" border around the edges.
4. Sprinkle feta evenly across dough and gently press into filling to secure. Roll lengthwise to form a log shape.
5. Cut the roll into twelve 1" pieces. Brush with egg. Place in the air fryer basket and cook 15 minutes, turning halfway through cooking time.
6. Let cool 5 minutes before serving.

Ricotta Veggie Potpie

Servings: 4
Cooking Time: 30 Minutes
Ingredients:
- 1 ¼ cup flour
- ¾ cup ricotta cheese
- 1 tbsp olive oil
- 1 potato, peeled and diced
- ¼ cup diced mushrooms
- ¼ cup diced carrots
- ¼ cup diced celery
- ¼ cup diced yellow onion
- 1 garlic clove, minced
- 1 tbsp unsalted butter
- 1 cup milk
- ½ tsp ground black pepper
- 1 tsp dried thyme
- 2 tbsp dill, chopped

Directions:
1. Preheat air fryer to 350°F. Combine 1 cup flour and ricotta cheese in a medium bowl and stir until the dough comes together. Heat oil over medium heat in a small skillet. Stir in potato, mushroom, carrots, dill, thyme, celery, onion, and garlic. Cook for 4-5 minutes, often stirring, until the onions are soft and translucent.
2. Add butter and melt, then stir in the rest of the flour. Slowly pour in the milk and keep stirring. Simmer for 5 minutes until the sauce has thickened, then stir in pepper and thyme. Spoon the vegetable mixture into four 6-ounce ramekins. Cut the dough into 4 equal sections and work it into rounds that fit over the size of the ramekins. Top the ramekins with the dough, then place the ramekins in the frying basket. Bake for 10 minutes until the crust is golden. Serve hot and enjoy.

Easy Baked Root Veggies

Servings:4
Cooking Time: 45 Minutes
Ingredients:
- ¼ cup olive oil
- 1 head broccoli, cut into florets
- 1 tablespoon dry onion powder
- 2 sweet potatoes, peeled and cubed
- 4 carrots, cut into chunks
- 4 zucchinis, sliced thickly
- salt and pepper to taste

Directions:
1. Preheat the air fryer to 400°F.
2. In a baking dish that can fit inside the air fryer, mix all the ingredients and bake for 45 minutes or until the vegetables are tender and the sides have browned.

Powerful Jackfruit Fritters

Servings: 4
Cooking Time: 30 Minutes
Ingredients:
- 1 can jackfruit, chopped
- 1 egg, beaten
- 1 tbsp Dijon mustard
- 1 tbsp mayonnaise
- 1 tbsp prepared horseradish
- 2 tbsp grated yellow onion
- 2 tbsp chopped parsley
- 2 tbsp chopped nori
- 2 tbsp flour
- 1 tbsp Cajun seasoning
- ¼ tsp garlic powder
- ¼ tsp salt
- 2 lemon wedges

Directions:
1. In a bowl, combine jackfruit, egg, mustard, mayonnaise, horseradish, onion, parsley, nori, flour, Cajun seasoning, garlic, and salt. Let chill in the fridge for 15 minutes. Preheat air fryer to 350°F. Divide the mixture into 12 balls. Place them in the frying basket and Air Fry for 10 minutes. Serve with lemon wedges.

Chili Tofu & Quinoa Bowls

Servings: 2
Cooking Time: 30 Minutes
Ingredients:
- 1 cup diced peeled sweet potatoes
- ¼ cup chopped mixed bell peppers
- 1/8 cup sprouted green lentils
- ½ onion, sliced
- 1 tsp avocado oil
- 1/8 cup chopped carrots
- 8 oz extra-firm tofu, cubed
- ½ tsp smoked paprika
- ½ tsp chili powder
- ¼ tsp salt
- 2 tsp lime zest
- 1 cup cooked quinoa
- 2 lime wedges

Directions:
1. Preheat air fryer at 350°F. Combine the onion, carrots, bell peppers, green lentils, sweet potato, and avocado oil in a bowl. In another bowl, mix the tofu, paprika, chili powder, and salt. Add veggie mixture to the frying basket and Air Fry for 8 minutes. Stir in tofu mixture and cook for 8 more minutes. Combine lime zest and quinoa. Divide into 2 serving bowls. Top each with the tofu mixture and squeeze a lime wedge over. Serve warm.

Pinto Taquitos

Servings: 4
Cooking Time: 8 Minutes
Ingredients:
- 12 corn tortillas (6- to 7-inch size)
- Filling
- ½ cup refried pinto beans
- ½ cup grated sharp Cheddar or Pepper Jack cheese
- ¼ cup corn kernels (if frozen, measure after thawing and draining)
- 2 tablespoons chopped green onion
- 2 tablespoons chopped jalapeño pepper (seeds and ribs removed before chopping)
- ½ teaspoon lime juice
- ½ teaspoon chile powder, plus extra for dusting
- ½ teaspoon cumin
- ½ teaspoon garlic powder
- oil for misting or cooking spray
- salsa, sour cream, or guacamole for dipping

Directions:
1. Mix together all filling Ingredients.
2. Warm refrigerated tortillas for easier rolling. (Wrap in damp paper towels and microwave for 30 to 60 seconds.)
3. Working with one at a time, place 1 tablespoon of filling on tortilla and roll up. Spray with oil or cooking spray and dust outside with chile powder to taste.
4. Place 6 taquitos in air fryer basket (4 on bottom layer, 2 stacked crosswise on top). Cook at 390°F for 8 minutes, until crispy and brown.
5. Repeat step 4 to cook remaining taquitos.
6. Serve plain or with salsa, sour cream, or guacamole for dipping.

Caprese-style Sandwiches

Servings: 2
Cooking Time: 20 Minutes
Ingredients:
- 2 tbsp balsamic vinegar
- 4 sandwich bread slices
- 2 oz mozzarella shreds
- 3 tbsp pesto sauce
- 2 tomatoes, sliced
- 8 basil leaves
- 8 baby spinach leaves
- 2 tbsp olive oil

Directions:
1. Preheat air fryer at 350°F. Drizzle balsamic vinegar on the bottom of bread slices and smear with pesto sauce. Then, layer mozzarella cheese, tomatoes, baby spinach leaves and basil leaves on top. Add top bread slices. Rub the outside top and bottom of each sandwich with olive oil. Place them in the frying basket and Bake for 5 minutes, flipping once. Serve right away.

Cauliflower Steaks Gratin

Servings: 2
Cooking Time: 13 Minutes
Ingredients:
- 1 head cauliflower
- 1 tablespoon olive oil
- salt and freshly ground black pepper
- ½ teaspoon chopped fresh thyme leaves
- 3 tablespoons grated Parmigiano-Reggiano cheese
- 2 tablespoons panko breadcrumbs

Directions:
1. Preheat the air-fryer to 370°F.
2. Cut two steaks out of the center of the cauliflower. To do this, cut the cauliflower in half and then cut one slice about 1-inch thick off each half. The rest of the cauliflower will fall apart into florets, which you can roast on their own or save for another meal.
3. Brush both sides of the cauliflower steaks with olive oil and season with salt, freshly ground black pepper and fresh thyme. Place the cauliflower steaks into the air fryer basket and air-fry for 6 minutes. Turn the steaks over and air-fry for another 4 minutes. Combine the Parmesan cheese and panko breadcrumbs and sprinkle the mixture over the tops of both steaks and air-fry for another 3 minutes until the cheese has melted and the breadcrumbs have browned. Serve this with some sautéed bitter greens and air-fried blistered tomatoes.

Arancini With Marinara

Servings: 6
Cooking Time: 15 Minutes
Ingredients:
- 2 cups cooked rice
- 1 cup grated Parmesan cheese
- 1 egg, whisked
- ¼ teaspoon dried thyme
- ½ teaspoon dried oregano
- ½ teaspoon dried basil
- ½ teaspoon dried parsley
- 1 teaspoon salt
- ¼ teaspoon paprika
- 1 cup breadcrumbs
- 4 ounces mozzarella, cut into 24 cubes
- 2 cups marinara sauce

Directions:
1. In a large bowl, mix together the rice, Parmesan cheese, and egg.
2. In another bowl, mix together the thyme, oregano, basil, parsley, salt, paprika, and breadcrumbs.
3. Form 24 rice balls with the rice mixture. Use your thumb to make an indentation in the center and stuff 1 cube of mozzarella in the center of the rice; close the ball around the cheese.
4. Roll the rice balls in the seasoned breadcrumbs until all are coated.
5. Preheat the air fryer to 400°F.
6. Place the rice balls in the air fryer basket and coat with cooking spray. Cook for 8 minutes, shake the basket, and cook another 7 minutes.
7. Heat the marinara sauce in a saucepan until warm. Serve sauce as a dip for arancini.

Fennel Tofu Bites

Servings: 4
Cooking Time: 35 Minutes
Ingredients:
- 1/3 cup vegetable broth
- 2 tbsp tomato sauce
- 2 tsp soy sauce
- 1 tbsp nutritional yeast
- 1 tsp Italian seasoning
- 1 tsp granulated sugar
- 1 tsp ginger grated
- ½ tsp fennel seeds
- ½ tsp garlic powder
- Salt and pepper to taste
- 14 oz firm tofu, cubed
- 2/3 cup bread crumbs
- 1 tsp Italian seasoning
- 2 tsp toasted sesame seeds
- 1 cup marinara sauce, warm

Directions:
1. In a large bowl, whisk the vegetable broth, soy sauce, ginger, tomato sauce, nutritional yeast, Italian seasoning, sugar, fennel seeds, garlic powder, salt and black pepper. Toss in tofu to coat. Let marinate covered in the fridge for 30 minutes, tossing once.
2. Preheat air fryer at 350°F. Mix the breadcrumbs, Italian seasoning, and salt in a bowl. Strain marinade from tofu cubes and dredge them in the breadcrumb mixture. Place tofu cubes in the greased frying basket and Air Fry for 10 minutes, turning once. Serve sprinkled with sesame seeds and marinara sauce on the side.

Tofu & Spinach Lasagna

Servings: 4
Cooking Time: 30 Minutes
Ingredients:
- 8 oz cooked lasagne noodles
- 1 tbsp olive oil
- 2 cups crumbled tofu
- 2 cups fresh spinach
- 2 tbsp cornstarch
- 1 tsp onion powder
- Salt and pepper to taste
- 2 garlic cloves, minced
- 2 cups marinara sauce
- ½ cup shredded mozzarella

Directions:
1. Warm the olive oil in a large pan over medium heat. Add the tofu and spinach and stir-fry for a minute. Add the cornstarch, onion powder, salt, pepper, and garlic. Stir until the spinach wilts. Remove from heat.
2. Preheat air fryer to 390°F. Pour a thin layer of pasta sauce in a baking pan. Layer 2-3 lasagne noodles on top of the marinara sauce. Top with a little more sauce and some of the tofu mix. Add another 2-3 noodles on top, then another layer of sauce, then another layer of tofu. Finish with a layer of noodles and a final layer of sauce. Sprinkle with mozzarella cheese on top. Place the pan in the air fryer and Bake for 15 minutes or until the noodle edges are browned and the cheese is melted. Cut and serve.

Roasted Vegetable Pita Pizza

Servings: 4
Cooking Time: 20 Minutes
Ingredients:
- 1 medium red bell pepper, seeded and cut into quarters
- 1 teaspoon extra-virgin olive oil
- ⅛ teaspoon black pepper
- ⅛ teaspoon salt
- Two 6-inch whole-grain pita breads
- 6 tablespoons pesto sauce
- ¼ small red onion, thinly sliced
- ½ cup shredded part-skim mozzarella cheese

Directions:
1. Preheat the air fryer to 400°F.
2. In a small bowl, toss the bell peppers with the olive oil, pepper, and salt.
3. Place the bell peppers in the air fryer and cook for 15 minutes, shaking every 5 minutes to prevent burning.
4. Remove the peppers and set aside. Turn the air fryer temperature down to 350°F.
5. Lay the pita bread on a flat surface. Cover each with half the pesto sauce; then top with even portions of the red bell peppers and onions. Sprinkle cheese over the top. Spray the air fryer basket with olive oil mist.
6. Carefully lift the pita bread into the air fryer basket with a spatula.
7. Cook for 5 to 8 minutes, or until the outer edges begin to brown and the cheese is melted.
8. Serve warm with desired sides.

Corn On The Cob

Servings: 2–4 Servings
Cooking Time: 20 Minutes
Ingredients:
- 2–4 ears of cleaned fresh corn
- 2 tablespoons of butter
- Pinch of salt and black pepper, to taste

Directions:
1. Preheat your air fryer to 370°F. Spray some oil inside the air fryer basket.
2. Wash the corn and dry them with a paper towel. Cut the corn in half to fit the size of the air fryer basket.
3. Grease all sides of corn with the melted butter. Season generously with pepper and salt around all sides of the corn.
4. Put in the air fryer and cook at 370°F for 12–16 minutes*, flipping halfway, until lightly browned and tender.
5. Top with grated Parmesan cheese and nutritional yeast for extra flavor.
6. Serve warm and enjoy your Corn on the Cob!

Nutrition:
- al yeast, grated Parmesan cheese, for serving

Cottage And Mayonnaise Stuffed Peppers

Servings: 2
Cooking Time: 20 Minutes
Ingredients:
- 1 red bell pepper, top and seeds removed
- 1 yellow bell pepper, top and seeds removed
- Salt and pepper, to taste
- 1 cup Cottage cheese
- 4 tablespoons mayonnaise
- 2 pickles, chopped

Directions:
1. Arrange the peppers in the lightly greased cooking basket. Cook in the preheated Air Fryer at 400°F for 15 minutes, turning them over halfway through the cooking time.
2. Season with salt and pepper.
3. Then, in a mixing bowl, combine the cream cheese with the mayonnaise and chopped pickles. Stuff the pepper with the cream cheese mixture and serve. Enjoy!

Crispy Avocados With Pico De Gallo

Servings:2
Cooking Time: 15 Minutes
Ingredients:
- 1 cup diced tomatoes
- 1 tbsp lime juice
- 1 tsp lime zest
- 2 tbsp chopped cilantro
- 1 serrano chiles, minced
- 2 cloves garlic, minced
- 1 tbsp diced white onions
- ½ tsp salt
- 2 avocados, halved and pitted
- 4 tbsp cheddar shreds

Directions:
1. Preheat air fryer to 350ºF. Combine all ingredients, except for avocados and cheddar cheese, in a bowl and let chill covered in the fridge. Place avocado halves, cut sides-up, in the frying basket, scatter cheese shreds over top of avocado halves, and Air Fry for 4 minutes. Top with pico de gallo and serve.

Mushroom Bolognese Casserole

Servings: 4
Cooking Time: 20 Minutes
Ingredients:
- 1 cup canned diced tomatoes
- 2 garlic cloves, minced
- 1 tsp onion powder
- ¾ tsp dried basil
- ¾ tsp dried oregano
- 1 cup chopped mushrooms
- 16 oz cooked spaghetti

Directions:
1. Preheat air fryer to 400°F. Whisk the tomatoes and their juices, garlic, onion powder, basil, oregano, and mushrooms in a baking pan. Cover with aluminum foil and Bake for 6 minutes. Slide out the pan and add the cooked spaghetti; stir to coat. Cover with aluminum foil and Bake for 3 minutes until and bubbly. Serve and enjoy!

Almond Flour Battered Wings

Servings: 4
Cooking Time: 25 Minutes
Ingredients:
- ¼ cup butter, melted
- ¾ cup almond flour
- 16 pieces chicken wings
- 2 tablespoons stevia powder
- 4 tablespoons minced garlic
- Salt and pepper to taste

Directions:
1. Preheat the air fryer for 5 minutes.
2. In a mixing bowl, combine the chicken wings, almond flour, stevia powder, and garlic Season with salt and pepper to taste.
3. Place in the air fryer basket and cook for 25 minutes at 400°F.
4. Halfway through the cooking time, make sure that you give the fryer basket a shake.
5. Once cooked, place in a bowl and drizzle with melted butter. Toss to coat.

Garlicky Brussel Sprouts With Saffron Aioli

Servings: 4
Cooking Time: 20 Minutes
Ingredients:
- 1 lb Brussels sprouts, halved
- 1 tsp garlic powder
- Salt and pepper to taste
- ½ cup mayonnaise
- ½ tbsp olive oil
- 1 tbsp Dijon mustard
- 1 tsp minced garlic
- Salt and pepper to taste
- ½ tsp liquid saffron

Directions:
1. Preheat air fryer to 380°F. Combine the Brussels sprouts, garlic powder, salt and pepper in a large bowl. Place in the fryer and spray with cooking oil. Bake for 12-14 minutes, shaking once, until just brown.
2. Meanwhile, in a small bowl, mix mayonnaise, olive oil, mustard, garlic, saffron, salt and pepper. When the Brussels sprouts are slightly cool, serve with aioli. Enjoy!

Vegan Buddha Bowls(2)

Servings: 4
Cooking Time: 20 Minutes
Ingredients:
- 1 carrot, peeled and julienned
- ½ onion, sliced into half-moons
- ¼ cup apple cider vinegar
- ½ tsp ground ginger
- ⅛ tsp cayenne pepper
- 1 parsnip, diced
- 1 tsp avocado oil
- 4 oz extra-firm tofu, cubed
- ½ tsp five-spice powder
- ½ tsp chili powder
- 2 tsp fresh lime zest
- 1 cup fresh arugula
- ½ cup cooked quinoa
- 2 tbsp canned kidney beans
- 2 tbsp canned sweetcorn
- 1 avocado, diced
- 2 tbsp pine nuts

Directions:
1. Preheat air fryer to 350°F. Combine carrot, vinegar, ginger, and cayenne in a bowl. In another bowl, combine onion, parsnip, and avocado oil. In a third bowl, mix the tofu, five-spice powder, and chili powder.
2. Place the onion mixture in the greased basket. Air Fry for 6 minutes. Stir in tofu mixture and cook for 8 more minutes. Mix in lime zest. Divide arugula, cooked quinoa, kidney beans, sweetcorn, drained carrots, avocado, pine nuts, and tofu mixture between 2 bowls. Serve.

Smoked Paprika Sweet Potato Fries

Servings: 4
Cooking Time: 35 Minutes
Ingredients:
- 2 sweet potatoes, peeled
- 1 ½ tbsp cornstarch
- 1 tbsp canola oil
- 1 tbsp olive oil
- 1 tsp smoked paprika
- 1 tsp garlic powder
- Salt and pepper to taste
- 1 cup cocktail sauce

Directions:
1. Cut the potatoes lengthwise to form French fries. Put in a resealable plastic bag and add cornstarch. Seal and shake to coat the fries. Combine the canola oil, olive oil, paprika, garlic powder, salt, and pepper fries in a large bowl. Add the sweet potato fries and mix to combine.
2. Preheat air fryer to 380°F. Place fries in the greased basket and fry for 20-25 minutes, shaking the basket once until crisp. Drizzle with Cocktail sauce to serve.

Bell Peppers Cups

Servings: 4
Cooking Time: 8 Minutes
Ingredients:
- 8 mini red bell peppers, tops and seeds removed
- 1 teaspoon fresh parsley, chopped
- ¾ cup feta cheese, crumbled
- ½ tablespoon olive oil
- Freshly ground black pepper, to taste

Directions:
1. Preheat the Air fryer to 390°F and grease an Air fryer basket.
2. Mix feta cheese, parsley, olive oil and black pepper in a bowl.
3. Stuff the bell peppers with feta cheese mixture and arrange in the Air fryer basket.
4. Cook for about 8 minutes and dish out to serve hot.

Cheesy Brussel Sprouts

Servings: 3
Cooking Time: 10 Minutes
Ingredients:
- 1 pound Brussels sprouts, trimmed and halved
- ¼ cup whole wheat breadcrumbs
- ¼ cup Parmesan cheese, shredded
- 1 tablespoon balsamic vinegar
- 1 tablespoon extra-virgin olive oil
- Salt and black pepper, to taste

Directions:
1. Preheat the Air fryer to 400°F and grease an Air fryer basket.
2. Mix Brussel sprouts, vinegar, oil, salt, and black pepper in a bowl and toss to coat well.
3. Arrange the Brussel sprouts in the Air fryer basket and cook for about 5 minutes.
4. Sprinkle with breadcrumbs and cheese and cook for about 5 more minutes.
5. Dish out and serve hot.

Garden Fresh Green Beans

Servings: 4
Cooking Time: 12 Minutes
Ingredients:
- 1 pound green beans, washed and trimmed
- 1 teaspoon butter, melted
- 1 tablespoon fresh lemon juice
- ¼ teaspoon garlic powder
- Salt and freshly ground pepper, to taste

Directions:
1. Preheat the Air fryer to 400°F and grease an Air fryer basket.
2. Put all the ingredients in a large bowl and transfer into the Air fryer basket.
3. Cook for about 8 minutes and dish out in a bowl to serve warm.

Lemony Green Beans

Servings: 3
Cooking Time: 12 Minutes
Ingredients:
- 1 pound green beans, trimmed and halved
- 1 teaspoon butter, melted
- 1 tablespoon fresh lemon juice
- ¼ teaspoon garlic powder

Directions:
1. Preheat the Air fryer to 400°F and grease an Air fryer basket.
2. Mix all the ingredients in a bowl and toss to coat well.
3. Arrange the green beans into the Air fryer basket and cook for about 12 minutes.
4. Dish out in a serving plate and serve hot.

Easy Glazed Carrots

Servings: 4
Cooking Time: 12 Minutes
Ingredients:
- 3 cups carrots, peeled and cut into large chunks
- 1 tablespoon olive oil
- 1 tablespoon honey
- Salt and black pepper, to taste

Directions:
1. Preheat the Air fryer to 390°F and grease an Air fryer basket.
2. Mix all the ingredients in a bowl and toss to coat well.
3. Transfer into the Air fryer basket and cook for about 12 minutes.
4. Dish out and serve hot.

Vegetarian Stuffed Bell Peppers

Servings: 3
Cooking Time: 40 Minutes
Ingredients:
- 1 cup mushrooms, chopped
- 1 tbsp allspice
- ¾ cup Alfredo sauce
- ½ cup canned diced tomatoes
- 1 cup cooked rice
- 2 tbsp dried parsley
- 2 tbsp hot sauce
- Salt and pepper to taste
- 3 large bell peppers

Directions:
1. Preheat air fryer to 375°F. Whisk mushrooms, allspice and 1 cup of boiling water until smooth. Stir in Alfredo sauce, tomatoes and juices, rice, parsley, hot sauce, salt, and black pepper. Set aside. Cut the top of each bell pepper, take out the core and seeds without breaking the pepper. Fill each pepper with the rice mixture and cover them with a 6-inch square of aluminum foil, folding the edges. Roast for 30 minutes until tender. Let cool completely before unwrapping. Serve immediately.

Vegetarian Eggplant "pizzas"

Servings: 4
Cooking Time: 25 Minutes
Ingredients:
- ½ cup diced baby bella mushrooms
- 3 tbsp olive oil
- ¼ cup diced onions
- ½ cup pizza sauce
- 1 eggplant, sliced
- 1 tsp salt
- 1 cup shredded mozzarella
- ¼ cup chopped oregano

Directions:
1. Warm 2 tsp of olive oil in a skillet over medium heat. Add in onion and mushrooms and stir-fry for 4 minutes until tender. Stir in pizza sauce. Turn the heat off.
2. Preheat air fryer to 375°F. Brush the eggplant slices with the remaining olive oil on both sides. Lay out slices on a large plate and season with salt. Then, top with the sauce mixture and shredded mozzarella. Place the eggplant pizzas in the frying basket and Air Fry for 5 minutes. Garnish with oregano to serve.

Spinach And Cheese Calzone

Servings: 2
Cooking Time: 10 Minutes
Ingredients:
- ⅔ cup frozen chopped spinach, thawed
- 1 cup grated mozzarella cheese
- 1 cup ricotta cheese
- ½ teaspoon Italian seasoning
- ½ teaspoon salt
- freshly ground black pepper
- 1 store-bought or homemade pizza dough* (about 12 to 16 ounces)
- 2 tablespoons olive oil
- pizza or marinara sauce (optional)

Directions:
1. Drain and squeeze all the water out of the thawed spinach and set it aside. Mix the mozzarella cheese, ricotta cheese, Italian seasoning, salt and freshly ground black pepper together in a bowl. Stir in the chopped spinach.
2. Divide the dough in half. With floured hands or on a floured surface, stretch or roll one half of the dough into a 10-inch circle. Spread half of the cheese and spinach mixture on half of the dough, leaving about one inch of dough empty around the edge.
3. Fold the other half of the dough over the cheese mixture, almost to the edge of the bottom dough to form a half moon. Fold the bottom edge of dough up over the top edge and crimp the dough around the edges in order to make the crust and seal the calzone. Brush the dough with olive oil. Repeat with the second half of dough to make the second calzone.
4. Preheat the air fryer to 360°F.
5. Brush or spray the air fryer basket with olive oil. Air-fry the calzones one at a time for 10 minutes, flipping the calzone over half way through. Serve with warm pizza or marinara sauce if desired.

Tex-mex Stuffed Sweet Potatoes

Servings: 2
Cooking Time: 40 Minutes
Ingredients:
- 2 medium sweet potatoes
- 1 can black beans
- 2 scallions, finely sliced
- 1 tbsp hot sauce
- 1 tsp taco seasoning
- 2 tbsp lime juice
- ¼ cup Ranch dressing

Directions:
1. Preheat air fryer to 400°F. Add in sweet potatoes and Roast for 30 minutes. Toss the beans, scallions, hot sauce, taco seasoning, and lime juice. Set aside. Once the potatoes are ready, cut them lengthwise, 2/3 through. Spoon 1/4 of the bean mixture into each half and drizzle Ranch dressing before serving.

Fried Potatoes With Bell Peppers

Servings: 4
Cooking Time: 30 Minutes
Ingredients:
- 3 russet potatoes, cubed
- 1 tbsp canola oil
- 1 tbsp olive oil
- 1 tsp paprika
- Salt and pepper to taste
- 1 chopped shallot
- ½ chopped red bell peppers
- ½ diced yellow bell peppers

Directions:
1. Preheat air fryer to 370°F. Whisk the canola oil, olive oil, paprika, salt, and pepper in a bowl. Toss in the potatoes to coat. Place the potatoes in the air fryer and Bake for 20 minutes, shaking the basket periodically. Top the potatoes with shallot and bell peppers and cook for an additional 3-4 minutes or until the potatoes are cooked through and the peppers are soft. Serve warm.

Roasted Vegetable Lasagna

Servings: 6
Cooking Time: 55 Minutes
Ingredients:
- 1 zucchini, sliced
- 1 yellow squash, sliced
- 8 ounces mushrooms, sliced
- 1 red bell pepper, cut into 2-inch strips
- 1 tablespoon olive oil
- 2 cups ricotta cheese
- 2 cups grated mozzarella cheese, divided
- 1 egg
- 1 teaspoon salt
- freshly ground black pepper
- ¼ cup shredded carrots
- ½ cup chopped fresh spinach
- 8 lasagna noodles, cooked
- Béchamel Sauce:
- 3 tablespoons butter
- 3 tablespoons flour
- 2½ cups milk
- ½ cup grated Parmesan cheese
- ½ teaspoon salt
- freshly ground black pepper
- pinch of ground nutmeg

Directions:
1. Preheat the air fryer to 400°F.
2. Toss the zucchini, yellow squash, mushrooms and red pepper in a large bowl with the olive oil and season with salt and pepper. Air-fry for 10 minutes, shaking the basket once or twice while the vegetables cook.
3. While the vegetables are cooking, make the béchamel sauce and cheese filling. Melt the butter in a medium saucepan over medium-high heat on the stovetop. Add the flour and whisk, cooking for a couple of minutes. Add the milk and whisk vigorously until smooth. Bring the mixture to a boil and simmer until the sauce thickens. Stir in the Parmesan cheese and season with the salt, pepper and nutmeg. Set the sauce aside.

4. Combine the ricotta cheese, 1¼ cups of the mozzarella cheese, egg, salt and pepper in a large bowl and stir until combined. Fold in the carrots and spinach.

5. When the vegetables have finished cooking, build the lasagna. Use a baking dish that is 6 inches in diameter and 4 inches high. Cover the bottom of the baking dish with a little béchamel sauce. Top with two lasagna noodles, cut to fit the dish and overlapping each other a little. Spoon a third of the ricotta cheese mixture and then a third of the roasted veggies on top of the noodles. Pour ½ cup of béchamel sauce on top and then repeat these layers two more times: noodles – cheese mixture – vegetables – béchamel sauce. Sprinkle the remaining mozzarella cheese over the top. Cover the dish with aluminum foil, tenting it loosely so the aluminum doesn't touch the cheese.

6. Lower the dish into the air fryer basket using an aluminum foil sling (fold a piece of aluminum foil into a strip about 2-inches wide by 24-inches long). Fold the ends of the aluminum foil over the top of the dish before returning the basket to the air fryer. Air-fry for 45 minutes, removing the foil for the last 2 minutes, to slightly brown the cheese on top.

7. Let the lasagna rest for at least 20 minutes to set up a little before slicing into it and serving.

Cheddar Stuffed Portobellos With Salsa

Servings: 4
Cooking Time: 20 Minutes
Ingredients:
- 8 portobello mushrooms
- 1/3 cup salsa
- ½ cup shredded cheddar
- 2 tbsp cilantro, chopped

Directions:
1. Preheat air fryer to 370°F. Remove the mushroom stems. Divide the salsa between the caps. Top with cheese and sprinkle with cilantro. Place the mushrooms in the greased frying basket and Bake for 8-10 minutes. Let cool slightly, then serve.

Fried Rice With Curried Tofu

Servings: 4
Cooking Time: 25 Minutes
Ingredients:
- 8 oz extra-firm tofu, cubed
- ½ cup canned coconut milk
- 2 tsp red curry paste
- 2 cloves garlic, minced
- 1 tbsp avocado oil
- 1 tbsp coconut oil
- 2 cups cooked rice
- 1 tbsp turmeric powder
- Salt and pepper to taste
- 4 lime wedges
- ¼ cup chopped cilantro

Directions:
1. Preheat air fryer to 350°F. Combine tofu, coconut milk, curry paste, garlic, and avocado oil in a bowl. Pour the mixture into a baking pan. Place the pan in the frying basket and Air Fry for 10 minutes, stirring once.

2. Melt the coconut oil in a skillet over medium heat. Add in rice, turmeric powder, salt, and black pepper, and cook for 2 minutes or until heated through. Divide the cooked rice between 4 medium bowls and top with tofu mixture and sauce. Top with cilantro and lime wedges to serve.

Chapter 6: Beef, pork & Lamb Recipes

Chili-lime Pork Loin

Servings: 4
Cooking Time: 30 Minutes
Ingredients:
- 1 tablespoon lime juice
- 1 tablespoon olive oil, plus more for spraying
- ½ tablespoon soy sauce
- ½ tablespoon chili powder
- ¼ tablespoon minced garlic
- 1 pound boneless pork tenderloin

Directions:
1. In a large zip-top plastic bag, mix together the lime juice, olive oil, soy sauce, chili powder, and garlic and mix well. Add the pork, seal, and refrigerate for at least 1 hour or overnight.
2. Spray a fryer basket lightly with olive oil.
3. Shake off any excess marinade from the pork and place it in the fryer basket.
4. Air fry for 15 minutes. Flip the tenderloin over and cook until the pork reaches an internal temperature of at least 145°F an additional 5 minutes. If necessary, continue to cook in 2- to 3-minute intervals until it reaches the proper temperature.
5. Let the tenderloin rest for 10 minutes before cutting into slices and serving.

Pork Tenderloins

Servings: 3
Cooking Time: 30 Minutes
Ingredients:
- 1 teaspoon salt
- ½ teaspoon pepper
- 1 lb. pork tenderloin
- 2 tablespoons minced fresh rosemary
- 2 tablespoons olive oil, divided
- 1 garlic cloves, minced
- Apricot Glaze Ingredients:
- 1 cup apricot preserves
- 3 garlic cloves, minced
- 4 tablespoons lemon juice

Directions:
1. After mixing the pepper, salt, garlic, oil, and rosemary well, brush the pork with them on all sides.
2. If needed, you can cut pork crosswise in half.
3. Arrange the pork to the sprayed cooking pan and cook at 390 degrees F/ 200 degrees C for 3 minutes on each side.
4. While cooking the pork, mix all of the glaze ingredients well.
5. Baste the pork every 5 minutes.
6. Cook at 330 degrees F/ 165 degrees C and cook for 20 minutes more.
7. When done, serve and enjoy.

Cheese Beef Roll

Servings: 4
Cooking Time: 15 Minutes
Ingredients:
- Black pepper and salt to taste
- 3 tablespoons pesto
- 6 slices cheese
- ¾ cup spinach, chopped
- 3 oz. bell pepper, deseeded and sliced

Directions:
1. At 400 degrees F/ 205 degrees C, preheat your air fryer.
2. Top the steak slices with pesto, cheese, spinach, bell pepper.
3. Roll up the steak slices and secure using a toothpick.
4. Season with black pepper and salt accordingly.
5. Place the prepared slices in your air fryer's cooking basket and cook for almost 15 minutes.
6. Serve and enjoy!

Lollipop Lamb Chops

Servings: 4
Cooking Time: 7 Minutes
Ingredients:
- ½ small clove garlic
- ¼ cup packed fresh parsley
- ¾ cup packed fresh mint
- ½ teaspoon lemon juice
- ¼ cup grated Parmesan cheese
- ⅓ cup shelled pistachios
- ¼ teaspoon salt
- ½ cup olive oil
- 8 lamb chops (1 rack)
- 2 tablespoons vegetable oil
- Salt and freshly ground black pepper, to taste
- 1 tablespoon dried rosemary, chopped
- 1 tablespoon dried thyme

Directions:
1. Make the pesto by combining the garlic, parsley and mint in a food processor and process until finely chopped. Add the lemon juice, Parmesan cheese, pistachios and salt. Process until all the ingredients have turned into a paste. With the processor running, slowly pour the olive oil in. Scrape the sides of the processor with a spatula and process for another 30 seconds.
2. Preheat the air fryer to 400°F (204°C).
3. Rub both sides of the lamb chops with vegetable oil and season with salt, pepper, rosemary and thyme, pressing the herbs into the meat gently with the fingers. Transfer the lamb chops to the air fryer basket.
4. Air fry the lamb chops for 5 minutes. Flip the chops over and air fry for an additional 2 minutes.
5. Serve the lamb chops with mint pesto drizzled on top.

Glazed Tender Pork Chops

Servings: 3
Cooking Time: 14 Minutes
Ingredients:
- 3 pork chops, rinsed and pat dry
- ¼ teaspoon smoked paprika
- ½ teaspoon garlic powder
- 2 teaspoons olive oil
- Black pepper
- Salt

Directions:
1. Coat pork chops with paprika, olive oil, garlic powder, black pepper, and salt.
2. Place the prepared pork chops in air fryer basket and cook at almost 380 degrees F/ 195 degrees C for almost 10-14 minutes. Turn halfway through the cooking time.
3. Serve and enjoy.

Provençal Grilled Rib-eye
Servings: 4
Cooking Time: 25 Minutes
Ingredients:
- 4 ribeye steaks
- 1 tbsp herbs de Provence
- Salt and pepper to taste

Directions:
1. Preheat air fryer to 360°F. Season the steaks with herbs, salt and pepper. Place them in the greased frying basket and cook for 8-12 minutes, flipping once. Use a thermometer to check for doneness and adjust time as needed. Let the steak rest for a few minutes and serve.

Spiced Pork Chops
Servings: 2
Cooking Time: 20 Minutes
Ingredients:
- 1 tablespoon olive oil
- ½ lb. pork chops
- ½ teaspoon dried oregano
- ¼ teaspoon red pepper flakes
- 1 teaspoon dried thyme
- ½ teaspoon salt
- ½ teaspoon pepper
- 6 large mushrooms, cleaned and sliced
- 1 large yellow onion, chopped
- 1 ½ tablespoons soy sauce
- 2 tablespoons fresh parsley, finely chopped

Directions:
1. Mix the pork chops with the onion, mushrooms, pepper, red pepper flakes, thyme, oregano, olive oil, soy sauce, and olive oil in a large bowl.
2. When coated, cook the pork chops and clean mushrooms in your air fryer at 390 degrees F/ 200 degrees C for 20 minutes.
3. Sprinkle with the fresh parsley, serve and enjoy!

Bacon With Shallot And Greens
Servings: 2
Cooking Time: 10 Minutes
Ingredients:
- 7 ounces mixed greens
- 8 thick slices pork bacon
- 2 shallots, peeled and diced
- Nonstick cooking spray

Directions:
1. Begin by preheating the air fryer to 345°F.
2. Now, add the shallot and bacon to the Air Fryer cooking basket; set the timer for 2 minutes. Spritz with a nonstick cooking spray.
3. After that, pause the Air Fryer; throw in the mixed greens; give it a good stir and cook an additional 5 minutes. Serve warm.

Sage Pork With Potatoes
Servings: 4
Cooking Time: 30 Minutes
Ingredients:
- 2 cups potatoes
- 2 tsp olive oil
- 1 lb pork tenderloin, cubed
- 1 onion, chopped
- 1 red bell pepper, chopped
- 2 garlic cloves, minced
- ½ tsp dried sage
- ½ tsp fennel seeds, crushed
- 2 tbsp chicken broth

Directions:
1. Preheat air fryer to 370°F. Add the potatoes and olive oil to a bowl and toss to coat. Transfer them to the frying basket and Air Fry for 15 minutes. Remove the bowl. Add the pork, onion, red bell pepper, garlic, sage, and fennel seeds, to the potatoes, add chicken broth and stir gently. Return the bowl to the frying basket and cook for 10 minutes. Be sure to shake the basket at least once. The pork should be cooked through and the potatoes soft and crispy. Serve immediately.

Stuffed Pork Chops
Servings: 4
Cooking Time: 12 Minutes
Ingredients:
- 4 boneless pork chops
- ½ teaspoon salt
- ½ teaspoon black pepper
- ¼ teaspoon paprika
- 1 cup frozen spinach, defrosted and squeezed dry
- 2 cloves garlic, minced
- 2 ounces cream cheese
- ¼ cup grated Parmesan cheese
- 1 tablespoon extra-virgin olive oil

Directions:
1. Pat the pork chops with a paper towel. Make a slit in the side of each pork chop to create a pouch.
2. Season the pork chops with the salt, pepper, and paprika.
3. In a small bowl, mix together the spinach, garlic, cream cheese, and Parmesan cheese.
4. Divide the mixture into fourths and stuff the pork chop pouches. Secure the pouches with toothpicks.
5. Preheat the air fryer to 400°F.
6. Place the stuffed pork chops in the air fryer basket and spray liberally with cooking spray. Cook for 6 minutes, flip and coat with more cooking spray, and cook another 6 minutes. Check to make sure the meat is cooked to an internal temperature of 145°F. Cook the pork chops in batches, as needed.

Juicy Spiced Rib-eye Steaks
Servings: 2
Cooking Time: 14 Minutes

Ingredients:
- 2 medium rib-eye steaks
- ¼ teaspoon garlic powder
- ¼ teaspoon onion powder
- 1 teaspoon olive oil
- Black pepper
- Salt

Directions:
1. Coat steaks with oil and season with garlic powder, onion powder, black pepper, and salt.
2. At 400 degrees F/ 205 degrees C, preheat your air fryer.
3. Place steaks into the air fryer basket and cook for 14 minutes. Turn halfway through.
4. Serve and enjoy.

Rice And Meatball Stuffed Bell Peppers

Servings: 4
Cooking Time: 11 To 17 Minutes

Ingredients:
- 4 bell peppers
- 1 tablespoon olive oil
- 1 small onion, chopped
- 2 cloves garlic, minced
- 1 cup frozen cooked rice, thawed
- 16 to 20 small frozen precooked meatballs, thawed
- ½ cup tomato sauce
- 2 tablespoons Dijon mustard

Directions:
1. To prepare the peppers, cut off about ½ inch of the tops. Carefully remove the membranes and seeds from inside the peppers. Set aside.
2. In a 6-by-6-by-2-inch pan, combine the olive oil, onion, and garlic. Bake in the air fryer for 2 to 4 minutes or until crisp and tender. Remove the vegetable mixture from the pan and set aside in a medium bowl.
3. Add the rice, meatballs, tomato sauce, and mustard to the vegetable mixture and stir to combine.
4. Stuff the peppers with the meat-vegetable mixture.
5. Place the peppers in the air fryer basket and bake for 9 to 13 minutes or until the filling is hot and the peppers are tender.

Beef And Broccoli Stir Fry

Servings: 4
Cooking Time: 15 Minutes

Ingredients:
- 3 tablespoons dry sherry
- ¼ cup soy sauce
- 4 garlic cloves, minced
- 1 tablespoon sesame oil
- ½ teaspoon red pepper flakes
- 1 pound flank or skirt steak, trimmed and cut into strips
- Olive oil
- ½ pound broccoli florets
- ¼ cup beef broth
- 2 teaspoons cornstarch

Directions:
1. In a small bowl, combine the sherry, soy sauce, garlic, sesame oil, and red pepper flakes to create a marinade.
2. Place the steak and 3 tablespoons of the marinade in a large zip-top plastic bag, seal, and refrigerate for at least 2 hours.
3. Spray a fryer basket lightly with olive oil.
4. Add half the steak to the fryer basket along with half the broccoli florets. Lightly spray with olive oil.
5. Air fry for 8 minutes. Shake the basket to redistribute and cook until cooked through, an additional 4 to 7 minutes. Repeat with the remaining steak and broccoli. Transfer the steak and broccoli to a large bowl.
6. While the steak is cooking, in a small saucepan over medium-high heat, combine the broth and remaining marinade and bring to a boil.
7. In a small bowl combine the cornstarch and 1 tablespoon of water to create a slurry. Add the slurry to the sauce pan and simmer, stirring, until the sauce starts to thicken, a few seconds to 1 minute.
8. Pour the sauce over the cooked steak and broccoli and toss to evenly coat.

Beefy Quesadillas

Servings: 4
Cooking Time: 45 Minutes

Ingredients:
- 2 cups grated cheddar
- 1 tsp chili powder
- ½ tsp smoked paprika
- ½ tsp ground cumin
- ½ tsp nutmeg
- ¼ tsp garlic powder
- Salt and pepper to taste
- 1 ribeye steak
- 2 tsp olive oil
- 1 red bell pepper, diced
- 1 grated carrot
- 1 green bell pepper, diced
- ½ red onion, sliced
- 1 cup corn kernels
- 3 tbsp butter, melted
- 8 tortillas

Directions:
1. Mix the chili powder, nutmeg, paprika, cumin, garlic powder, salt, and pepper in a bowl. Toss in ribeye until fully coated and let marinate covered in the fridge for 30 minutes. Preheat air fryer at 400ºF. Place ribeye in the greased frying basket and Bake for 6 minutes until rare, flipping once. Let rest onto a cutting board for 5 minutes before slicing thinly against the grain.
2. Warm the olive oil in a skillet over high heat. Add in bell peppers, carrot and onion and cook for 6-8 minutes until the peppers are tender. Stir in corn. Set aside. Preheat air fryer at 350ºF. Brush on one side of a tortilla lightly with melted butter. Layer ¼ beef strips, ¼ bell pepper mixture, and finally, ¼ of the grated cheese. Top with a second tortilla and lightly brush with butter on top. Repeat with the remaining ingredients. Place quesadillas, butter side down, in the frying basket and Bake for 3 minutes. Cut them into 6 sections and serve.

Baby Back Ribs

Servings: 4
Cooking Time: 36 Minutes
Ingredients:
- 2¼ pounds Pork baby back rib rack(s)
- 1 tablespoon Dried barbecue seasoning blend or rub (gluten-free, if a concern)
- 1 cup Water
- 3 tablespoons Purchased smooth barbecue sauce (gluten-free, if a concern)

Directions:
1. Preheat the air fryer to 350°F.
2. Cut the racks into 4- to 5-bone sections, about two sections for the small batch, three for the medium, and four for the large. Sprinkle both sides of these sections with the seasoning blend.
3. Pour the water into the bottom of the air-fryer drawer or into a tray placed under the rack. Set the rib sections in the basket so that they're not touching. Air-fry for 30 minutes, turning once.
4. If using a tray with water, check it a couple of times to make sure it still has water in it or hasn't overflowed from the rendered fat.
5. Brush half the barbecue sauce on the exposed side of the ribs. Air-fry undisturbed for 3 minutes. Turn the racks over, brush with the remaining sauce, and air-fry undisturbed for 3 minutes more, or until sizzling and brown.
6. Use kitchen tongs to transfer the racks to a cutting board. Let stand for 5 minutes, then slice between the bones to serve.

Rib Eye Steak Seasoned With Italian Herb

Servings: 4
Cooking Time: 45 Minutes
Ingredients:
- 1 packet Italian herb mix
- 1 tablespoon olive oil
- 2 pounds bone-in rib eye steak
- Salt and pepper to taste

Directions:
1. Preheat the air fryer to 390°F.
2. Place the grill pan accessory in the air fryer.
3. Season the steak with salt, pepper, Italian herb mix, and olive oil. Cover top with foil.
4. Grill for 45 minutes and flip the steak halfway through the cooking time.

Paprika Pork Chops

Servings: 6
Cooking Time: 12 Minutes
Ingredients:
- 1 ½ pounds pork chops, boneless
- 1 teaspoon paprika
- 1 teaspoon creole seasoning
- 1 teaspoon garlic powder
- ¼ cup parmesan cheese, grated
- ⅓ cup almond flour

Directions:
1. At 360 degrees F/ 180 degrees C, preheat your Air fryer.
2. Add all the recipe ingredients except pork chops in a zip-lock bag.
3. Add pork chops in the bag. Seal this bag and shake well to coat pork chops.
4. Remove pork chops from zip-lock bag and place in the air fryer basket.
5. Cook pork chops for almost 10-12 minutes.
6. Serve and enjoy.

Cheese-stuffed Steak Burgers

Servings: 4
Cooking Time: 10 Minutes
Ingredients:
- 1 pound 80/20 ground sirloin
- 4 ounces mild Cheddar cheese, cubed
- ½ teaspoon salt
- ¼ teaspoon ground black pepper

Directions:
1. Form ground sirloin into four equal balls, then separate each ball in half and flatten into two thin patties, for eight total patties. Place 1 ounce Cheddar into center of one patty, then top with a second patty and press edges to seal burger closed. Repeat with remaining patties and Cheddar to create four burgers.
2. Sprinkle salt and pepper over both sides of burgers and carefully place burgers into ungreased air fryer basket. Adjust the temperature to 350°F and set the timer for 10 minutes. Burgers will be done when browned on the edges and top. Serve warm.

Italian-style Honey Pork

Servings: 3
Cooking Time: 50 Minutes
Ingredients:
- 1 teaspoon Celtic sea salt
- ½-teaspoon black pepper, freshly cracked
- ¼ cup red wine
- 1 tablespoon mustard
- 1 tablespoon honey
- 2 garlic cloves, minced
- 1 lb. pork top loin
- 1 tablespoon Italian herb seasoning blend

Directions:
1. Prepare a suitable bowl, mix up the salt, black pepper, red wine, mustard, honey, garlic and the pork top loin, then marinate the pork top loin at least 30 minutes.
2. Spray the cooking basket of your air fryer with the non-stick cooking spray.
3. Sprinkle the Italian herb on the top of the pork top loin after transfer it to the basket.
4. Cook the pork top loin at 370 degrees F/ 185 degrees C for 10 minutes, flipping and spraying with cooking oil halfway through.
5. When cooked, serve and enjoy.

Panko-breaded Pork Chops

Servings: 5
Cooking Time: 15 Minutes
Ingredients:
- 5 (3½- to 5-ounce) pork chops (bone-in or boneless)
- Seasoning salt
- Pepper
- ¼ cup all-purpose flour
- 2 tablespoons panko bread crumbs
- Cooking oil

Directions:
1. Season the pork chops with the seasoning salt and pepper to taste.
2. Sprinkle the flour on both sides of the pork chops, then coat both sides with panko bread crumbs.
3. Place the pork chops in the air fryer. Stacking them is okay. (See Air fryer cooking tip.) Spray the pork chops with cooking oil. Cook for 6 minutes.
4. Open the air fryer and flip the pork chops. Cook for an additional 6 minutes
5. Cool before serving.

Thai Burgers

Servings:4
Cooking Time: 15 Minutes
Ingredients:
- ½ cup soft bread crumbs
- ¼ cup Thai chili sauce
- 2 minced green onions
- 2 cloves garlic, minced
- 1¼ pounds 93 percent lean ground beef
- 4 onion rolls, split in half
- 1 large beefsteak tomato, sliced
- ⅓ cup commercial peanut sauce

Directions:
1. In a large bowl, combine the bread crumbs, Thai chili sauce, green onions, and garlic, and mix well. Add the ground beef and mix gently but thoroughly until combined.
2. Form the beef mixture into four patties. Make an indentation in the center of each patty with your thumb so the burgers don't puff up when they cook.
3. Cook for 12 minutes, and then test the burgers. If they aren't at least 165°F, cook for 3 minutes until they reach that temperature.
4. Assemble burgers with the onion rolls, sliced tomato, and peanut sauce.

Roasted Garlic Ribeye With Mayo

Servings: 3
Cooking Time: 20 Minutes
Ingredients:
- 1 ½ lbs. ribeye, bone-in
- 1 tablespoon butter, room temperature
- Salt, to taste
- ½-teaspoon crushed black pepper
- ½-teaspoon dried dill
- ½-teaspoon cayenne pepper
- ½-teaspoon garlic powder
- ½-teaspoon onion powder
- 1 teaspoon ground coriander
- 1 tablespoon mayonnaise
- 1 teaspoon garlic, minced

Directions:
1. Use the kitchen towel to pat the ribeye dry, then rub it with the softened butter on all sides.
2. Transfer the ribeye to the basket of your air fryer after sprinkling with the seasonings.
3. Cook the ribeye at 400 degrees F/ 205 degrees C for 15 minutes, flipping halfway through.
4. Meanwhile, mix the mayonnaise and garlic well, and refrigerate the mixture until the ribeye cooked.
5. When ready, serve and enjoy!

Quick & Easy Meatballs

Servings: 4
Cooking Time: 12 Minutes
Ingredients:
- 4 oz lamb meat, minced
- 1 tbsp oregano, chopped
- ½ tbsp lemon zest
- 1 egg, lightly beaten
- Pepper
- Salt

Directions:
1. Add all ingredients into the bowl and mix until well combined.
2. Spray air fryer basket with cooking spray.
3. Make balls from bowl mixture and place into the air fryer basket and cook at 400°F for 12 minutes.
4. Serve and enjoy.

Spice Meatloaf

Servings: 8
Cooking Time: 20 Minutes
Ingredients:
- 1-pound ground beef
- ½ teaspoon dried tarragon
- 1 teaspoon Italian seasoning
- 1 tablespoon Worcestershire sauce
- ¼ cup ketchup
- ¼ cup coconut flour
- ½ cup almond flour
- 1 garlic clove, minced
- ¼ cup onion, chopped
- 2 eggs, lightly beaten
- ¼ teaspoon black pepper
- ½ teaspoon salt

Directions:
1. Add all the recipe ingredients into the mixing bowl and mix until well combined.
2. Make the equal shape of patties from mixture and place on a plate. Place in refrigerator for 10 minutes.
3. Grease its air fryer basket with cooking spray.
4. At 360 degrees F/ 180 degrees C, preheat your air fryer.
5. Place prepared patties in air fryer basket and cook for 10 minutes.
6. Serve and enjoy.

Chipotle Pork Meatballs

Servings: 4
Cooking Time: 35 Minutes
Ingredients:
- 1 lb ground pork
- 1 egg
- ¼ cup chipotle sauce
- ¼ cup grated celery
- ¼ cup chopped parsley
- ¼ cup chopped cilantro
- ¼ cup flour
- ¼ tsp salt

Directions:
1. Preheat air fryer to 350°F. In a large bowl, combine the ground pork, egg, chipotle sauce, celery, parsley, cilantro, flour, and salt. Form mixture into 16 meatballs. Place the meatballs in the lightly greased frying basket and Air Fry for 8-10 minutes, flipping once. Serve immediately!

Italian Lamb Chops With Avocado Mayo

Servings: 2
Cooking Time: 12 Minutes
Ingredients:
- 2 lamp chops
- 2 teaspoons Italian herbs
- 2 avocados
- ½ cup mayonnaise
- 1 tablespoon lemon juice

Directions:
1. Season the lamb chops with the Italian herbs, then set aside for 5 minutes.
2. Preheat the air fryer to 400°F (204°C) and place the rack inside.
3. Put the chops on the rack and air fry for 12 minutes.
4. In the meantime, halve the avocados and open to remove the pits. Spoon the flesh into a blender.
5. Add the mayonnaise and lemon juice and pulse until a smooth consistency is achieved.
6. Take care when removing the chops from the air fryer, then plate up and serve with the avocado mayo.

Buttery Pork Chops

Servings: 4
Cooking Time: 12 Minutes
Ingredients:
- 4 boneless pork chops
- 1 teaspoon salt
- ½ teaspoon ground black pepper
- 4 tablespoons salted butter, sliced into 8 (½-tablespoon) pats, divided

Directions:
1. Preheat the air fryer to 400°F.
2. Sprinkle pork chops with salt and pepper. Top each pork chop with a ½-tablespoon butter pat.
3. Place chops in the air fryer basket and cook 12 minutes, turning halfway through cooking time, until tops and edges are golden brown and internal temperature reaches at least 145°F.
4. Use remaining butter pats to top each pork chop while hot, then let cool 5 minutes before serving warm.

Mozzarella-stuffed Meatloaf

Servings: 6
Cooking Time: 30 Minutes
Ingredients:
- 1 pound 80/20 ground beef
- ½ medium green bell pepper, seeded and chopped
- ¼ medium yellow onion, peeled and chopped
- ½ teaspoon salt
- ¼ teaspoon ground black pepper
- 2 ounces mozzarella cheese, sliced into ¼"-thick slices
- ¼ cup low-carb ketchup

Directions:
1. In a large bowl, combine ground beef, bell pepper, onion, salt, and black pepper. Cut a piece of parchment to fit air fryer basket. Place half beef mixture on ungreased parchment and form a 9" × 4" loaf, about ½" thick.
2. Center mozzarella slices on beef loaf, leaving at least ¼" around each edge.
3. Press remaining beef into a second 9" × 4" loaf and place on top of mozzarella, pressing edges of loaves together to seal.
4. Place parchment with meatloaf into air fryer basket. Adjust the temperature to 350°F and set the timer for 30 minutes, carefully turning loaf and brushing top with ketchup halfway through cooking. Loaf will be browned and have an internal temperature of at least 180°F when done. Slice and serve warm.

Sriracha Pork Strips With Rice

Servings: 4
Cooking Time: 30 Minutes + Chilling Time
Ingredients:
- ½ cup lemon juice
- 2 tbsp lemon marmalade
- 1 tbsp avocado oil
- 1 tbsp tamari
- 2 tsp sriracha
- 1 tsp yellow mustard
- 1 lb pork shoulder strips
- 4 cups cooked white rice
- ¼ cup chopped cilantro
- 1 tsp black pepper

Directions:
1. Whisk the lemon juice, lemon marmalade, avocado oil, tamari, sriracha, and mustard in a bowl. Reserve half of the marinade. Toss pork strips with half of the marinade and let marinate covered in the fridge for 30 minutes.
2. Preheat air fryer at 350°F. Place pork strips in the frying basket and Air Fry for 17 minutes, tossing twice. Transfer them to a bowl and stir in the remaining marinade. Serve over cooked rice and scatter with cilantro and pepper.

Lamb Burgers

Servings: 2
Cooking Time: 16 Minutes
Ingredients:
- 8 oz lamb, minced
- ½ teaspoon salt
- ½ teaspoon ground black pepper
- ½ teaspoon dried cilantro
- 1 tablespoon water
- Cooking spray

Directions:
1. In the mixing bowl mix up minced lamb, salt, ground black pepper, dried cilantro, and water.
2. Stir the meat mixture carefully with the help of the spoon and make 2 burgers.
3. Preheat the air fryer to 375°F.
4. Spray the air fryer basket with cooking spray and put the burgers inside.
5. Cook them for 8 minutes from each side.

Garlic Fillets

Servings: 4
Cooking Time: 15 Minutes
Ingredients:
- 1-pound beef filet mignon
- 1 teaspoon minced garlic
- 1 tablespoon peanut oil
- ½ teaspoon salt
- 1 teaspoon dried oregano

Directions:
1. Chop the beef into the medium size pieces and sprinkle with salt and dried oregano. Then add minced garlic and peanut oil and mix up the meat well. Place the bowl with meat in the fridge for 10 minutes to marinate. Meanwhile, preheat the air fryer to 400°F. Put the marinated beef pieces in the air fryer and cook them for 10 minutes Then flip the beef on another side and cook for 5 minutes more.

Garlic Beef With Egg And Bell Pepper

Servings: 4
Cooking Time: 30 Minutes
Ingredients:
- 1 pound ground beef
- 6 eggs, beaten
- 1 green bell pepper, seeded and chopped
- 1 onion, chopped
- 3 cloves of garlic, minced
- 3 tablespoons olive oil
- Salt and pepper

Directions:
1. Stir the ground beef well with the olive oil, onion, garlic, and bell pepper in the cooking basket of your air fryer.
2. Dress with salt and pepper, then pour in the beaten eggs and mix.
3. Cook at 330 degrees F/ 165 degrees C for 30 minutes.
4. When done, serve and enjoy.

Ritzy Skirt Steak Fajitas

Servings: 4
Cooking Time: 30 Minutes
Ingredients:
- 2 tablespoons olive oil
- ¼ cup lime juice
- 1 clove garlic, minced
- ½ teaspoon ground cumin
- ½ teaspoon hot sauce
- ½ teaspoon salt
- 2 tablespoons chopped fresh cilantro
- 1 pound (454 g) skirt steak
- 1 onion, sliced
- 1 teaspoon chili powder
- 1 red pepper, sliced
- 1 green pepper, sliced
- Salt and freshly ground black pepper, to taste
- 8 flour tortillas
- Toppings:
- Shredded lettuce
- Crumbled Queso Fresco (or grated Cheddar cheese)
- Sliced black olives
- Diced tomatoes
- Sour cream
- Guacamole

Directions:
1. Combine the olive oil, lime juice, garlic, cumin, hot sauce, salt and cilantro in a shallow dish. Add the skirt steak and turn it over several times to coat all sides. Pierce the steak with a needle-style meat tenderizer or paring knife. Marinate the steak in the refrigerator for at least 3 hours, or overnight. When you are ready to cook, remove the steak from the refrigerator and let it sit at room temperature for 30 minutes.
2. Preheat the air fryer to 400ºF (204ºC).
3. Toss the onion slices with the chili powder and a little olive oil and transfer them to the air fryer basket. Air fry for 5 minutes. Add the red and green peppers to the air fryer basket with the onions, season with salt and pepper and air fry for 8 more minutes, until the onions and peppers are soft. Transfer the vegetables to a dish and cover with aluminum foil to keep warm.
4. Put the skirt steak in the air fryer basket and pour the marinade over the top. Air fry at 400ºF (204ºC) for 12 minutes. Flip the steak over and air fry for an additional 5 minutes. Transfer the cooked steak to a cutting board and let the steak rest for a few minutes. If the peppers and onions need to be heated, return them to the air fryer for just 1 to 2 minutes.
5. Thinly slice the steak at an angle, cutting against the grain of the steak. Serve the steak with the onions and peppers, the warm tortillas and the fajita toppings on the side.
6. Serve immediately.

Homemade Ham Cheese Sandwiches

Servings: 4
Cooking Time: 10 Minutes
Ingredients:
- 4 slices lean pork ham
- 4 slices cheese
- 8 slices tomato

Directions:
1. At 360 degrees F/ 180 degrees C, preheat your Air fryer.
2. Spread 4 slices of bread on a flat surface.
3. Spread the slices with cheese, tomato, turkey and ham.
4. Cover with the remaining pork slices to form sandwiches.
5. Add the sandwiches to the air fryer basket and cook for almost 10 minutes.
6. Serve.

Meatloaf

Servings: 4
Cooking Time: 40 Minutes
Ingredients:
- 1 pound 80/20 lean ground beef
- 1 large egg
- 3 tablespoons Italian bread crumbs
- 1 teaspoon salt
- 2 tablespoons ketchup
- 2 tablespoons brown sugar

Directions:
1. Preheat the air fryer to 350°F.
2. In a large bowl, combine beef, egg, bread crumbs, and salt.
3. In a small bowl, mix ketchup and brown sugar.
4. Form meat mixture into a 6" × 3" loaf and brush with ketchup mixture.
5. Place in the air fryer basket and cook 40 minutes until internal temperature reaches at least 160°F. Serve warm.

Homemade Toad In The Hole

Servings: 4
Cooking Time: 40 Minutes
Ingredients:
- 6 beef sausages
- 1 tablespoon butter, melted
- 1 cup plain flour
- A pinch of salt
- 2 eggs
- 1 cup semi-skimmed milk

Directions:
1. Cook the sausages in your Air Fryer at about 380 degrees F/ 195 degrees C for almost 15 minutes, shaking halfway through the cooking time.
2. Meanwhile, make up the batter mix.
3. Tip the flour into a bowl with salt; make a well in the middle and crack the eggs into it.
4. Mix with an electric whisk; now, slowly and gradually pour in the milk, whisking all the time.
5. Place the sausages in a lightly greased baking pan.
6. Pour the prepared batter over the sausages.
7. Cook in the preheated Air Fryer at about 370 degrees F/ 185 degrees C approximately 25 minutes, until golden and risen.
8. Serve.

Marinated Beef And Vegetable Stir Fry

Servings: 4
Cooking Time: 35 Minutes
Ingredients:
- 2 lbs. top round, cut into bite-sized strips
- 2 garlic cloves, sliced
- 1 teaspoon dried marjoram
- ¼ cup red wine
- 1 tablespoon tamari sauce
- Salt and black pepper, to taste
- ½ tablespoon olive oil
- 1 red onion, sliced
- 2 bell peppers, sliced
- 1 carrot, sliced

Directions:
1. In a suitable bowl, add the top round, marjoram, red wine, garlic, tamari sauce, salt, and pepper in a bowl; cover and marinate for 1 hour.
2. Oil the cooking tray of your air fryer.
3. Take the marinated beef out of the marinade and arrange to the tray.
4. Cook at 390 degrees F/200 degrees C for 15 minutes.
5. After that, add the garlic, onion, peppers and carrot, cook for 15 minutes more or until tender.
6. Open the Air Fryer every 5 minutes and baste the meat with the remaining marinade.
7. When done, serve and enjoy.

Pesto Coated Rack Of Lamb

Servings: 4
Cooking Time: 15 Minutes
Ingredients:
- ½ bunch fresh mint
- 1 rack of lamb
- 1 garlic clove
- ¼ cup extra-virgin olive oil
- ½ tablespoon honey
- Salt and black pepper, to taste

Directions:
1. Preheat the Air fryer to 200°F and grease an Air fryer basket.
2. Put the mint, garlic, oil, honey, salt, and black pepper in a blender and pulse until smooth to make pesto.
3. Coat the rack of lamb with this pesto on both sides and arrange in the Air fryer basket.
4. Cook for about 15 minutes and cut the rack into individual chops to serve.

Tacos Norteños

Servings: 4
Cooking Time: 25 Minutes
Ingredients:
- ½ cup minced purple onions
- 5 radishes, julienned
- 2 tbsp white wine vinegar
- ½ tsp granulated sugar
- Salt and pepper to taste
- ¼ cup olive oil
- ½ tsp ground cumin
- 1 flank steak
- 10 mini flour tortillas
- 1 cup shredded red cabbage
- ½ cup cucumber slices
- ½ cup fresh radish slices

Directions:
1. Combine the radishes, vinegar, sugar, and salt in a bowl. Let sit covered in the fridge until ready to use. Whisk the olive oil, salt, black pepper and cumin in a bowl. Toss in flank steak and let marinate in the fridge for 30 minutes.
2. Preheat air fryer at 325ºF. Place flank steak in the frying basket and Bake for 18-20 minutes, tossing once. Let rest onto a cutting board for 5 minutes before slicing thinly against the grain. Add steak slices to flour tortillas along with red cabbage, chopped purple onions, cucumber slices, radish slices and fresh radish slices. Serve warm.

Pork Burgers With Cheddar Cheese

Servings: 2
Cooking Time: 20 Minutes
Ingredients:
- 1 medium onion, chopped
- 1 tablespoon mixed herbs
- 2 teaspoons garlic powder
- 1 teaspoon dried basil
- 1 tablespoon tomato puree
- 1 teaspoon mustard
- Black pepper and salt to taste
- 2 bread buns, halved
- Assembling:
- 1 large onion, sliced in 2-inch rings
- 1 large tomato, sliced in 2-inch rings
- 2 small lettuce leaves, cleaned
- 4 slices Cheddar cheese

Directions:
1. In a suitable bowl, add pork, chopped onion, mixed herbs, garlic powder, dried basil, tomato puree, mustard, salt, and black pepper.
2. Use hands to mix evenly. Form 2 patties out of the mixture and place on a flat plate.
3. At 370 degrees F/ 185 degrees C, preheat your air fryer.
4. Place the pork patties in the fryer basket, and cook for almost 15 minutes.
5. Slide-out the basket and turn the patties with a spatula.
6. Reduce its temperature to 350 degrees F/ 175 degrees C and continue cooking for 5 minutes.
7. Once ready, remove them onto a plate and start assembling the burger.
8. Place 2 halves of the bun on a clean flat surface.
9. Add the lettuce in both, then a patty each, followed by an onion ring each, a tomato ring each, and then 2 slices of cheddar cheese each.
10. Cover the buns with their other halves.
11. Serve with ketchup and French fries.

Tender Steak With Salsa Verde

Servings: 4
Cooking Time: 20 Minutes
Ingredients:
- 1 flank steak, halved
- 1 ½ cups salsa verde
- ½ tsp black pepper

Directions:
1. Toss steak and 1 cup of salsa verde in a bowl and refrigerate covered for 2 hours. Preheat air fryer to 400ºF. Add steaks to the lightly greased frying basket and Air Fry for 10-12 minutes or until you reach your desired doneness, flipping once. Let sit onto a cutting board for 5 minutes. Thinly slice against the grain and divide between 4 plates. Spoon over the remaining salsa verde and serve sprinkled with black pepper to serve.

Beef & Sauerkraut Spring Rolls

Servings: 4
Cooking Time: 20 Minutes
Ingredients:
- 5 Colby cheese slices, cut into strips
- 2 tbsp Thousand Island Dressing for dipping
- 10 spring roll wrappers
- 1/3 lb corned beef
- 2 cups sauerkraut
- 1 tsp ground cumin
- ½ tsp ground nutmeg
- 1 egg, beaten
- 1 tsp corn starch

Directions:
1. Preheat air fryer to 360°F. Mix the egg and cornstarch in a bowl to thicken. Lay out the spring roll wrappers on a clean surface. Place a few strips of the cut-up corned beef in the middle of the wraps. Sprinkle with Colby cheese, cumin, and nutmeg and top with 1-2 tablespoons of sauerkraut. Roll up and seal the seams with the egg and cornstarch mixture. Place the rolls in the greased frying basket. Bake for 7 minutes, shaking the basket several times until the spring rolls are golden brown. Serve warm with Thousand Island for dipping.

Carne Asada Tacos

Servings: 4
Cooking Time: 14 Minutes
Ingredients:
- ⅓ cup olive oil
- 1½ pounds (680 g) flank steak
- Salt and freshly ground black pepper, to taste
- ⅓ cup freshly squeezed lime juice
- ½ cup chopped fresh cilantro
- 4 teaspoons minced garlic
- 1 teaspoon ground cumin
- 1 teaspoon chili powder

Directions:
1. Brush the air fryer basket with olive oil.
2. Put the flank steak in a large mixing bowl. Season with salt and pepper.
3. Add the lime juice, cilantro, garlic, cumin, and chili powder and toss to coat the steak.
4. For the best flavor, let the steak marinate in the refrigerator for about 1 hour.
5. Preheat the air fryer to 400ºF (204ºC)
6. Put the steak in the air fryer basket. Air fry for 7 minutes. Flip the steak. Air fry for 7 minutes more or until an internal temperature reaches at least 145ºF (63ºC).
7. Let the steak rest for about 5 minutes, then cut into strips to serve.

Vietnamese Beef Lettuce Wraps

Servings: 4
Cooking Time: 12 Minutes
Ingredients:
- ⅓ cup low-sodium soy sauce*
- 2 teaspoons fish sauce*
- 2 teaspoons brown sugar
- 1 tablespoon chili paste
- juice of 1 lime
- 2 cloves garlic, minced
- 2 teaspoons fresh ginger, minced
- 1 pound beef sirloin
- Sauce
- ⅓ cup low-sodium soy sauce*
- juice of 2 limes
- 1 tablespoon mirin wine
- 2 teaspoons chili paste
- Serving
- 1 head butter lettuce
- ½ cup julienned carrots
- ½ cup julienned cucumber
- ½ cup sliced radishes, sliced into half moons
- 2 cups cooked rice noodles
- ⅓ cup chopped peanuts

Directions:
1. Combine the soy sauce, fish sauce, brown sugar, chili paste, lime juice, garlic and ginger in a bowl. Slice the beef into thin slices, then cut those slices in half. Add the beef to the marinade and marinate for 1 to 3 hours in the refrigerator. When you are ready to cook, remove the steak from the refrigerator and let it sit at room temperature for 30 minutes.
2. Preheat the air fryer to 400°F.
3. Transfer the beef and marinade to the air fryer basket. Air-fry at 400°F for 12 minutes, shaking the basket a few times during the cooking process.
4. While the beef is cooking, prepare a wrap-building station. Combine the soy sauce, lime juice, mirin wine and chili paste in a bowl and transfer to a little pouring vessel. Separate the lettuce leaves from the head of lettuce and put them in a serving bowl. Place the carrots, cucumber, radish, rice noodles and chopped peanuts all in separate serving bowls.
5. When the beef has finished cooking, transfer it to another serving bowl and invite your guests to build their wraps. To build the wraps, place some beef in a lettuce leaf and top with carrots, cucumbers, some rice noodles and chopped peanuts. Drizzle a little sauce over top, fold the lettuce around the ingredients and enjoy!

Pork Kabobs With Pineapple

Servings: 4
Cooking Time: 30 Minutes
Ingredients:
- 2 cans juice-packed pineapple chunks, juice reserved
- 1 green bell pepper, cut into ½-inch chunks
- 1 red bell pepper, cut into ½-inch chunks
- 1 lb pork tenderloin, cubed
- Salt and pepper to taste
- 1 tbsp honey
- ½ tsp ground ginger
- ½ tsp ground coriander
- 1 red chili, minced

Directions:
1. Preheat the air fryer to 375°F. Mix the coriander, chili, salt, and pepper in a bowl. Add the pork and toss to coat. Then, thread the pork pieces, pineapple chunks, and bell peppers onto skewers. Combine the pineapple juice, honey, and ginger and mix well. Use all the mixture as you brush it on the kebabs. Put the kebabs in the greased frying basket and Air Fry for 10-14 minutes or until cooked through. Serve and enjoy!

Tasty Pork Chops

Servings: 4
Cooking Time: 9 Minutes
Ingredients:
- 4 pork chops, boneless
- 1 teaspoon onion powder
- 1 teaspoon smoked paprika
- ½ cup parmesan cheese, grated
- 2 tablespoons olive oil
- ½ teaspoon black pepper
- 1 teaspoon kosher salt

Directions:
1. Brush pork chops with olive oil.
2. In a suitable bowl, mix together parmesan cheese and spices.
3. Grease its air fryer basket with cooking spray.

4. Coat pork chops with parmesan cheese mixture and place in the air fryer basket.
5. Cook pork chops at 375 degrees F/ 190 degrees C for 9 minutes. Turn halfway through the cooking time.
6. Serve and enjoy.

Greek Lamb Rack

Servings: 4
Cooking Time: 10 Minutes
Ingredients:
- ¼ cup freshly squeezed lemon juice
- 1 teaspoon oregano
- 2 teaspoons minced fresh rosemary
- 1 teaspoon minced fresh thyme
- 2 tablespoons minced garlic
- Salt and freshly ground black pepper, to taste
- 2 to 4 tablespoons olive oil
- 1 lamb rib rack (7 to 8 ribs)

Directions:
1. Preheat the air fryer to 360°F (182°C).
2. In a small mixing bowl, combine the lemon juice, oregano, rosemary, thyme, garlic, salt, pepper, and olive oil and mix well.
3. Rub the mixture over the lamb, covering all the meat. Put the rack of lamb in the air fryer. Roast for 10 minutes. Flip the rack halfway through.
4. After 10 minutes, measure the internal temperature of the rack of lamb reaches at least 145°F (63°C).
5. Serve immediately.

Rib Eye Cheesesteaks With Fried Onions

Servings: 2
Cooking Time: 20 Minutes
Ingredients:
- 1 (12-ounce) rib eye steak
- 2 tablespoons Worcestershire sauce
- salt and freshly ground black pepper
- ½ onion, sliced
- 2 tablespoons butter, melted
- 4 ounces sliced Cheddar or provolone cheese
- 2 long hoagie rolls, lightly toasted

Directions:
1. Place the steak in the freezer for 30 minutes to make it easier to slice. When it is well-chilled, thinly slice the steak against the grain and transfer it to a bowl. Pour the Worcestershire sauce over the steak and season it with salt and pepper. Allow the meat to come to room temperature.
2. Preheat the air fryer to 400°F.
3. Toss the sliced onion with the butter and transfer it to the air fryer basket. Air-fry at 400°F for 12 minutes, shaking the basket a few times during the cooking process. Place the steak on top of the onions and air-fry for another 6 minutes, stirring the meat and onions together halfway through the cooking time.
4. When the air fryer has finished cooking, divide the steak and onions in half in the air fryer basket, pushing each half to one side of the air fryer basket. Place the cheese on top of each half, push the drawer back into the turned off air fryer and let it sit for 2 minutes, until the cheese has melted.
5. Transfer each half of the cheesesteak mixture into a toasted roll with the cheese side up and dig in!

Italian-style Cheeseburgers With Cheese Slices

Servings: 4
Cooking Time: 12 Minutes
Ingredients:
- 1-pound ground beef
- 4 cheddar cheese slices
- ½ teaspoon Italian seasoning
- Black pepper
- Salt

Directions:
1. Grease its air fryer basket with cooking spray.
2. In a suitable bowl, mix together ground beef, Italian seasoning, black pepper, and salt.
3. Make 4 equal shapes of patties from meat mixture and place into the air fryer basket.
4. Cook at almost 375 degrees F/ 190 degrees C for 5 minutes. Turn patties to another side and cook for 5 minutes more.
5. Place cheese slices on top of each patty and cook for 2 minutes more.
6. Serve and enjoy.

Delicious Cheeseburgers

Servings: 4
Cooking Time: 12 Minutes
Ingredients:
- 1 lb ground beef
- 4 cheddar cheese slices
- 1/2 tsp Italian seasoning
- Pepper
- Salt
- Cooking spray

Directions:
1. Spray air fryer basket with cooking spray.
2. In a bowl, mix together ground beef, Italian seasoning, pepper, and salt.
3. Make four equal shapes of patties from meat mixture and place into the air fryer basket.
4. Cook at 375°F for 5 minutes. Turn patties to another side and cook for 5 minutes more.
5. Place cheese slices on top of each patty and cook for 2 minutes more.
6. Serve and enjoy.

Chapter 7: Fish And Seafood Recipes

Parmesan Tilapia With Parsley
Servings: 4
Cooking Time: 10 Minutes
Ingredients:
- 1 pound tilapia fillets
- ¾ cup parmesan cheese, grated
- 1 tablespoon parsley, chopped
- 2 teaspoons paprika
- 1 tablespoon olive oil
- Black pepper and salt to taste

Directions:
1. At 400 degrees F/ 205 degrees C, preheat your air fryer.
2. In a shallow dish, combine together the paprika, grated cheese, black pepper, salt and parsley.
3. Pour a little olive oil over the tilapia fillets.
4. Cover the fillets with the paprika and cheese mixture.
5. Lay the fillets on a sheet of aluminum foil and transfer to the Air Fryer basket.
6. Air fry for almost 10 minutes. Serve hot.

Crispy Parmesan Lobster Tails
Servings: 4
Cooking Time: 7 Minutes
Ingredients:
- 4 lobster tails
- 2 tablespoons salted butter, melted
- 1½ teaspoons Cajun seasoning, divided
- ¼ teaspoon salt
- ¼ teaspoon ground black pepper
- ¼ cup grated Parmesan cheese
- ½ ounce plain pork rinds, finely crushed

Directions:
1. Cut lobster tails open carefully with a pair of scissors and gently pull meat away from shells, resting meat on top of shells.
2. Brush lobster meat with butter and sprinkle with 1 teaspoon Cajun seasoning, ¼ teaspoon per tail.
3. In a small bowl, mix remaining Cajun seasoning, salt, pepper, Parmesan, and pork rinds. Gently press ¼ mixture onto meat on each lobster tail.
4. Carefully place tails into ungreased air fryer basket. Adjust the temperature to 400°F and set the timer for 7 minutes. Lobster tails will be crispy and golden on top and have an internal temperature of at least 145°F when done. Serve warm.

Sesame-glazed Salmon
Servings: 4
Cooking Time: 16 Minutes
Ingredients:
- 3 tablespoons soy sauce
- 1 tablespoon rice wine or dry sherry
- 1 tablespoon brown sugar
- 1 tablespoon toasted sesame oil
- 1 teaspoon minced garlic
- ¼ teaspoon minced ginger
- 4 (6 ounce) salmon fillets, skin-on
- Olive oil
- ½ tablespoon sesame seeds

Directions:
1. In a small bowl, mix together the soy sauce, rice wine, brown sugar, toasted sesame oil, garlic, and ginger.
2. Place the salmon in a shallow baking dish and pour the marinade over the fillets. Cover and refrigerate for at least 1 hour, turning the fillets occasionally to coat in the marinade.
3. Spray a fryer basket lightly with olive oil.
4. Shake off as much marinade as possible and place the fillets, skin side down, in the fryer basket in a single layer. Reserve the marinade. You may need to cook them in batches.
5. Air fry for 8 to 10 minutes. Brush the tops of the salmon fillets with the reserved marinade and sprinkle with sesame seeds.
6. Increase the fryer temperature to 400°F and cook for 2 to 5 more minutes for medium, 1 to 3 minutes for medium rare, or 4 to 6 minutes for well done.

Spiced Shrimp With Zucchini
Servings: 4
Cooking Time: 25 Minutes
Ingredients:
- 2 zucchinis
- 30 shrimp
- 7 cherry tomatoes
- Black pepper and salt to taste
- 1 garlic clove

Directions:
1. Pour the oil in the air fryer, add the garlic clove and diced zucchini.
2. Cook for almost 15 minutes at 300 degrees F/ 150 degrees C.
3. Add the shrimp and the pieces of tomato, salt, and spices.
4. Cook for another 5 to 10 minutes or until the shrimp water evaporates.

Spicy Orange Shrimp
Servings: 4
Cooking Time: 15 Minutes
Ingredients:
- Olive oil
- ⅓ cup orange juice
- 3 teaspoons minced garlic
- 1 teaspoon Old Bay seasoning
- ¼ to ½ teaspoon cayenne pepper
- 1 pound medium shrimp, thawed, deveined, peeled, with tails off

Directions:
1. Spray a fryer basket lightly with olive oil.
2. In a medium bowl, combine the orange juice, garlic, Old Bay seasoning, and cayenne pepper.
3. Dry the shrimp with paper towels to remove excess water.
4. Add the shrimp to the marinade and stir to evenly coat. Cover with plastic wrap and place in the refrigerator for 30 minutes so the shrimp can soak up the marinade.
5. Place the shrimp into the fryer basket. Air fry for 5 minutes. Shake the basket and lightly spray with olive oil. Cook until the shrimp are opaque and crisp, 5 to 10 more minutes.

Fish Piccata With Crispy Potatoes

Servings: 4
Cooking Time: 30 Minutes
Ingredients:
- 4 cod fillets
- 1 tbsp butter
- 2 tsp capers
- 1 garlic clove, minced
- 2 tbsp lemon juice
- ½ lb asparagus, trimmed
- 2 large potatoes, cubed
- 1 tbsp olive oil
- Salt and pepper to taste
- ¼ tsp garlic powder
- 1 tsp dried rosemary
- 1 tsp dried parsley
- 1 tsp chopped dill

Directions:
1. Preheat air fryer to 380°F. Place each fillet on a large piece of foil. Top each fillet with butter, capers, dill, garlic, and lemon juice. Fold the foil over the fish and seal the edges to make a pouch. Mix asparagus, parsley, potatoes, olive oil, salt, rosemary, garlic powder, and pepper in a large bowl. Place asparagus in the frying basket. Roast for 4 minutes, then shake the basket. Top vegetable with foil packets and Roast for another 8 minutes. Turn off air fryer and let it stand for 5 minutes. Serve warm and enjoy.

Classic Crab Cakes

Servings: 4
Cooking Time: 10 Minutes
Ingredients:
- 10 ounces Lump crabmeat, picked over for shell and cartilage
- 6 tablespoons Plain panko bread crumbs (gluten-free, if a concern)
- 6 tablespoons Chopped drained jarred roasted red peppers
- 4 Medium scallions, trimmed and thinly sliced
- ¼ cup Regular or low-fat mayonnaise (not fat-free; gluten-free, if a concern)
- ¼ teaspoon Dried dill
- ¼ teaspoon Dried thyme
- ¼ teaspoon Onion powder
- ¼ teaspoon Table salt
- ⅛ teaspoon Celery seeds
- Up to ⅛ teaspoon Cayenne
- Vegetable oil spray

Directions:
1. Preheat the air fryer to 400°F.
2. Gently mix the crabmeat, bread crumbs, red pepper, scallion, mayonnaise, dill, thyme, onion powder, salt, celery seeds, and cayenne in a bowl until well combined.
3. Use clean and dry hands to form ½ cup of this mixture into a tightly packed 1-inch-thick, 3- to 4-inch-wide patty. Coat the top and bottom of the patty with vegetable oil spray and set it aside. Continue making 1 more patty for a small batch, 3 more for a medium batch, or 5 more for a larger one, coating them with vegetable oil spray on both sides.
4. Set the patties in one layer in the basket and air-fry undisturbed for 10 minutes, or until lightly browned and cooked through.
5. Use a nonstick-safe spatula to transfer the crab cakes to a serving platter or plates. Wait a couple of minutes before serving.

Shrimp Teriyaki

Servings: 10
Cooking Time: 6 Minutes
Ingredients:
- 1 tablespoon Regular or low-sodium soy sauce or gluten-free tamari sauce
- 1 tablespoon Mirin or a substitute (see here)
- 1 teaspoon Ginger juice (see the headnote)
- 10 Large shrimp (20–25 per pound), peeled and deveined
- ⅔ cup Plain panko bread crumbs (gluten-free, if a concern)
- 1 Large egg
- Vegetable oil spray

Directions:
1. Whisk the soy or tamari sauce, mirin, and ginger juice in an 8- or 9-inch square baking pan until uniform. Add the shrimp and toss well to coat. Cover and refrigerate for 1 hour, tossing the shrimp in the marinade at least twice.
2. Preheat the air fryer to 400°F.
3. Thread a marinated shrimp on a 4-inch bamboo skewer by inserting the pointy tip at the small end of the shrimp, then guiding the skewer along the shrimp so that the tip comes out the thick end and the shrimp is flat along the length of the skewer. Repeat with the remaining shrimp. (You'll need eight 4-inch skewers for the small batch, 10 skewers for the medium batch, and 12 for the large.)
4. Pour the bread crumbs onto a dinner plate. Whisk the egg in the baking pan with any marinade that stayed behind. Lay the skewers in the pan, in as close to a single layer as possible. Turn repeatedly to make sure the shrimp is coated in the egg mixture.
5. One at a time, take a skewered shrimp out of the pan and set it in the bread crumbs, turning several times and pressing gently until the shrimp is evenly coated on all sides. Coat the shrimp with vegetable oil spray and set the skewer aside. Repeat with the remainder of the shrimp.
6. Set the skewered shrimp in the basket in one layer. Air-fry undisturbed for 6 minutes, or until pink and firm.
7. Transfer the skewers to a wire rack. Cool for only a minute or two before serving.

Feta & Shrimp Pita

Servings: 4
Cooking Time: 15 Minutes
Ingredients:
- 1 lb peeled shrimp, deveined
- 2 tbsp olive oil

- 1 tsp dried oregano
- ½ tsp dried thyme
- ½ tsp garlic powder
- ¼ tsp shallot powder
- ¼ tsp tarragon powder
- Salt and pepper to taste
- 4 whole-wheat pitas
- 4 oz feta cheese, crumbled
- 1 cup grated lettuce
- 1 tomato, diced
- ¼ cup black olives, sliced
- 1 lemon

Directions:
1. Preheat the oven to 380°F. Mix the shrimp with olive oil, oregano, thyme, garlic powder, shallot powder, tarragon powder salt, and pepper in a bowl. Pour shrimp in a single layer in the frying basket and Bake for 6-8 minutes or until no longer pink and cooked through. Divide the shrimp into warmed pitas with feta, lettuce, tomato, olives, and a squeeze of lemon. Serve and enjoy!

Mahi-mahi "burrito" Fillets

Servings: 3
Cooking Time: 10 Minutes
Ingredients:
- 1 Large egg white
- 1½ cups Crushed corn tortilla chips (gluten-free, if a concern)
- 1 tablespoon Chile powder
- 3 5-ounce skinless mahi-mahi fillets
- 6 tablespoons Canned refried beans
- Vegetable oil spray

Directions:
1. Preheat the air fryer to 400°F.
2. Set up and fill two shallow soup plates or small pie plates on your counter: one with the egg white, beaten until foamy; and one with the crushed tortilla chips.
3. Gently rub ½ teaspoon chile powder on each side of each fillet.
4. Spread 1 tablespoon refried beans over both sides and the edges of a fillet. Dip the fillet in the egg white, turning to coat it on both sides. Let any excess egg white slip back into the rest, then set the fillet in the crushed tortilla chips. Turn several times, pressing gently to coat it evenly. Coat the fillet on all sides with the vegetable oil spray, then set it aside. Prepare the remaining fillet(s) in the same way.
5. When the machine is at temperature, set the fillets in the basket with as much air space between them as possible. Air-fry undisturbed for 10 minutes, or until crisp and browned.
6. Use a nonstick-safe spatula to transfer the fillets to a serving platter or plates. Cool for only a minute or so, then serve hot.

Shrimp "scampi"

Servings: 4
Cooking Time: 5 Minutes
Ingredients:
- 1½ pounds Large shrimp, peeled and deveined
- ¼ cup Olive oil
- 2 tablespoons Minced garlic
- 1 teaspoon Dried oregano
- Up to 1 teaspoon Red pepper flakes
- ½ teaspoon Table salt
- 2 tablespoons White balsamic vinegar

Directions:
1. Preheat the air fryer to 400°F.
2. Stir the shrimp, olive oil, garlic, oregano, red pepper flakes, and salt in a large bowl until the shrimp are well coated.
3. When the machine is at temperature, transfer the shrimp to the basket. They will overlap and even sit on top of each other. Air-fry for 5 minutes, tossing and rearranging the shrimp twice to make sure the covered surfaces are exposed, until pink and firm.
4. Pour the contents of the basket into a serving bowl. Pour the vinegar over the shrimp while hot and toss to coat.

Ginger Salmon Fillet

Servings: 4
Cooking Time: 22 Minutes
Ingredients:
- 2 salmon fillets
- 60g cane sugar
- 4 tablespoons soy sauce
- 50g sesame seeds
- Unlimited Ginger

Directions:
1. Preheat the air fryer at about 360 degrees F/ 180 degrees C for 5 minutes.
2. Put the sugar and soy sauce in the basket.
3. Cook everything for 5 minutes.
4. In the meantime, wash the fish well, pass it through sesame to cover it completely and place it inside the tank and add the fresh ginger.
5. Cook for 12 minutes.
6. Flip the salmon fillets and finish cooking for another 8 minutes.

Lemon-roasted Salmon Fillets

Servings: 3
Cooking Time: 7 Minutes
Ingredients:
- 3 6-ounce skin-on salmon fillets
- Olive oil spray
- 9 Very thin lemon slices
- ¾ teaspoon Ground black pepper
- ¼ teaspoon Table salt

Directions:
1. Preheat the air fryer to 400°F.
2. Generously coat the skin of each of the fillets with olive oil spray. Set the fillets skin side down on your work surface. Place three overlapping lemon slices down the length of each salmon fillet. Sprinkle them with the pepper and salt. Coat lightly with olive oil spray.

3. Use a nonstick-safe spatula to transfer the fillets one by one to the basket, leaving as much air space between them as possible. Air-fry undisturbed for 7 minutes, or until cooked through.
4. Use a nonstick-safe spatula to transfer the fillets to serving plates. Cool for only a minute or two before serving.

Honey-glazed Salmon

Servings: 4
Cooking Time: 30 Minutes
Ingredients:
- 2 tablespoons soy sauce
- 1 teaspoon sriracha
- ½ teaspoon minced garlic
- 4 skin-on salmon fillets
- 2 teaspoons honey

Directions:
1. In a large bowl, whisk together soy sauce, sriracha, and garlic. Place salmon in bowl. Cover and let marinate in refrigerator at least 20 minutes.
2. Preheat the air fryer to 375°F.
3. Place salmon in the air fryer basket and cook 8 minutes. Open air fryer and brush honey on salmon. Continue cooking 2 more minutes until salmon flakes easily and internal temperature reaches at least 145°F. Serve warm.

Hearty Lemon Salmon

Servings: 2
Cooking Time: 12 Minutes
Ingredients:
- 2 salmon steaks
- Coarse salt, to taste
- 1 tablespoon sesame oil
- Zest of 1 lemon
- ¼ teaspoon black pepper
- 1 tablespoon fresh lemon juice
- 1 teaspoon garlic, minced
- ½ teaspoon smoked cayenne pepper
- ½ teaspoon dried dill

Directions:
1. At 380 degrees F/ 195 degrees C, preheat your air fryer. Pat dry the salmon steaks with a kitchen towel.
2. In a ceramic dish, combine the remaining ingredients until everything is well whisked.
3. Add the salmon steaks to the ceramic dish and let them sit in the refrigerator for 1 hour. Now, place the salmon steaks in the cooking basket. Reserve the marinade.
4. Cook for 12 minutes, flipping halfway through the cooking time.
5. Meanwhile, cook the marinade in a small sauté pan over a moderate flame. Cook until the sauce has thickened.
6. Pour the prepared spicy sauce over the steaks and serve.

Lemon-basil On Cod Filet

Servings: 4
Cooking Time: 15 Minutes
Ingredients:
- ¼ cup olive oil
- 4 cod fillets
- A bunch of basil, torn
- Juice from 1 lemon, freshly squeezed
- Salt and pepper to taste

Directions:
1. Preheat the air fryer for 5 minutes.
2. Season the cod fillets with salt and pepper to taste. Place on lightly greased air fryer baking pan.
3. Mix the rest of the ingredients in a bowl and toss to combine. Pour over fish.
4. Cook for 15 minutes at 330°F.
5. Serve and enjoy.

Tuna And Fruit Kebabs

Servings: 4
Cooking Time: 8 To 12 Minutes
Ingredients:
- 1 pound tuna steaks, cut into 1-inch cubes
- ½ cup canned pineapple chunks, drained, juice reserved
- ½ cup large red grapes
- 1 tablespoon honey
- 2 teaspoons grated fresh ginger
- 1 teaspoon olive oil
- Pinch cayenne pepper

Directions:
1. Thread the tuna, pineapple, and grapes on 8 bamboo (see Tip) or 4 metal skewers that fit in the air fryer.
2. In a small bowl, whisk the honey, 1 tablespoon of reserved pineapple juice, the ginger, olive oil, and cayenne. Brush this mixture over the kebabs. Let them stand for 10 minutes.
3. Grill the kebabs for 8 to 12 minutes, or until the tuna reaches an internal temperature of at least 145°F on a meat thermometer, and the fruit is tender and glazed, brushing once with the remaining sauce. Discard any remaining marinade. Serve immediately.

Fish Sticks With Tartar Sauce

Servings: 2
Cooking Time: 6 Minutes
Ingredients:
- 12 ounces cod or flounder
- ½ cup flour
- ½ teaspoon paprika
- 1 teaspoon salt
- lots of freshly ground black pepper
- 2 eggs, lightly beaten
- 1½ cups panko breadcrumbs
- 1 teaspoon salt
- vegetable oil
- Tartar Sauce:
- ¼ cup mayonnaise
- 2 teaspoons lemon juice
- 2 tablespoons finely chopped sweet pickles
- salt and freshly ground black pepper

Directions:
1. Cut the fish into ¾-inch wide sticks or strips. Set up a dredging station. Combine the flour, paprika, salt and pepper in a shallow dish. Beat the eggs lightly in a second shallow dish. Finally, mix the breadcrumbs and salt in a third shallow dish. Coat the fish sticks by dipping the fish into the flour, then the egg and finally the breadcrumbs, coating on all sides in each step and pressing the crumbs firmly onto the fish. Place the finished sticks on a plate or baking sheet while you finish all the sticks.
2. Preheat the air fryer to 400°F.
3. Spray the fish sticks with the oil and spray or brush the bottom of the air fryer basket. Place the fish into the basket and air-fry at 400°F for 4 minutes, turn the fish sticks over, and air-fry for another 2 minutes.
4. While the fish is cooking, mix the tartar sauce ingredients together.
5. Serve the fish sticks warm with the tartar sauce and some French fries on the side.

Cod Nuggets

Servings: 4
Cooking Time: 12 Minutes
Ingredients:
- 2 boneless, skinless cod fillets
- 1 ½ teaspoons salt, divided
- ¾ teaspoon ground black pepper, divided
- 2 large eggs
- 1 cup plain bread crumbs

Directions:
1. Preheat the air fryer to 350°F.
2. Cut cod fillets into sixteen even-sized pieces. In a large bowl, add cod nuggets and sprinkle with 1 teaspoon salt and ½ teaspoon pepper.
3. In a small bowl, whisk eggs. In another small bowl, mix bread crumbs with remaining ½ teaspoon salt and ¼ teaspoon pepper.
4. One by one, dip nuggets in the eggs, shaking off excess before rolling in the bread crumb mixture. Repeat to make sixteen nuggets.
5. Place nuggets in the air fryer basket and spritz with cooking spray. Cook 12 minutes, turning halfway through cooking time. Nuggets will be done when golden brown and have an internal temperature of at least 145°F. Serve warm.

Baltimore Crab Cakes

Servings: 4
Cooking Time: 35 Minutes
Ingredients:
- ½ lb lump crabmeat, shells discarded
- 2 tbsp mayonnaise
- ½ tsp yellow mustard
- ½ tsp lemon juice
- ½ tbsp minced shallot
- ¼ cup bread crumbs
- 1 egg
- Salt and pepper to taste
- 4 poached eggs
- ½ cup bechamel sauce
- 2 tsp chopped chives
- 1 lemon, cut into wedges

Directions:
1. Preheat air fryer at 400ºF. Combine all ingredients, except eggs, sauce, and chives, in a bowl. Form mixture into 4 patties. Place crab cakes in the greased frying basket and Air Fry for 10 minutes, flipping once. Transfer them to a serving dish. Top each crab cake with 1 poached egg, drizzle with Bechamel sauce and scatter with chives and lemon wedges. Serve and enjoy!

Asparagus & Salmon Spring Rolls

Servings: 4
Cooking Time: 30 Minutes
Ingredients:
- ½ lb salmon fillets
- 1 tsp toasted sesame oil
- 1 onion, sliced
- 8 rice paper wrappers
- 4 asparagus, thinly sliced
- 1 carrot, shredded
- 1/3 cup chopped parsley
- ¼ cup chopped fresh basil

Directions:
1. Preheat air fryer to 370°F. Lay the salmon in the frying basket and pour some sesame oil over, then toss in the onion. Air Fry for 8-10 minutes. The salmon should flake when poked with a fork and the onion is soft. Pour warm water into a shallow bowl, then one at a time wet the rice paper wrappers and put them on a clean workspace. Put an eighth of salmon/onion mix on each wrapper as well as asparagus, carrot, parsley, and basil. Fold the wrappers and roll up, sealing the ingredients inside. Air Fry in the fryer for 7-9 minutes until crispy and golden. Serve hot.

Grouper With Miso-honey Sauce

Servings: 2
Cooking Time: 10 Minutes
Ingredients:
- ¾ pound grouper fillets
- Salt and white pepper, to taste
- 1 tablespoon sesame oil
- 1 teaspoon water
- 1 teaspoon deli mustard or Dijon mustard
- ¼ cup white miso
- 1 tablespoon mirin
- 1 tablespoon honey
- 1 tablespoon Shoyu sauce

Directions:
1. Sprinkle salt and white pepper on the grouper fillets, then drizzle them with a nonstick cooking oil.
2. Arrange the fillets to the air fryer and cook them at 400 degrees F/ 205 degrees C for 10 minutes, flipping halfway through.
3. Meanwhile, whisk the other ingredients to make the sauce.
4. Serve the warm fish with the miso-honey sauce on the side. Bon appétit!

Lemon Shrimp And Zucchinis

Servings: 4
Cooking Time: 15 Minutes
Ingredients:
- 1 pound shrimp, peeled and deveined
- A pinch of salt and black pepper
- 2 zucchinis, cut into medium cubes
- 1 tablespoon lemon juice
- 1 tablespoon olive oil
- 1 tablespoon garlic, minced

Directions:
1. In a pan that fits the air fryer, combine all the ingredients, toss, put the pan in the machine and cook at 370°F for 15 minutes. Divide between plates and serve right away.

Pancetta-wrapped Scallops With Pancetta Slices

Servings: 3
Cooking Time: 10 Minutes
Ingredients:
- 1 pound sea scallops
- 1 tablespoon deli mustard
- 2 tablespoons soy sauce
- ¼ teaspoon shallot powder
- ¼ teaspoon garlic powder
- ½ teaspoon dried dill
- Sea salt, to taste
- Ground black pepper, to taste
- 4 ounces' pancetta slices

Directions:
1. Transfer the sea scallops that have patted dry in advance to a mixing bowl, the add the deli mustard, soy sauce, shallot powder, garlic powder, dill, salt, black pepper and toss well.
2. Use a bacon slice to wrap one scallop, when finished, transfer the scallop wraps to the cooking basket.
3. Cook the scallop wraps in your Air Fryer at 400 degrees F/ 205 degrees C for 7 minutes.
4. After 4 minutes of cooking time, turn them over and cook an additional 3 minutes.
5. Serve with hot sauce for dipping if desired. Bon appétit!

Easy Marinated Salmon Fillets

Servings:4
Cooking Time: 20 Minutes
Ingredients:
- 1 tablespoon olive oil, plus more for spraying
- ¼ cup soy sauce
- ¼ cup rice wine vinegar
- 1 tablespoon brown sugar
- 1 teaspoon mustard powder
- 1 teaspoon ground ginger
- ½ teaspoon freshly ground black pepper
- ½ teaspoon minced garlic
- 4 (6 ounce) salmon fillets, skin-on

Directions:
1. Spray a fryer basket lightly with olive oil.
2. In a small bowl combine the soy sauce, rice wine vinegar, brown sugar, 1 tablespoon of olive oil, mustard powder, ginger, black pepper, and garlic to make a marinade.
3. Place the fillets in a shallow baking dish and pour the marinade over them. Cover the baking dish and marinate for at least 1 hour in the refrigerator, turning the fillets occasionally to keep them coated in the marinade.
4. Shake off as much marinade as possible from the fillets and place them, skin side down, in the fryer basket in a single layer. You may need to cook the fillets in batches.
5. Air fry for 10 to 15 minutes for medium-rare to medium done salmon or 15 to 20 minutes for well done. The minimum internal temperature should be 145°F at the thickest part of the fillet.

Spanish Garlic Shrimp

Servings:4
Cooking Time: 15 Minutes
Ingredients:
- 2 teaspoons olive oil plus more for spraying
- 2 teaspoons minced garlic
- 2 teaspoons lemon juice
- ½ to 1 teaspoon crushed red pepper
- 12 ounces medium cooked shrimp, thawed, and deveined, with tails on

Directions:
1. Spray a fryer basket lightly with olive oil.
2. In a medium bowl, mix together the garlic, lemon juice, 2 teaspoons of olive oil, and crushed red pepper to make a marinade.
3. Add the shrimp and toss to coat in the marinade. Cover with plastic wrap and place the bowl in the refrigerator for 30 minutes.
4. Place the shrimp in the fryer basket. Air fry for 5 minutes. Shake the basket and cook until the shrimp are cooked through and nicely browned, an additional 5 to 10 minutes.

Salty German-style Shrimp Pancakes

Servings: 4
Cooking Time: 15 Minutes
Ingredients:
- 1 tbsp butter
- 3 eggs, beaten
- ½ cup flour
- ½ cup milk
- ⅛ tsp salt
- 1 cup salsa
- 1 cup cooked shrimp, minced
- 2 tbsp cilantro, chopped

Directions:
1. Preheat air fryer to 390°F. Mix the eggs, flour, milk, and salt in a bowl until frothy. Pour the batter into a greased baking pan and place in the air fryer. Bake for 15 minutes or until the pancake is puffed and golden. Flip the pancake onto a plate. Mix salsa, shrimp, and cilantro. Top the pancake and serve.

Scallops And Spring Veggies

Servings: 4
Cooking Time: 7 To 10 Minutes
Ingredients:
- ½ pound asparagus, ends trimmed, cut into 2-inch pieces
- 1 cup sugar snap peas
- 1 pound sea scallops
- 1 tablespoon lemon juice
- 2 teaspoons olive oil
- ½ teaspoon dried thyme
- Pinch salt
- Freshly ground black pepper

Directions:
1. Place the asparagus and sugar snap peas in the air fryer basket. Cook for 2 to 3 minutes or until the vegetables are just starting to get tender.
2. Meanwhile, check the scallops for a small muscle attached to the side, and pull it off and discard.
3. In a medium bowl, toss the scallops with the lemon juice, olive oil, thyme, salt, and pepper. Place into the air fryer basket on top of the vegetables.
4. Steam for 5 to 7 minutes, tossing the basket once during cooking time, until the scallops are just firm when tested with your finger and are opaque in the center, and the vegetables are tender. Serve immediately.

Spicy Prawns

Servings: 2
Cooking Time: 8 Minutes
Ingredients:
- 6 prawns
- 1/4 tsp pepper
- 1/2 tsp chili powder
- 1 tsp chili flakes
- 1/4 tsp salt

Directions:
1. Preheat the air fryer to 350°F.
2. In a bowl, mix together spices add prawns.
3. Spray air fryer basket with cooking spray.
4. Transfer prawns into the air fryer basket and cook for 8 minutes.
5. Serve and enjoy.

Parmesan Fish Bites

Servings: 2
Cooking Time: 30 Minutes
Ingredients:
- 1 haddock fillet, cut into bite-sized pieces
- 1 tbsp shredded cheddar
- 2 tbsp shredded Parmesan
- 2 eggs, beaten
- ½ cup breadcrumbs
- Salt and pepper to taste
- ½ cup mayoracha sauce

Directions:
1. Preheat air fryer to 350°F. Dip the strips in the beaten eggs. Place the bread crumbs, Parmesan, cheddar, salt and pepper in a bowl and mix well. Coat the fish strips in the dry mixture and place them on the foil-lined frying basket. Air Fry for 14-16 minutes. Halfway through the cooking time, shake the basket. When the cooking time is over, the fish will be cooked through and crust golden brown. Serve with mayoracha sauce (mixed mayo with sriracha) for dipping and enjoy!

Restaurant-style Flounder Cutlets

Servings: 2
Cooking Time: 15 Minutes
Ingredients:
- 1 egg
- 1 cup Pecorino Romano cheese, grated
- Sea salt and white pepper, to taste
- 1/2 teaspoon cayenne pepper
- 1 teaspoon dried parsley flakes
- 2 flounder fillets

Directions:
1. To make a breading station, whisk the egg until frothy.
2. In another bowl, mix Pecorino Romano cheese, and spices.
3. Dip the fish in the egg mixture and turn to coat evenly; then, dredge in the cracker crumb mixture, turning a couple of times to coat evenly.
4. Cook in the preheated Air Fryer at 390°F for 5 minutes; turn them over and cook another 5 minutes. Enjoy!

Catfish Fillets With Tortilla Chips

Servings: 4
Cooking Time: 30 Minutes
Ingredients:
- 2 catfish fillets [catfish]
- 1 medium egg, beaten
- 1 cup bread crumbs
- 1 cup tortilla chips
- 1 lemon, juiced and peeled
- 1 teaspoon parsley
- Salt and pepper to taste

Directions:
1. Slice the catfish fillets neatly and then drizzle lightly with the lemon juice.
2. Mix up the bread crumbs with the lemon rind, parsley, tortillas, salt and pepper in a bowl, then pour into your food processor and pulse.
3. Distributes the fillets evenly on the base of the cooking tray.
4. Cover the fish fillets well with the prepared mixture.
5. Arrange the tray to your air fryer and cook the fillets at 350 degrees F/ 175 degrees C for 15 minutes.
6. When done, serve with chips and a refreshing drink.

Teriyaki Salmon

Servings: 4
Cooking Time: 27 Minutes
Ingredients:
- ½ cup teriyaki sauce
- ¼ teaspoon salt
- 1 teaspoon ground ginger

- ½ teaspoon garlic powder
- 4 boneless, skinless salmon fillets
- 2 tablespoons toasted sesame seeds

Directions:
1. In a large bowl, whisk teriyaki sauce, salt, ginger, and garlic powder. Add salmon to the bowl, being sure to coat each side with marinade. Cover and let marinate in refrigerator 15 minutes.
2. Preheat the air fryer to 375°F.
3. Spritz fillets with cooking spray and place in the air fryer basket. Cook 12 minutes, turning halfway through cooking time, until glaze has caramelized to a dark brown color, salmon flakes easily, and internal temperature reaches at least 145°F. Sprinkle sesame seeds on salmon and serve warm.

Sweet And Sour Glazed Cod

Servings: 2
Cooking Time: 12 Minutes

Ingredients:
- 1 teaspoon water
- 4 cod fillets
- 1/3 cup soy sauce
- 1/3 cup honey
- 3 teaspoons rice wine vinegar

Directions:
1. Preheat the Air fryer to 355°F and grease an Air fryer basket.
2. Mix the soy sauce, honey, vinegar and water in a small bowl.
3. Reserve about half of the mixture in another bowl.
4. Stir the cod fillets in the remaining mixture until well coated.
5. Cover and refrigerate to marinate for about 3 hours.
6. Arrange the cod fillets into the Air fryer basket and cook for about 12 minutes, flipping once in between.
7. Coat with the reserved marinade and dish out the cod to serve hot.

Tuna-stuffed Tomatoes

Servings: 2
Cooking Time: 5 Minutes

Ingredients:
- 2 medium beefsteak tomatoes, tops removed, seeded, membranes removed
- 2 pouches tuna packed in water, drained
- 1 medium stalk celery, trimmed and chopped
- 2 tablespoons mayonnaise
- ¼ teaspoon salt
- ¼ teaspoon ground black pepper
- 2 teaspoons coconut oil
- ¼ cup shredded mild Cheddar cheese

Directions:
1. Scoop pulp out of each tomato, leaving ½" shell.
2. In a medium bowl, mix tuna, celery, mayonnaise, salt, and pepper. Drizzle with coconut oil. Spoon ½ mixture into each tomato and top each with 2 tablespoons Cheddar.
3. Place tomatoes into ungreased air fryer basket. Adjust the temperature to 320°F and set the timer for 5 minutes. Cheese will be melted when done. Serve warm.

Pecan-crusted Tilapia

Servings: 4
Cooking Time: 8 Minutes

Ingredients:
- 1 pound skinless, boneless tilapia filets
- ¼ cup butter, melted
- 1 teaspoon minced fresh or dried rosemary
- 1 cup finely chopped pecans
- 1 teaspoon sea salt
- ¼ teaspoon paprika
- 2 tablespoons chopped parsley
- 1 lemon, cut into wedges

Directions:
1. Pat the tilapia filets dry with paper towels.
2. Pour the melted butter over the filets and flip the filets to coat them completely.
3. In a medium bowl, mix together the rosemary, pecans, salt, and paprika.
4. Preheat the air fryer to 350°F.
5. Place the tilapia filets into the air fryer basket and top with the pecan coating. Cook for 6 to 8 minutes. The fish should be firm to the touch and flake easily when fully cooked.
6. Remove the fish from the air fryer. Top the fish with chopped parsley and serve with lemon wedges.

Salmon

Servings: 4
Cooking Time: 8 Minutes

Ingredients:
- Marinade
- 3 tablespoons low-sodium soy sauce
- 3 tablespoons rice vinegar
- 3 tablespoons ketchup
- 3 tablespoons olive oil
- 3 tablespoons brown sugar
- 1 teaspoon garlic powder
- ½ teaspoon ground ginger
- 4 salmon fillets (½-inch thick, 3 to 4 ounces each)
- cooking spray

Directions:
1. Mix all marinade ingredients until well blended.
2. Place salmon in sealable plastic bag or shallow container with lid. Pour marinade over fish and turn to coat well. Refrigerate for 30minutes.
3. Drain marinade, and spray air fryer basket with cooking spray.
4. Place salmon in basket, skin-side down.
5. Cook at 360°F for 10 minutes, watching closely to avoid overcooking. Salmon is done when just beginning to flake and still very moist.

Crusty Catfish With Parmesan Cheese
Servings: 2
Cooking Time: 50 Minutes
Ingredients:
- ½ lb. catfish
- ½ cup bran cereal
- ¼ cup Parmesan cheese, grated
- Sea salt, to taste
- Ground black pepper, to taste
- 1 teaspoon smoked paprika
- ½ teaspoon garlic powder
- ¼-teaspoon ground bay leaf
- 1 egg
- ½ tablespoon butter, melted
- 4 sweet potatoes, cut French fries

Directions:
1. Use the kitchen towel to pat the catfish dry.
2. In a shallow bowl, combine the bran cereal with the Parmesan cheese and all spices in a shallow bowl.
3. In another shallow bowl, whisk the egg.
4. Coat the fish evenly and completely with the egg mixture, then dredge in the bran cereal mixture, turning a couple of times to coat evenly.
5. Arrange the catfish to the basket that has been sprayed and cook at 390 degrees F/ 200 degrees C for 10 minutes; flip them and cook for 4 minutes more.
6. After that, drizzle the melted butter all over the sweet potatoes; cook them at 380 degrees F/ 195 degrees C for 30 minutes, shaking occasionally.
7. Serve over the warm fish fillets. Bon appétit!

Garlic-lemon Steamer Clams
Servings: 2
Cooking Time: 30 Minutes
Ingredients:
- 25 Manila clams, scrubbed
- 2 tbsp butter, melted
- 1 garlic clove, minced
- 2 lemon wedges

Directions:
1. Add the clams to a large bowl filled with water and let sit for 10 minutes. Drain. Pour more water and let sit for 10 more minutes. Drain. Preheat air fryer to 350°F. Place clams in the basket and Air Fry for 7 minutes. Discard any clams that don´t open. Remove clams from shells and place them into a large serving dish. Drizzle with melted butter and garlic and squeeze lemon on top. Serve.

Spicy Salmon And Fennel Salad
Servings: 3
Cooking Time: 20 Minutes
Ingredients:
- 1 pound salmon
- 1 fennel, quartered
- 1 teaspoon olive oil
- Sea salt, to taste
- Ground black pepper, to taste
- ½ teaspoon paprika
- 1 tablespoon balsamic vinegar
- 1 tablespoon lime juice
- 1 tablespoon extra-virgin olive oil
- 1 tomato, sliced
- 1 cucumber, sliced
- 1 tablespoon sesame seeds, lightly toasted

Directions:
1. Combine the olive oil, salt, black pepper and paprika well, then stir the salmon and fennel with the spice mixture.
2. Cook the salmon at 380 degrees F/ 195 degrees C for 12 minutes, shaking the basket once or twice for even cooking.
3. After cutting the salmon into bite-sized strips, transfer them to a nice salad bowl.
4. In the same bowl, add in the fennel, balsamic vinegar, lime juice, 1 tablespoon of extra-virgin olive oil, tomato and cucumber, then combine well.
5. Serve garnished with lightly toasted sesame seeds. Enjoy!

Cajun Salmon
Servings: 2
Cooking Time: 7 Minutes
Ingredients:
- 2 boneless, skinless salmon fillets
- 2 tablespoons salted butter, softened
- ⅛ teaspoon cayenne pepper
- ½ teaspoon garlic powder
- 1 teaspoon paprika
- ¼ teaspoon ground black pepper

Directions:
1. Brush both sides of each fillet with butter. In a small bowl, mix remaining ingredients and rub into fish on both sides.
2. Place fillets into ungreased air fryer basket. Adjust the temperature to 390°F and set the timer for 7 minutes. Internal temperature will be 145°F when done. Serve warm.

Shrimp Sliders With Avocado
Servings: 4
Cooking Time: 10 Minutes
Ingredients:
- 16 raw jumbo shrimp, peeled, deveined and tails removed (about 1 pound)
- 1 rib celery, finely chopped
- 2 carrots, grated (about ½ cup) 2 teaspoons lemon juice
- 2 teaspoons Dijon mustard
- ¼ cup chopped fresh basil or parsley
- ½ cup breadcrumbs
- ½ teaspoon salt
- freshly ground black pepper
- vegetable or olive oil, in a spray bottle
- 8 slider buns
- mayonnaise
- butter lettuce
- 2 avocados, sliced and peeled

Directions:
1. Put the shrimp into a food processor and pulse it a few times to rough chop the shrimp. Remove three quarters of the shrimp and transfer it to a bowl. Continue to process the remaining shrimp in the food processor until it is a smooth purée. Transfer the purée to the bowl with the chopped shrimp.
2. Add the celery, carrots, lemon juice, mustard, basil, breadcrumbs, salt and pepper to the bowl and combine well.
3. Preheat the air fryer to 380°F.
4. While the air fryer Preheats, shape the shrimp mixture into 8 patties. Spray both sides of the patties with oil and transfer one layer of patties to the air fryer basket. Air-fry for 10 minutes, flipping the patties over halfway through the cooking time.
5. Prepare the slider rolls by toasting them and spreading a little mayonnaise on both halves. Place a piece of butter lettuce on the bottom bun, top with the shrimp slider and then finish with the avocado slices on top. Pop the top half of the bun on top and enjoy!

Snow Crab Legs

Servings: 6
Cooking Time: 15 Minutes Per Batch
Ingredients:
- 8 pounds fresh shell-on snow crab legs
- 2 tablespoons olive oil
- 2 teaspoons Old Bay Seasoning
- 4 tablespoons salted butter, melted
- 2 teaspoons lemon juice

Directions:
1. Preheat the air fryer to 400°F.
2. Drizzle crab legs with oil and sprinkle with Old Bay. Place in the air fryer basket, working in batches as necessary. Cook 15 minutes, turning halfway through cooking time, until crab turns a bright red-orange.
3. In a small bowl, whisk together butter and lemon juice. Serve as a dipping sauce with warm crab legs.

Nutty Shrimp With Amaretto Glaze

Servings: 10
Cooking Time: 10 Minutes
Ingredients:
- 1 cup flour
- ½ teaspoon baking powder
- 1 teaspoon salt
- 2 eggs, beaten
- ½ cup milk
- 2 tablespoons olive or vegetable oil
- 2 cups sliced almonds
- 2 pounds large shrimp (about 32 to 40 shrimp), peeled and deveined, tails left on
- 2 cups amaretto liqueur

Directions:
1. Combine the flour, baking powder and salt in a large bowl. Add the eggs, milk and oil and stir until it forms a smooth batter. Coarsely crush the sliced almonds into a second shallow dish with your hands.
2. Dry the shrimp well with paper towels. Dip the shrimp into the batter and shake off any excess batter, leaving just enough to lightly coat the shrimp. Transfer the shrimp to the dish with the almonds and coat completely. Place the coated shrimp on a plate or baking sheet and when all the shrimp have been coated, freeze the shrimp for an 1 hour, or as long as a week before air-frying.
3. Preheat the air fryer to 400°F.
4. Transfer 8 frozen shrimp at a time to the air fryer basket. Air-fry for 6 minutes. Turn the shrimp over and air-fry for an additional 4 minutes. Repeat with the remaining shrimp.
5. While the shrimp are cooking, bring the Amaretto to a boil in a small saucepan on the stovetop. Lower the heat and simmer until it has reduced and thickened into a glaze – about 10 minutes.
6. Remove the shrimp from the air fryer and brush both sides with the warm amaretto glaze. Serve warm.

Bacon-wrapped Scallops

Servings: 4
Cooking Time: 8 Minutes
Ingredients:
- 16 large scallops
- 8 bacon strips
- ½ teaspoon black pepper
- ¼ teaspoon smoked paprika

Directions:
1. Pat the scallops dry with a paper towel. Slice each of the bacon strips in half. Wrap 1 bacon strip around 1 scallop and secure with a toothpick. Repeat with the remaining scallops. Season the scallops with pepper and paprika.
2. Preheat the air fryer to 350°F.
3. Place the bacon-wrapped scallops in the air fryer basket and cook for 4 minutes, shake the basket, cook another 3 minutes, shake the basket, and cook another 1 to 3 to minutes. When the bacon is crispy, the scallops should be cooked through and slightly firm, but not rubbery. Serve immediately.

Basil Mushroom & Shrimp Spaghetti

Servings: 6
Cooking Time: 20 Minutes
Ingredients:
- 8 oz baby Bella mushrooms, sliced
- ½ cup grated Parmesan
- 1 lb peeled shrimp, deveined
- 3 tbsp olive oil
- ¼ tsp garlic powder
- ¼ tsp shallot powder
- ¼ tsp cayenne
- 1 lb cooked pasta spaghetti
- 5 garlic cloves, minced
- Salt and pepper to taste
- ½ cup dill

Directions:

1. Preheat air fryer to 380°F. Toss the shrimp, 1 tbsp of olive oil, garlic powder, shallot powder and cayenne in a bowl. Put the shrimp into the frying basket and Roast for 5 minutes. Remove and set aside.
2. Warm the remaining olive oil in a large skillet over medium heat. Add the garlic and mushrooms and cook for 5 minutes. Pour in the pasta, ½ cup of water, Parmesan, salt, pepper, and dill and stir to coat the pasta. Stir in the shrimp. Remove from heat, then let the mixture rest for 5 minutes. Serve and enjoy!

Fish Sticks

Servings: 4
Cooking Time: 20 Minutes
Ingredients:
- 1 lb. tilapia fillets, cut into strips
- 1 large egg, beaten
- 2 tsp. Old Bay seasoning
- 1 tbsp. olive oil
- 1 cup friendly bread crumbs

Directions:
1. Pre-heat the Air Fryer at 400°F.
2. In a shallow dish, combine together the bread crumbs, Old Bay, and oil. Put the egg in a small bowl.
3. Dredge the fish sticks in the egg. Cover them with bread crumbs and put them in the fryer's basket.
4. Cook the fish for 10 minutes or until they turn golden brown.
5. Serve hot.

Glazed Salmon With Soy Sauce

Servings: 2
Cooking Time: 14 Minutes
Ingredients:
- 1 teaspoon water
- 2 3½-ounce salmon fillets
- ⅓ cup soy sauce
- ⅓ cup honey
- 3 teaspoons rice wine vinegar

Directions:
1. At 355 degrees F/ 180 degrees C, preheat your air fryer. and grease an air fryer grill pan.
2. Mix all the recipe ingredients in a suitable bowl except salmon.
3. Reserve ½ of the mixture in a suitable bowl and coat the salmon in remaining mixture.
4. Refrigerate, covered for about 2 hours and place the salmon in the air fryer basket.
5. Cook for about 13 minutes, flipping once in between and coat with reserved marinade.
6. Place the leftover salmon marinade in a small pan and cook for about 1 minute.
7. Serve salmon with marinade sauce and enjoy.

Garlic-lemon Scallops

Servings: 4
Cooking Time: 12 Minutes
Ingredients:
- ¼ teaspoon salt
- ¼ teaspoon ground black pepper
- 8 sea scallops, rinsed and patted dry
- 4 tablespoons salted butter, melted
- 4 teaspoons finely minced garlic
- Zest and juice of ½ small lemon

Directions:
1. Preheat the air fryer to 375°F.
2. Sprinkle salt and pepper evenly over scallops. Spritz scallops lightly with cooking spray. Place in the air fryer basket in a single layer and cook 12 minutes, turning halfway through cooking time, until scallops are opaque and firm and internal temperature reaches at least 130°F.
3. While scallops are cooking, in a small bowl, mix butter, garlic, lemon zest, and juice. Set aside.
4. When scallops are done, drizzle with garlic–lemon butter. Serve warm.

Salmon Croquettes

Servings: 4
Cooking Time: 8 Minutes
Ingredients:
- 1 tablespoon oil
- ½ cup breadcrumbs
- 1 14.75-ounce can salmon, drained and all skin and fat removed
- 1 egg, beaten
- ⅓ cup coarsely crushed saltine crackers (about 8 crackers)
- ½ teaspoon Old Bay Seasoning
- ½ teaspoon onion powder
- ½ teaspoon Worcestershire sauce

Directions:
1. Preheat air fryer to 390°F.
2. In a shallow dish, mix oil and breadcrumbs until crumbly.
3. In a large bowl, combine the salmon, egg, cracker crumbs, Old Bay, onion powder, and Worcestershire. Mix well and shape into 8 small patties about ½-inch thick.
4. Gently dip each patty into breadcrumb mixture and turn to coat well on all sides.
5. Cook at 390°F for 8minutes or until outside is crispy and browned.

Chapter 8: Poultry Recipes

Piri-piri Chicken Thighs

Servings: 4
Cooking Time: 25 Minutes
Ingredients:
- ¼ cup piri-piri sauce
- 1 tablespoon freshly squeezed lemon juice
- 2 tablespoons brown sugar, divided
- 2 cloves garlic, minced
- 1 tablespoon extra-virgin olive oil
- 4 bone-in, skin-on chicken thighs, each weighing approximately 7 to 8 ounces (198 to 227 g)
- ½ teaspoon cornstarch

Directions:
1. To make the marinade, whisk together the piri-piri sauce, lemon juice, 1 tablespoon of brown sugar, and the garlic in a small bowl. While whisking, slowly pour in the oil in a steady stream and continue to whisk until emulsified. Using a skewer, poke holes in the chicken thighs and place them in a small glass dish. Pour the marinade over the chicken and turn the thighs to coat them with the sauce. Cover the dish and refrigerate for at least 15 minutes and up to 1 hour.
2. Preheat the air fryer to 375ºF (191ºC). Remove the chicken thighs from the dish, reserving the marinade, and place them skin-side down in the air fryer basket. Air fry until the internal temperature reaches 165ºF (74ºC), 15 to 20 minutes.
3. Meanwhile, whisk the remaining brown sugar and the cornstarch into the marinade and microwave it on high power for 1 minute until it is bubbling and thickened to a glaze.
4. Once the chicken is cooked, turn the thighs over and brush them with the glaze. Air fry for a few additional minutes until the glaze browns and begins to char in spots.
5. Remove the chicken to a platter and serve with additional piri-piri sauce, if desired.

Chicken Burgers With Blue Cheese Sauce

Servings: 4
Cooking Time: 40 Minutes
Ingredients:
- ¼ cup crumbled blue cheese
- ¼ cup sour cream
- 2 tbsp mayonnaise
- 1 tbsp red hot sauce
- Salt to taste
- 3 tbsp buffalo wing sauce
- 1 lb ground chicken
- 2 tbsp grated carrot
- 2 tbsp diced celery
- 1 egg white

Directions:
1. Whisk the blue cheese, sour cream, mayonnaise, red hot sauce, salt, and 1 tbsp of buffalo sauce in a bowl. Let sit covered in the fridge until ready to use.
2. Preheat air fryer at 350ºF. In another bowl, combine the remaining ingredients. Form mixture into 4 patties, making a slight indentation in the middle of each. Place patties in the greased frying basket and Air Fry for 13 minutes until you reach your desired doneness, flipping once. Serve with the blue cheese sauce.

Basic Chicken Breasts.

Servings: 4
Cooking Time: 15 Minutes
Ingredients:
- 2 tsp olive oil
- 2 chicken breasts
- Salt and pepper to taste
- ½ tsp garlic powder
- ½ tsp rosemary

Directions:
1. Preheat air fryer to 350ºF. Rub the chicken breasts with olive oil over tops and bottom and sprinkle with garlic powder, rosemary, salt, and pepper. Place the chicken in the frying basket and Air Fry for 9 minutes, flipping once. Let rest onto a serving plate for 5 minutes before cutting into cubes. Serve and enjoy!

Chicken With 20 Cloves Of Garlic

Servings: 4
Cooking Time: 25 Minutes
Ingredients:
- 4 (5-ounce) low-sodium bone-in skinless chicken breasts (see Tip)
- 1 tablespoon olive oil
- 1 tablespoon freshly squeezed lemon juice
- 3 tablespoons cornstarch
- 1 teaspoon dried basil leaves
- ⅛ teaspoon freshly ground black pepper
- 20 garlic cloves, unpeeled

Directions:
1. Rub the chicken with the olive oil and lemon juice on both sides and sprinkle with the cornstarch, basil, and pepper.
2. Place the seasoned chicken in the air fryer basket and top with the garlic cloves. Roast for about 25 minutes, or until the garlic is soft and the chicken reaches an internal temperature of 165°F on a meat thermometer. Serve immediately.

Crispy Italian Chicken Thighs

Servings: 4
Cooking Time: 25 Minutes
Ingredients:
- ½ cup mayonnaise
- 4 bone-in, skin-on chicken thighs
- 1 teaspoon salt
- ½ teaspoon ground black pepper
- 2 teaspoons Italian seasoning
- 1 cup Italian bread crumbs

Directions:
1. Preheat the air fryer to 370°F.
2. Brush mayonnaise over chicken thighs on both sides.
3. Sprinkle thighs with salt, pepper, and Italian seasoning.
4. Place bread crumbs into a resealable plastic bag and add thighs. Shake to coat.
5. Remove thighs from bag and spritz with cooking spray. Place in the air fryer basket and cook 25 minutes, turning thighs after 15 minutes, until skin is golden and crispy and internal temperature reaches at least 165°F.
6. Serve warm.

Fajita Chicken Strips

Servings: 4
Cooking Time: 15 Minutes
Ingredients:
- 1 pound (454 g) boneless, skinless chicken tenderloins, cut into strips
- 3 bell peppers, any color, cut into chunks
- 1 onion, cut into chunks
- 1 tablespoon olive oil
- 1 tablespoon fajita seasoning mix
- Cooking spray

Directions:
1. Preheat the air fryer to 370ºF (188ºC).
2. In a large bowl, mix together the chicken, bell peppers, onion, olive oil, and fajita seasoning mix until completely coated.
3. Spray the air fryer basket lightly with cooking spray.
4. Place the chicken and vegetables in the air fryer basket and lightly spray with cooking spray.
5. Air fry for 7 minutes. Shake the basket and air fry for an additional 5 to 8 minutes, until the chicken is cooked through and the veggies are starting to char.
6. Serve warm.

Za'atar Chicken Thighs

Servings: 4
Cooking Time: 35 Minutes
Ingredients:
- 4 chicken thighs
- 2 sprigs thyme
- 1 onion, cut into chunks
- 2 ½ tablespoons za'atar
- ½ teaspoon cinnamon
- 2 garlic cloves, smashed
- 1 lemon juice
- 1 lemon zest
- ¼ cup olive oil
- ¼ teaspoon black pepper
- 1 teaspoon salt

Directions:
1. Add oil, lemon juice, lemon zest, cinnamon, garlic, black pepper, 2 tablespoon za'atar, and salt in a large ziplock bag and shake well.
2. Add chicken, thyme, and onion to bag and shake well to coat. Place in refrigerator for overnight.
3. At 380 degrees F/ 195 degrees C, preheat your air fryer.
4. Add marinated chicken in air fryer basket and cook at 380 degrees F/ 195 degrees C for 15 minutes.
5. Turn chicken to another side and sprinkle with remaining za'atar spice, then cook for 15-18 minutes more.
6. Serve and enjoy.

Nutty Chicken Tenders

Servings: 4
Cooking Time: 12 Minutes
Ingredients:
- 1 pound (454 g) chicken tenders
- 1 teaspoon kosher salt
- 1 teaspoon black pepper
- ½ teaspoon smoked paprika
- ¼ cup coarse mustard
- 2 tablespoons honey
- 1 cup finely crushed pecans

Directions:
1. Preheat the air fryer to 350ºF (177ºC).
2. Place the chicken in a large bowl. Sprinkle with the salt, pepper, and paprika. Toss until the chicken is coated with the spices. Add the mustard and honey and toss until the chicken is coated.
3. Place the pecans on a plate. Working with one piece of chicken at a time, roll the chicken in the pecans until both sides are coated. Lightly brush off any loose pecans. Place the chicken in the air fryer basket.
4. Bake for 12 minutes, or until the chicken is cooked through and the pecans are golden brown.
5. Serve warm.

Celery Chicken

Servings: 4
Cooking Time: 15 Minutes
Ingredients:
- ½ cup soy sauce
- 2 tablespoons hoisin sauce
- 4 teaspoons minced garlic
- 1 teaspoon freshly ground black pepper
- 8 boneless, skinless chicken tenderloins
- 1 cup chopped celery
- 1 medium red bell pepper, diced
- Olive oil spray

Directions:
1. Preheat the air fryer to 375ºF (191ºC). Spray the air fryer basket lightly with olive oil spray.
2. In a large bowl, mix together the soy sauce, hoisin sauce, garlic, and black pepper to make a marinade. Add the chicken, celery, and bell pepper and toss to coat.
3. Shake the excess marinade off the chicken, place it and the vegetables in the air fryer basket, and lightly spray with olive oil spray. You may need to cook them in batches. Reserve the remaining marinade.
4. Air fry for 8 minutes. Turn the chicken over and brush with some of the remaining marinade. Air fry for an additional 5 to 7 minutes, or until the chicken reaches an internal temperature of at least 165ºF (74ºC). Serve.

Southwest Gluten-free Turkey Meatloaf

Servings: 8
Cooking Time: 35 Minutes
Ingredients:
- 1 pound lean ground turkey
- ¼ cup corn grits
- ¼ cup diced onion
- 1 teaspoon minced garlic
- ½ teaspoon black pepper
- ½ teaspoon salt
- 1 large egg
- ½ cup ketchup

- 4 teaspoons chipotle hot sauce
- ⅓ cup shredded cheddar cheese

Directions:
1. Preheat the air fryer to 350°F.
2. In a large bowl, mix together the ground turkey, corn grits, onion, garlic, black pepper, and salt.
3. In a small bowl, whisk the egg. Add the egg to the turkey mixture and combine.
4. In a small bowl, mix the ketchup and hot sauce. Set aside.
5. Liberally spray a 9-x-4-inch loaf pan with olive oil spray. Depending on the size of your air fryer, you may need to use 2 or 3 mini loaf pans.
6. Spoon the ground turkey mixture into the loaf pan and evenly top with half of the ketchup mixture. Cover with foil and place the meatloaf into the air fryer. Cook for 30 minutes; remove the foil and discard. Check the internal temperature (it should be nearing 165°F).
7. Coat the top of the meatloaf with the remaining ketchup mixture, and sprinkle the cheese over the top. Place the meatloaf back in the air fryer for the remaining 5 minutes (or until the internal temperature reaches 165°F).
8. Remove from the oven and let cool 5 minutes before serving. Serve warm with desired sides.

Cornflake Chicken Nuggets

Servings: 4
Cooking Time: 25 Minutes
Ingredients:
- 1 egg white
- 1 tbsp lemon juice
- ½ tsp dried basil
- ½ tsp ground paprika
- 1 lb chicken breast fingers
- ½ cup ground cornflakes
- 2 slices bread, crumbled

Directions:
1. Preheat air fryer to 400°F. Whisk the egg white, lemon juice, basil, and paprika, then add the chicken and stir. Combine the cornflakes and breadcrumbs on a plate, then put the chicken fingers in the mix to coat. Put the nuggets in the frying basket and Air Fry for 10-13 minutes, turning halfway through, until golden, crisp and cooked through. Serve hot!

Party Buffalo Chicken Drumettes

Servings: 6
Cooking Time: 30 Minutes
Ingredients:
- 16 chicken drumettes
- 1 tsp garlic powder
- 1 tbsp chicken seasoning
- Black pepper to taste
- ¼ cup Buffalo wings sauce
- 2 spring onions, sliced
- Cooking spray

Directions:
1. Preheat air fryer to 400°F. Sprinkle garlic, chicken seasoning, and black pepper on the drumettes. Place them in the fryer and spray with cooking oil. Air Fry for 10 minutes, shaking the basket once. Transfer the drumettes to a large bowl. Drizzle with Buffalo wing sauce and toss to coat. Place in the fryer and Fry for 7-8 minutes, until crispy. Allow to cool slightly. Top with spring onions and serve warm.

Grilled Cajun Chicken

Servings: 2
Cooking Time: 20 Minutes
Ingredients:
- 2 medium skinless, boneless chicken breasts
- ½ teaspoon salt
- 3 tablespoons Cajun spice
- 1 tablespoon olive oil

Directions:
1. Before cooking, heat your air fryer to 370 degrees F/ 185 degrees C.
2. Rub the chicken breasts with Cajun sauce and salt. Drizzle olive oil over the chicken breast.
3. Transfer the chicken breasts in an air fryer basket.
4. Cook in the preheated air fryer for 7 minutes.
5. When the cooking time is over, flip the both chicken breasts to the other side and cook again for 3 to 4 minutes.
6. When cooked, remove onto a cutting board and slice into your desired size.
7. Serve and enjoy!

Chicken Pigs In Blankets

Servings: 4
Cooking Time: 40 Minutes
Ingredients:
- 8 chicken drumsticks, boneless, skinless
- 2 tbsp light brown sugar
- 2 tbsp ketchup
- 1 tbsp grainy mustard
- 8 smoked bacon slices
- 1 tsp chopped fresh sage

Directions:
1. Preheat the air fryer to 350°F. Mix brown sugar, sage, ketchup, and mustard in a bowl and brush the chicken with it. Wrap slices of bacon around the drumsticks and brush with the remaining mix. Line the frying basket with round parchment paper with holes. Set 4 drumsticks on the paper, add a raised rack and set the other drumsticks on it. Bake for 25-35 minutes, moving the bottom drumsticks to the top, top to the bottom, and flipping at about 14-16 minutes. Sprinkle with sage and serve.

Teriyaki Chicken Bites

Servings: 4
Cooking Time: 30 Minutes
Ingredients:
- 1 lb boneless, skinless chicken thighs, cubed
- 1 green onion, sliced diagonally
- 1 large egg
- 1 tbsp teriyaki sauce
- 4 tbsp flour

- 1 tsp sesame oil
- 2 tsp balsamic vinegar
- 2 tbsp tamari
- 3 cloves garlic, minced
- 2 tsp grated fresh ginger
- 2 tsp chili garlic sauce
- 2 tsp granular honey
- Salt and pepper to taste

Directions:
1. Preheat air fryer to 400ºF. Beat the egg, teriyaki sauce, and flour in a bowl. Stir in chicken pieces until fully coated. In another bowl, combine the remaining ingredients, except for the green onion. Reserve. Place chicken pieces in the frying basket lightly greased with olive oil and Air Fry for 15 minutes, tossing every 5 minutes. Remove them to the bowl with the sauce and toss to coat. Scatter with green onions to serve. Enjoy!

Roasted Chicken And Vegetable Salad

Servings: 4
Cooking Time: 10 To 13 Minutes
Ingredients:
- 3 (4-ounce / 113-g) low-sodium boneless, skinless chicken breasts, cut into 1-inch cubes
- 1 small red onion, sliced
- 1 red bell pepper, sliced
- 1 cup green beans, cut into 1-inch pieces
- 2 tablespoons low-fat ranch salad dressing
- 2 tablespoons freshly squeezed lemon juice
- ½ teaspoon dried basil
- 4 cups mixed lettuce

Directions:
1. Preheat the air fryer to 400ºF (204ºC).
2. In the air fryer basket, roast the chicken, red onion, red bell pepper, and green beans for 10 to 13 minutes, or until the chicken reaches an internal temperature of 165ºF (74ºC) on a meat thermometer, tossing the food in the basket once during cooking.
3. While the chicken cooks, in a serving bowl, mix the ranch dressing, lemon juice, and basil.
4. Transfer the chicken and vegetables to a serving bowl and toss with the dressing to coat. Serve immediately on lettuce leaves.

Pecan-crusted Turkey Cutlets

Servings: 4
Cooking Time: 10 To 12 Minutes
Ingredients:
- ¾ cup panko bread crumbs
- ¼ teaspoon salt
- ¼ teaspoon pepper
- ¼ teaspoon dry mustard
- ¼ teaspoon poultry seasoning
- ½ cup pecans
- ¼ cup cornstarch
- 1 egg, beaten
- 1 pound (454 g) turkey cutlets, ½-inch thick
- Salt and pepper, to taste
- Cooking spray

Directions:
1. Preheat the air fryer to 360ºF (182ºC).
2. Place the panko crumbs, salt, pepper, mustard, and poultry seasoning in a food processor. Process until crumbs are finely crushed. Add pecans and process just until nuts are finely chopped.
3. Place cornstarch in a shallow dish and beaten egg in another. Transfer coating mixture from food processor into a third shallow dish.
4. Sprinkle turkey cutlets with salt and pepper to taste.
5. Dip cutlets in cornstarch and shake off excess, then dip in beaten egg and finally roll in crumbs, pressing to coat well. Spray both sides with cooking spray.
6. Place 2 cutlets in air fryer basket in a single layer and air fry for 10 to 12 minutes. Repeat with the remaining cutlets.
7. Serve warm.

Basil Turkey With Chili Mayo

Servings: 4
Cooking Time: 40 Minutes
Ingredients:
- 3 teaspoons olive oil
- ½ teaspoon marjoram
- 1 teaspoon basil
- ½ teaspoon garlic powder
- 1 teaspoon shallot powder
- Coarse salt, to taste
- Ground black pepper, to taste
- 2 pounds turkey breast, boneless
- Chili mayo:
- ¼ cup mayonnaise
- ¼ cup sour cream
- 1 tablespoon chili sauce
- ½ teaspoon stone-ground mustard

Directions:
1. Before cooking, heat your air fryer to 360 degrees F/ 180 degrees C.
2. Combine thoroughly the spices with olive oil in a mixing bowl.
3. Using the spice mixture, rub the turkey to coat the turkey on all sides.
4. Cook in your air fryer for 40 minutes. Flip the turkey halfway through cooking. When cooked, the internal temperature should be 165 degrees F/ 75 degrees C.
5. To make the chili mayo, mix all the ingredients. Cool the sauce in the refrigerator until ready to serve.
6. Slice the turkey breast against the grain skin-side up.
7. Serve the meal with chili mayo. Enjoy your meal.

Garlic Parmesan Drumsticks

Servings: 4
Cooking Time: 25 Minutes
Ingredients:
- 8 chicken drumsticks
- ½ teaspoon salt
- ⅛ teaspoon ground black pepper
- ½ teaspoon garlic powder

- 2 tablespoons salted butter, melted
- ½ cup grated Parmesan cheese
- 1 tablespoon dried parsley

Directions:
1. Sprinkle drumsticks with salt, pepper, and garlic powder. Place drumsticks into ungreased air fryer basket.
2. Adjust the temperature to 400°F and set the timer for 25 minutes, turning drumsticks halfway through cooking. Drumsticks will be golden and have an internal temperature of at least 165°F when done.
3. Transfer drumsticks to a large serving dish. Pour butter over drumsticks, and sprinkle with Parmesan and parsley. Serve warm.

Hoisin Turkey Burgers

Servings:4
Cooking Time: 20 Minutes
Ingredients:
- Olive oil
- 1 pound lean ground turkey
- ¼ cup whole-wheat bread crumbs
- ¼ cup hoisin sauce
- 2 tablespoons soy sauce
- 4 whole-wheat buns

Directions:
1. Spray a fryer basket lightly with olive oil.
2. In a large bowl, mix together the turkey, bread crumbs, hoisin sauce, and soy sauce.
3. Form the mixture into 4 equal patties. Cover with plastic wrap and refrigerate the patties for 30 minutes.
4. Place the patties in the fryer basket in a single layer. Spray the patties lightly with olive oil.
5. Air fry for 10 minutes. Flip the patties over, lightly spray with olive oil, and cook until golden brown, an additional 5 to 10 minutes.
6. Place the patties on buns and top with your choice of low-calorie burger toppings like sliced tomatoes, onions, and cabbage slaw.

Parmesan Chicken Tenderloins

Servings: 6
Cooking Time: 12 Minutes
Ingredients:
- 1 lime
- 2 pounds' chicken tenderloins, cut up
- ½ cup pork rinds, crushed
- ½ cup Parmesan cheese, grated
- 1 tablespoon olive oil
- Salt and black pepper, to taste
- 1 teaspoon cayenne pepper
- ⅓ teaspoon ground cumin
- 1 teaspoon chili powder
- 1 egg

Directions:
1. Squeeze and rub the lime juice all over the chicken.
2. Spritz the cooking basket with a nonstick cooking spray.
3. In a suitable mixing bowl, thoroughly combine the pork rinds, Parmesan, olive oil, salt, black pepper, cayenne pepper, cumin, and chili powder.
4. In a suitable shallow bowl, whisk the egg until well beaten.
5. Dip the chicken tenders in the egg, then in pork rind mixture.
6. Transfer the coated and breaded chicken to the prepared cooking basket.
7. Cook in the preheated Air Fryer at 380 degrees F/ 195 degrees C for 12 minutes almost.
8. Turn them once cooked halfway through.
9. Serve immediately.

Chicken Skewers

Servings: 4
Cooking Time: 55 Minutes
Ingredients:
- 1 lb boneless skinless chicken thighs, cut into pieces
- 1 sweet onion, cut into 1-inch pieces
- 1 zucchini, cut into 1-inch pieces
- 1 red bell pepper, cut into 1-inch pieces
- ¼ cup olive oil
- 1 tsp garlic powder
- 1 tsp shallot powder
- 1 tsp ground cumin
- ½ tsp dried oregano
- ½ tsp dried thyme
- ¼ cup lemon juice
- 1 tbsp apple cider vinegar
- 12 grape tomatoes

Directions:
1. Combine the olive oil, garlic powder, shallot powder, cumin, oregano, thyme, lemon juice, and vinegar in a bowl; mix well. Alternate skewering the chicken, bell pepper, onion, zucchini, and tomatoes. Once all of the skewers are prepared, place them in a greased baking dish and pour the olive oil marinade over the top. Turn to coat. Cover with plastic wrap and refrigerate.
2. Preheat air fryer to 380°F. Remove the skewers from the marinade and arrange them in a single layer on the frying basket. Bake for 25 minutes, rotating once. Let the skewers sit for 5 minutes. Serve and enjoy!

Herb-buttermilk Chicken Breast

Servings:2
Cooking Time: 40 Minutes
Ingredients:
- 1 large bone-in, skin-on chicken breast
- 1 cup buttermilk
- 1½ teaspoons dried parsley
- 1½ teaspoons dried chives
- ¾ teaspoon kosher salt
- ½ teaspoon dried dill
- ½ teaspoon onion powder
- ¼ teaspoon garlic powder
- ¼ teaspoon dried tarragon
- Cooking spray

Directions:

1. Place the chicken breast in a bowl and pour over the buttermilk, turning the chicken in it to make sure it's completely covered. Let the chicken stand at room temperature for at least 20 minutes or in the refrigerator for up to 4 hours.
2. Meanwhile, in a bowl, stir together the parsley, chives, salt, dill, onion powder, garlic powder, and tarragon.
3. Preheat the air fryer to 300ºF (149ºC).
4. Remove the chicken from the buttermilk, letting the excess drip off, then place the chicken skin-side up directly in the air fryer. Sprinkle the seasoning mix all over the top of the chicken breast, then let stand until the herb mix soaks into the buttermilk, at least 5 minutes.
5. Spray the top of the chicken with cooking spray. Bake for 10 minutes, then increase the temperature to 350ºF (177ºC) and bake until an instant-read thermometer inserted into the thickest part of the breast reads 160ºF (71ºC) and the chicken is deep golden brown, 30 to 35 minutes.
6. Transfer the chicken breast to a cutting board, let rest for 10 minutes, then cut the meat off the bone and cut into thick slices for serving.

Cheesy Chicken Tenders
Servings: 4
Cooking Time: 25 Minutes
Ingredients:
- 1 cup grated Parmesan cheese
- ¼ cup grated cheddar
- 1 ¼ lb chicken tenders
- 1 egg, beaten
- 2 tbsp milk
- Salt and pepper to taste
- ½ tsp garlic powder
- 1 tsp dried thyme
- ¼ tsp shallot powder

Directions:
1. Preheat the air fryer to 400°F. Stir the egg and milk until combined. Mix the salt, pepper, garlic, thyme, shallot, cheddar cheese, and Parmesan cheese on a plate. Dip the chicken in the egg mix, then in the cheese mix, and press to coat. Lay the tenders in the frying basket in a single layer. Add a raised rack to cook more at one time. Spray all with oil and Bake for 12-16 minutes, flipping once halfway through cooking. Serve hot.

Gruyère Asparagus & Chicken Quiche
Servings: 4
Cooking Time: 30 Minutes
Ingredients:
- 1 grilled chicken breasts, diced
- ½ cup shredded Gruyère cheese
- 1 premade pie crust
- 2 eggs, beaten
- ¼ cup milk
- Salt and pepper to taste
- ½ lb asparagus, sliced
- 1 lemon, zested

Directions:
1. Preheat air fryer to 360°F. Carefully press the crust into a baking dish, trimming the edges. Prick the dough with a fork a few times. Add the eggs, milk, asparagus, salt, pepper, chicken, lemon zest, and half of Gruyère cheese to a mixing bowl and stir until completely blended. Pour the mixture into the pie crust. Bake in the air fryer for 15 minutes. Sprinkle the remaining Gruyère cheese on top of the quiche filling. Bake for 5 more minutes until the quiche is golden brown. Remove and allow to cool for a few minutes before cutting. Serve sliced and enjoy!

Air Fryer Naked Chicken Tenders
Servings: 4
Cooking Time: 7 Minutes
Ingredients:
- Seasoning:
- 1 teaspoon kosher salt
- ½ teaspoon garlic powder
- ½ teaspoon onion powder
- ½ teaspoon chili powder
- ¼ teaspoon sweet paprika
- ¼ teaspoon freshly ground black pepper
- Chicken:
- 8 chicken breast tenders (1 pound / 454 g total)
- 2 tablespoons mayonnaise

Directions:
1. Preheat the air fryer to 375ºF (191ºC).
2. For the seasoning: In a small bowl, combine the salt, garlic powder, onion powder, chili powder, paprika, and pepper.
3. For the chicken: Place the chicken in a medium bowl and add the mayonnaise. Mix well to coat all over, then sprinkle with the seasoning mix.
4. Working in batches, arrange a single layer of the chicken in the air fryer basket. Air fry for 6 to 7 minutes, flipping halfway, until cooked through in the center. Serve immediately.

Cranberry Turkey Quesadillas
Servings: 4
Cooking Time: 4 To 8 Minutes
Ingredients:
- 6 low-sodium whole-wheat tortillas
- ⅓ cup shredded low-sodium low-fat Swiss cheese
- ¾ cup shredded cooked low-sodium turkey breast
- 2 tablespoons cranberry sauce
- 2 tablespoons dried cranberries
- ½ teaspoon dried basil
- Olive oil spray, for spraying the tortillas

Directions:
1. Put 3 tortillas on a work surface.
2. Evenly divide the Swiss cheese, turkey, cranberry sauce, and dried cranberries among the tortillas. Sprinkle with the basil and top with the remaining tortillas.
3. Spray the outsides of the tortillas with olive oil spray.
4. One at a time, grill the quesadillas in the air fryer for 4 to 8 minutes, or until crisp and the cheese is melted. Cut into quarters and serve.

Healthy Chicken With Veggies

Servings: 4 Servings
Cooking Time: 20 Minutes
Ingredients:
- 1 pound of chopped chicken breast
- 1 chopped zucchini
- 1 cup of broccoli florets
- 1 cup of chopped bell peppers
- ½ chopped onion
- 2 minced garlic cloves
- 2 tablespoons of olive oil
- 1 tablespoon of Italian seasonings
- ½ teaspoon of garlic powder
- ½ teaspoon of chili powder (optional)
- Pinch of salt and black pepper, to taste

Directions:
1. Preheat your air fryer to 400ºF.
2. Put the chopped vegetables with chicken breast into a large mixing bowl. Add seasonings with oil and mix it well.
3. Transfer all the ingredients into the air fry basket and cook at 400ºF for 10 minutes. Toss halfway through cooking. If it's not ready, cook for 3–5 minutes more.
4. Serve warm and enjoy your Healthy Chicken with Veggies!

Chicken Tenders With Basil-strawberry Glaze

Servings: 4
Cooking Time: 20 Minutes
Ingredients:
- 1 lb chicken tenderloins
- ¼ cup strawberry preserves
- 3 tbsp chopped basil
- 1 tsp orange juice
- ½ tsp orange zest
- Salt and pepper to taste

Directions:
1. Combine all ingredients, except for 1 tbsp of basil, in a bowl. Marinade in the fridge covered for 30 minutes.
2. Preheat air fryer to 350ºF. Place the chicken tenders in the frying basket and Air Fry for 4-6 minutes. Shake gently the basket and turn over the chicken. Cook for 5 more minutes. Top with the remaining basil to serve.

Yogurt-marinated Chicken Legs

Servings: 4
Cooking Time: 50 Minutes
Ingredients:
- 1 cup Greek yogurt
- 1 tbsp Dijon mustard
- 1 tsp smoked paprika
- 1 tbsp crushed red pepper
- 1 tsp garlic powder
- 1 tsp dried oregano
- 1 tsp dried thyme
- 1 teaspoon ground cumin
- ¼ cup lemon juice
- Salt and pepper to taste
- 1 ½ lb chicken legs
- 3 tbsp butter, melted

Directions:
1. Combine all ingredients, except chicken and butter, in a bowl. Fold in chicken legs and toss until coated. Let sit covered in the fridge for 60 minutes up to overnight.
2. Preheat air fryer at 375ºF. Shake excess marinade from chicken; place them in the greased frying basket and Air Fry for 18 minutes, brush melted butter and flip once. Let chill for 5 minutes before serving.

Garlic Turkey With Tomato Mix

Servings: 4
Cooking Time: 25 Minutes
Ingredients:
- 1 pound turkey meat, cubed and browned
- A pinch of salt and black pepper
- 1 green bell pepper, chopped
- 3 garlic cloves, chopped
- 1 and ½ tsps. cumin, ground
- 12 ounces veggies stock
- 1 cup tomatoes, chopped

Directions:
1. Mix the turkey, salt, black pepper, green bell pepper, garlic cloves, ground cumin, veggies stock, and the chopped tomatoes together in a baking pan that fits in your air fryer.
2. Toss well to season.
3. Cook in your air fryer at 380 degrees F/ 195 degrees C for 25 minutes.
4. When the cooking time runs out, remove from the air fryer.
5. Serve hot on plates and enjoy!

Indian Chicken Tandoori

Servings: 2
Cooking Time: 35 Minutes
Ingredients:
- 2 chicken breasts, cubed
- ½ cup hung curd
- 1 tsp turmeric powder
- 1 tsp red chili powder
- 1 tsp chaat masala powder
- Pinch of salt

Directions:
1. Preheat air fryer to 350°F. Mix the hung curd, turmeric, red chili powder, chaat masala powder, and salt in a mixing bowl. Stir until the mixture is free of lumps. Coat the chicken with the mixture, cover, and refrigerate for 30 minutes to marinate. Place the marinated chicken chunks in a baking pan and drizzle with the remaining marinade. Bake for 25 minutes until the chicken is juicy and spiced. Serve warm.

Thai Turkey And Zucchini Meatballs
Servings: 4
Cooking Time: 12 Minutes
Ingredients:
- 1½ cups grated zucchini,
- squeezed dry in a clean kitchen towel (about 1 large zucchini)
- 3 scallions, finely chopped
- 2 cloves garlic, minced
- 1 tablespoon grated fresh ginger
- 1 tablespoon finely chopped fresh cilantro
- zest of 1 lime
- 1 teaspoon salt
- freshly ground black pepper
- 1½ pounds ground turkey (a mix of light and dark meat)
- 2 eggs, lightly beaten
- 1 cup Thai sweet chili sauce (spring roll sauce)
- lime wedges, for serving

Directions:
1. Combine the zucchini, scallions, garlic, ginger, cilantro, lime zest, salt, pepper, ground turkey and eggs in a bowl and mix the ingredients together. Gently shape the mixture into 24 balls, about the size of golf balls.
2. Preheat the air fryer to 380°F.
3. Working in batches, air-fry the meatballs for 12 minutes, turning the meatballs over halfway through the cooking time. As soon as the meatballs have finished cooking, toss them in a bowl with the Thai sweet chili sauce to coat.
4. Serve the meatballs over rice noodles or white rice with the remaining Thai sweet chili sauce and lime wedges to squeeze over the top.

Turkey Sausage With Veggies
Servings: 2
Cooking Time: 15 Minutes
Ingredients:
- 4 turkey sausages
- ½ pound Brussels sprouts, trimmed and halved
- 1 teaspoon olive oil
- Sea salt, to taste
- Ground black pepper, to taste
- ½ teaspoon cayenne pepper
- ½ teaspoon shallot powder
- ¼ teaspoon dried dill weed

Directions:
1. Arrange the turkey sausage in the air fryer basket.
2. Mix the Brussels sprouts, spices, and olive oil together in a mixing dish and toss well. Spread the Brussels sprouts around the sausages.
3. Cook in your air fryer at 380 degrees F/ 195 degrees C for 15 minutes. Halfway through cooking, shake the basket.
4. Enjoy!

Yummy Stuffed Chicken Breast
Servings: 4
Cooking Time: 15 Minutes
Ingredients:
- 2 chicken fillets, skinless and boneless, each cut into 2 pieces
- 4 brie cheese slices
- 1 tablespoon chive, minced
- 4 cured ham slices
- Salt and black pepper, to taste

Directions:
1. Preheat the Air fryer to 355°F and grease an Air fryer basket.
2. Make a slit in each chicken piece horizontally and season with the salt and black pepper.
3. Insert cheese slice in the slits and sprinkle with chives.
4. Wrap each chicken piece with one ham slice and transfer into the Air fryer basket.
5. Cook for about 15 minutes and dish out to serve warm.

Sage & Paprika Turkey Cutlets
Servings: 4
Cooking Time: 15 Minutes
Ingredients:
- ½ cup bread crumbs
- ¼ tsp paprika
- Salt and pepper to taste
- ⅛ tsp dried sage
- ⅛ tsp garlic powder
- ¼ tsp ground cumin
- 1 egg
- 4 turkey breast cutlets
- 2 tbsp chopped chervil

Directions:
1. Preheat air fryer to 380°F. Combine the bread crumbs, paprika, salt, black pepper, sage, cumin, and garlic powder in a bowl and mix well. Beat the egg in another bowl until frothy. Dip the turkey cutlets into the egg mixture, then coat them in the bread crumb mixture. Put the breaded turkey cutlets in the frying basket. Bake for 4 minutes. Turn the cutlets over, then Bake for 4 more minutes. Decorate with chervil and serve.

Barbecued Chicken Thighs
Servings: 4
Cooking Time: 15 To 18 Minutes
Ingredients:
- 6 boneless, skinless chicken thighs
- ¼ cup store-bought gluten-free barbecue sauce
- 2 cloves garlic, minced
- 2 tablespoons lemon juice

Directions:
1. In a medium bowl, combine the chicken, barbecue sauce, cloves, and lemon juice, and mix well. Let marinate for 10 minutes.
2. Remove the chicken thighs from the bowl and shake off excess sauce. Put the chicken pieces in the air fryer, leaving a bit of space between each one.
3. Grill for 15 to 18 minutes or until the chicken is 165°F on an instant-read meat thermometer.

Dill Chicken Strips

Servings: 4
Cooking Time: 10 Minutes
Ingredients:
- 2 whole boneless, skinless chicken breasts, halved lengthwise
- 1 cup Italian dressing
- 3 cups finely crushed potato chips
- 1 tablespoon dried dill weed
- 1 tablespoon garlic powder
- 1 large egg, beaten
- Cooking spray

Directions:
1. In a large resealable bag, combine the chicken and Italian dressing. Seal the bag and refrigerate to marinate at least 1 hour.
2. In a shallow dish, stir together the potato chips, dill, and garlic powder. Place the beaten egg in a second shallow dish.
3. Remove the chicken from the marinade. Roll the chicken pieces in the egg and the potato chip mixture, coating thoroughly.
4. Preheat the air fryer to 325ºF (163ºC). Line the air fryer basket with parchment paper.
5. Place the coated chicken on the parchment and spritz with cooking spray.
6. Bake for 5 minutes. Flip the chicken, spritz it with cooking spray, and bake for 5 minutes more until the outsides are crispy and the insides are no longer pink. Serve immediately.

Herb Seasoned Turkey Breast

Servings: 4
Cooking Time: 35 Minutes
Ingredients:
- 2 lbs turkey breast
- 1 tsp fresh sage, chopped
- 1 tsp fresh rosemary, chopped
- 1 tsp fresh thyme, chopped
- Pepper
- Salt

Directions:
1. Spray air fryer basket with cooking spray.
2. In a small bowl, mix together sage, rosemary, and thyme.
3. Season turkey breast with pepper and salt and rub with herb mixture.
4. Place turkey breast in air fryer basket and cook at 390°F for 30-35 minutes.
5. Slice and serve.

Jerk Chicken Wings

Servings: 4
Cooking Time: 1 Hour 20 Minutes
Ingredients:
- ¼ cup Jamaican jerk marinade
- 1 teaspoon onion powder
- 1 teaspoon garlic powder
- 1 teaspoon salt
- 2 pounds chicken wings, flats and drums separated

Directions:
1. In a large bowl, combine jerk seasoning, onion powder, garlic powder, and salt. Add chicken wings and toss to coat well. Cover and let marinate in refrigerator at least 1 hour.
2. Preheat the air fryer to 400°F.
3. Place wings in the air fryer basket in a single layer, working in batches as necessary. Cook wings 20 minutes, turning halfway through cooking time, until internal temperature reaches at least 165°F. Cool 5 minutes before serving.

Honey Rosemary Chicken

Servings: 4
Cooking Time: 20 Minutes
Ingredients:
- ¼ cup balsamic vinegar
- ¼ cup honey
- 2 tablespoons olive oil
- 1 tablespoon dried rosemary leaves
- 1 teaspoon salt
- ½ teaspoon freshly ground black pepper
- 2 whole boneless, skinless chicken breasts (about 1 pound / 454 g each), halved
- Cooking spray

Directions:
1. In a large resealable bag, combine the vinegar, honey, olive oil, rosemary, salt, and pepper. Add the chicken pieces, seal the bag, and refrigerate to marinate for at least 2 hours.
2. Preheat the air fryer to 325ºF (163ºC). Line the air fryer basket with parchment paper.
3. Remove the chicken from the marinade and place it on the parchment. Spritz with cooking spray.
4. Bake for 10 minutes. Flip the chicken, spritz it with cooking spray, and bake for 10 minutes more until the internal temperature reaches 165ºF (74ºC) and the chicken is no longer pink inside. Let sit for 5 minutes before serving.

Cheese Turkey Meatloaf

Servings: 6
Cooking Time: 47 Minutes
Ingredients:
- 2 pounds' turkey mince
- ½ cup scallions, chopped
- 2 garlic cloves, finely minced
- 1 teaspoon dried thyme
- ½ teaspoon dried basil
- ¾ cup Colby cheese, shredded
- 1 tablespoon tamari sauce
- Black pepper and salt, to your liking
- ¼ cup roasted red pepper tomato sauce
- ¾ tablespoons olive oil
- 1 medium-sized egg, well beaten

Directions:

1. In a nonstick skillet, that is preheated over a moderate heat, sauté the turkey mince, scallions, garlic, thyme, and basil until just tender and fragrant.
2. Then set your Air Fryer to cook at almost 360 degrees F/ 180 degrees C.
3. Combine sautéed mixture with the cheese and tamari sauce; then form the mixture into a loaf shape.
4. Mix the remaining items and pour them over the meatloaf.
5. Cook in the preheated air fryer basket for 45 to 47 minutes.
6. Serve warm.

Crispy Parmesan Chicken Breasts
Servings: 3
Cooking Time: 15 Minutes
Ingredients:
- 2 6-ounces boneless chicken breasts, cut into tenders
- ¾ cup buttermilk
- 1½ teaspoons Worcestershire sauce, divided
- ½ teaspoon smoked paprika, divided
- Salt and black pepper, as required
- ½ cup all-purpose flour
- 1½ cups panko breadcrumbs
- ¼ cup Parmesan cheese, finely grated
- 2 tablespoons butter, melted
- 2 large eggs

Directions:
1. In a suitable bowl, mix together buttermilk, ¾ teaspoon of Worcestershire sauce, ¼ teaspoon of paprika, salt, and black pepper.
2. Add in the chicken tenders and refrigerate overnight.
3. In a suitable bowl, mix the flour, remaining paprika, salt, and black pepper.
4. Place the remaining Worcestershire sauce and eggs in a third bowl and beat until well combined.
5. Mix well the panko, Parmesan, and butter in a fourth bowl.
6. Remove the chicken tenders from bowl and discard the buttermilk.
7. Coat the chicken tenders with flour mixture, then dip into egg mixture and finally coat with the panko mixture.
8. At 400 degrees F/ 205 degrees C, preheat your Air Fryer. Oil its air fryer basket.
9. Arrange chicken tenders into the prepared air fryer basket in 2 batches in a single layer.
10. Air fry for about 13-15 minutes, flipping once halfway through.
11. Remove from Air Fryer and transfer the chicken tenders onto a serving platter.
12. Serve hot.

Buttered Chicken Thighs
Servings: 4
Cooking Time: 30 Minutes
Ingredients:
- 4 bone-in chicken thighs, skinless
- 2 tbsp butter, melted
- 1 tsp garlic powder
- 1 tsp lemon zest
- Salt and pepper to taste
- 1 lemon, sliced

Directions:
1. Preheat air fryer to 380°F. Stir the chicken thighs in the butter, lemon zest, garlic powder, and salt. Divide the chicken thighs between 4 pieces of foil and sprinkle with black pepper, and then top with slices of lemon. Bake in the air fryer for 20-22 minutes until golden. Serve.

The Ultimate Chicken Bulgogi
Servings: 4
Cooking Time: 30 Minutes
Ingredients:
- 1 ½ lb boneless, skinless chicken thighs, cubed
- 1 cucumber, thinly sliced
- ¼ cup apple cider vinegar
- 4 garlic cloves, minced
- ¼ tsp ground ginger
- ⅛ tsp red pepper flakes
- 2 tsp honey
- ⅛ tsp salt
- 2 tbsp tamari
- 2 tsp sesame oil
- 2 tsp granular honey
- 2 tbsp lemon juice
- ½ tsp lemon zest
- 3 scallions, chopped
- 2 cups cooked white rice
- 2 tsp roasted sesame seeds

Directions:
1. In a bowl, toss the cucumber, vinegar, half of the garlic, half of the ginger, pepper flakes, honey, and salt and store in the fridge covered. Combine the tamari, sesame oil, granular honey, lemon juice, remaining garlic, remaining ginger, and chicken in a large bowl. Toss to coat and marinate in the fridge for 10 minutes.
2. Preheat air fryer to 350ºF. Place chicken in the frying basket, do not discard excess marinade. Air Fry for 11 minutes, shaking once and pouring excess marinade over. Place the chicken bulgogi over the cooked rice and scatter with scallion greens, pickled cucumbers, and sesame seeds. Serve and enjoy!

Turkey Scotch Eggs
Servings: 4
Cooking Time: 30 Minutes
Ingredients:
- 1 ½ lb ground turkey
- 1 tbsp ground cumin
- 1 tsp ground coriander
- 2 garlic cloves, minced
- 3 raw eggs
- 1 ½ cups bread crumbs
- 6 hard-cooked eggs, peeled
- ½ cup flour

Directions:
1. Preheat air fryer to 370°F. Place the ground turkey, cumin, coriander, garlic, one egg, and ½ cup of bread crumbs in a large bowl and mix until well incorporated.

2. Divide into 6 equal portions, then flatten each into long ovals. Set aside. In a shallow bowl, beat the remaining raw eggs. In another shallow bowl, add flour. Do the same with another plate for bread crumbs. Roll each cooked egg in flour, then wrap with one oval of chicken sausage until completely covered.

3. Roll again in flour, then coat in the beaten egg before rolling in bread crumbs. Arrange the eggs in the greased frying basket. Air Fry for 12-14 minutes, flipping once until the sausage is cooked and the eggs are brown. Serve.

Air Fried Chicken Tenderloin

Servings: 8
Cooking Time: 15 Minutes
Ingredients:
- ½ cup almond flour
- 1 egg, beaten
- 2 tablespoons coconut oil
- 8 chicken tenderloins
- Salt and pepper to taste

Directions:
1. Preheat the air fryer for 5 minutes.
2. Season the chicken tenderloin with salt and pepper to taste.
3. Soak in beaten eggs then dredge in almond flour.
4. Place in the air fryer and brush with coconut oil.
5. Cook for 15 minutes at 375°F.
6. Halfway through the cooking time, give the fryer basket a shake to cook evenly.

Yummy Shredded Chicken

Servings: 2
Cooking Time: 15 Minutes
Ingredients:
- 2 large chicken breasts
- ¼ tsp Pepper
- 1 tsp garlic puree
- 1 tsp mustard
- Salt

Directions:
1. Add all ingredients to the bowl and toss well.
2. Transfer chicken into the air fryer basket and cook at 360°F for 15 minutes.
3. Remove chicken from air fryer and shred using a fork.
4. Serve and enjoy.

Turkey Burgers

Servings: 4
Cooking Time: 13 Minutes
Ingredients:
- 1 pound ground turkey
- ¼ cup diced red onion
- 1 tablespoon grilled chicken seasoning
- ½ teaspoon dried parsley
- ½ teaspoon salt
- 4 slices provolone cheese
- 4 whole-grain sandwich buns
- Suggested toppings: lettuce, sliced tomatoes, dill pickles, and mustard

Directions:
1. Combine the turkey, onion, chicken seasoning, parsley, and salt and mix well.
2. Shape into 4 patties.
3. Cook at 360°F for 11 minutes or until turkey is well done and juices run clear.
4. Top each burger with a slice of cheese and cook 2 minutes to melt.
5. Serve on buns with your favorite toppings.

Goat Cheese Stuffed Turkey Roulade

Servings: 4
Cooking Time: 55 Minutes
Ingredients:
- 1 boneless turkey breast, skinless
- Salt and pepper to taste
- 4 oz goat cheese
- 1 tbsp marjoram
- 1 tbsp sage
- 2 garlic cloves, minced
- 2 tbsp olive oil
- 2 tbsp chopped cilantro

Directions:
1. Preheat air fryer to 380°F. Butterfly the turkey breast with a sharp knife and season with salt and pepper. Mix together the goat cheese, marjoram, sage, and garlic in a bowl. Spread the cheese mixture over the turkey breast, then roll it up tightly, tucking the ends underneath.
2. Put the turkey breast roulade onto a piece of aluminum foil, wrap it up, and place it into the air fryer. Bake for 30 minutes. Turn the turkey breast, brush the top with oil, and then continue to cook for another 10-15 minutes. Slice and serve sprinkled with cilantro.

Chapter 9: Vegetable Side Dishes Recipes

Mashed Potato Tots

Servings: 18
Cooking Time: 10 Minutes
Ingredients:
- 1 medium potato or 1 cup cooked mashed potatoes
- 1 tablespoon real bacon bits
- 2 tablespoons chopped green onions, tops only
- ¼ teaspoon onion powder
- 1 teaspoon dried chopped chives
- salt
- 2 tablespoons flour
- 1 egg white, beaten
- ½ cup panko breadcrumbs
- oil for misting or cooking spray

Directions:
1. If using cooked mashed potatoes, jump to step 4.
2. Peel potato and cut into ½-inch cubes. (Small pieces cook more quickly.) Place in saucepan, add water to cover, and heat to boil. Lower heat slightly and continue cooking just until tender, about 10minutes.
3. Drain potatoes and place in ice cold water. Allow to cool for a minute or two, then drain well and mash.
4. Preheat air fryer to 390°F.
5. In a large bowl, mix together the potatoes, bacon bits, onions, onion powder, chives, salt to taste, and flour. Add egg white and stir well.
6. Place panko crumbs on a sheet of wax paper.
7. For each tot, use about 2 teaspoons of potato mixture. To shape, drop the measure of potato mixture onto panko crumbs and push crumbs up and around potatoes to coat edges. Then turn tot over to coat other side with crumbs.
8. Mist tots with oil or cooking spray and place in air fryer basket, crowded but not stacked.
9. Cook at 390°F for 10 minutes, until browned and crispy.
10. Repeat steps 8 and 9 to cook remaining tots.

Cheddar Tomatillos With Lettuce

Servings: 4
Cooking Time: 4 Minutes
Ingredients:
- 2 tomatillos
- ¼ cup coconut flour
- 2 eggs, beaten
- ¼ teaspoon ground nutmeg
- ¼ teaspoon chili flakes
- 1 ounce Cheddar cheese, shredded
- 4 lettuce leaves

Directions:
1. Cut the tomatillos into slices.
2. Mix ground nutmeg, chili flakes, and beaten eggs in a bowl.
3. Brush the tomatillo slices with the egg mixture. Then coat with coconut flour.
4. Repeat above steps with the rest slices.
5. Before cooking, heat your air fryer to 400 degrees F/ 205 degrees C.
6. Place the coated tomatillo slices in the air fryer basket in a single layer.
7. Cook in your air fryer for 2 minutes from each side.
8. When cooked, add the lettuce leaves on the top of the tomatillos.
9. To serve, sprinkle with shredded cheese.

Tuna Platter

Servings: 4
Cooking Time: 9 Minutes
Ingredients:
- 4 new potatoes, boiled in their jackets
- ½ cup vinaigrette dressing, plus 2 tablespoons
- ½ pound fresh green beans, cut in half-inch pieces and steamed
- 1 tablespoon Herbes de Provence
- 1 tablespoon minced shallots
- 1½ tablespoons tarragon vinegar
- 4 tuna steaks, each ¾-inch thick, about 1 pound
- salt and pepper
- Salad
- 8 cups chopped romaine lettuce
- 12 grape tomatoes, halved lengthwise
- ½ cup pitted olives (black, green, nicoise, or combination)
- 2 boiled eggs, peeled and halved lengthwise

Directions:
1. Quarter potatoes and toss with 1 tablespoon salad dressing.
2. Toss the warm beans with the other tablespoon of salad dressing. Set both aside while you prepare the tuna.
3. Mix together the herbs, shallots, and vinegar and rub into all sides of tuna. Season fish to taste with salt and pepper.
4. Cook tuna at 390°F for 7minutes and check. If needed, cook 2 minutes longer, until tuna is barely pink in the center.
5. Spread the lettuce over a large platter.
6. Slice the tuna steaks in ½-inch pieces and arrange them in the center of the lettuce.
7. Place the remaining ingredients around the tuna. Diners create their own plates by selecting what they want from the platter. Pass remainder of salad dressing at the table.

Garlicky Brussels Sprouts

Servings: 4
Cooking Time: 35 Minutes
Ingredients:
- 1 lb Brussels sprouts, halved lengthwise
- 1 tbsp olive oil
- 1 tbsp lemon juice
- ½ tsp sea salt
- ⅛ tsp garlic powder
- 4 garlic cloves, sliced
- 2 tbsp parsley, chopped
- ½ tsp red chili flakes

Directions:
1. Preheat the air fryer to 375°F. Combine the olive oil, lemon juice, salt, and garlic powder in a bowl and mix well. Add the Brussels sprouts and toss to coat. Put the Brussels sprouts in the frying basket. Air Fry for 15-20 minutes, shaking the basket once until golden and crisp. Sprinkle with garlic slices, parsley, and chili flakes. Toss and cook for 2-4 minutes more until the garlic browns a bit.

Corn Muffins

Servings: 12
Cooking Time: 10 Minutes
Ingredients:
- ½ cup all-purpose flour
- ½ cup cornmeal
- ¼ cup granulated sugar
- ½ teaspoon baking powder
- ¼ cup salted butter, melted
- ½ cup buttermilk
- 1 large egg

Directions:
1. Preheat the air fryer to 350°F.
2. In a large bowl, whisk together flour, cornmeal, sugar, and baking powder.
3. Add butter, buttermilk, and egg to dry mixture. Stir until well combined.
4. Divide batter evenly among twelve silicone or aluminum muffin cups, filling cups about halfway. Working in batches as needed, place in the air fryer and cook 10 minutes until golden brown. Let cool 5 minutes before serving.

Lemony Cabbage Slaw

Servings: 4
Cooking Time: 20 Minutes
Ingredients:
- 1 green cabbage head, shredded
- Juice of ½ lemon
- A pinch of salt and black pepper
- ½ cup coconut cream
- ½ teaspoon fennel seeds
- 1 tablespoon mustard

Directions:
1. Combine all the ingredients in a suitable baking pan.
2. Cook in your air fryer at 350 degrees F/ 175 degrees C for 20 minutes.
3. Serve on plates as a side dish.

Sesame Taj Tofu

Servings: 4
Cooking Time: 25 Minutes
Ingredients:
- 1 block firm tofu, pressed and cut into 1-inch thick cubes
- 2 tablespoons soy sauce
- 2 teaspoons toasted sesame seeds
- 1 teaspoon rice vinegar
- 1 tablespoon cornstarch

Directions:
1. Preheat the air fryer to 400°F (204°C).
2. Add the tofu, soy sauce, sesame seeds, and rice vinegar in a bowl together and mix well to coat the tofu cubes. Then cover the tofu in cornstarch and put it in the air fryer basket.
3. Air fry for 25 minutes, giving the basket a shake at five-minute intervals to ensure the tofu cooks evenly.
4. Serve immediately.

Mushroom Mozzarella Risotto

Servings: 4
Cooking Time: 20 Minutes
Ingredients:
- 1-pound white mushrooms, sliced
- ¼ cup mozzarella, shredded
- 1 cauliflower head, florets separated and riced
- 1 cup chicken stock
- 1 tablespoon thyme, chopped
- 1 teaspoon Italian seasoning
- A pinch of salt and black pepper
- 2 tablespoons olive oil

Directions:
1. Grease a suitable baking pan with oil and then heat to medium heat.
2. Add the cauliflower rice and mushrooms. Toss and cook for a few minutes.
3. Add the shredded mozzarella, chicken stock, Italian seasoning, salt, and black pepper in the pan.
4. Cook in your air fryer at 360 degrees F/ 180 degrees C for 20 minutes.
5. To serve, sprinkle the chopped thyme on the top.

Cheesy Zucchini Tots

Servings: 4
Cooking Time: 6 Minutes
Ingredients:
- 1 zucchini, grated
- ½ cup Mozzarella, shredded
- 1 egg, beaten
- 2 tablespoons almond flour
- ½ teaspoon ground black pepper
- 1 teaspoon coconut oil, melted

Directions:
1. Before cooking, heat your air fryer to 385 degrees F/ 195 degrees C.
2. Brush the coconut oil over the inside of the air fryer basket.
3. Mix the shredded Mozzarella, almond flour, egg, ground black pepper, and grated zucchini in a mixing bowl. Make small zucchini tots. Arrange evenly the zucchini tots on the air fryer basket.
4. Cook in your air fryer at 385 degrees F/ 195 degrees C for 3 minutes from each side or until golden brown.

Garlic Kale Mash

Servings: 4
Cooking Time: 20 Minutes
Ingredients:
- 1 cauliflower head, florets separated
- 4 teaspoons butter, melted
- 4 garlic cloves, minced
- 3 cups kale, chopped
- 2 scallions, chopped
- A pinch of black pepper and salt
- ⅓ cup coconut cream
- 1 tablespoon parsley, chopped

Directions:

1. In a pan that fits the air fryer, combine the cauliflower with the butter, garlic, scallions, salt, black pepper and the cream, toss, introduce the pan in the machine and cook at almost 380 degrees F/ 195 degrees C for 20 minutes.
2. Mash the mix well, add the remaining ingredients, whisk, divide between plates and serve.

Open-faced Sandwich

Servings: 4
Cooking Time: 25 Minutes
Ingredients:
- 1 can chickpeas, drained and rinsed
- 1 medium-sized head of cauliflower
- 1 tbsp. extra-virgin olive oil
- 2 ripe avocados, mashed
- 2 tbsps. lemon juice
- 4 flatbreads, toasted
- salt and pepper to taste

Directions:
1. Before cooking, heat your air fryer to 425 degrees F/ 220 degrees C.
2. Cut the cauliflower head into florets. Combine chickpea, olive oil, lemon juice, and the cauliflower together in a mixing bowl.
3. Transfer the mixture inside the air fryer basket.
4. Cook in your air fryer for 25 minutes.
5. When cooked, spread the mixture on half of the flatbread and then add avocado mash.
6. To season, add more salt and pepper as you like.
7. Serve the meal with hot sauce.

Potato And Broccoli With Tofu Scramble

Servings: 3
Cooking Time: 30 Minutes
Ingredients:
- 2½ cups chopped red potato
- 2 tablespoons olive oil, divided
- 1 block tofu, chopped finely
- 2 tablespoons tamari
- 1 teaspoon turmeric powder
- ½ teaspoon onion powder
- ½ teaspoon garlic powder
- ½ cup chopped onion
- 4 cups broccoli florets

Directions:
1. Preheat the air fryer to 400ºF (204ºC).
2. Toss together the potatoes and 1 tablespoon of the olive oil.
3. Air fry the potatoes in a baking dish for 15 minutes, shaking once during the cooking time to ensure they fry evenly.
4. Combine the tofu, the remaining 1 tablespoon of the olive oil, turmeric, onion powder, tamari, and garlic powder together, stirring in the onions, followed by the broccoli.
5. Top the potatoes with the tofu mixture and air fry for an additional 15 minutes. Serve warm.

Dauphinoise (potatoes Au Gratin)

Servings: 4
Cooking Time: 30 Minutes
Ingredients:
- ½ cup grated cheddar cheese
- 3 peeled potatoes, sliced
- ½ cup milk
- ½ cup heavy cream
- Salt and pepper to taste
- 1 tsp ground nutmeg

Directions:
1. Preheat air fryer to 350°F. Place the milk, heavy cream, salt, pepper, and nutmeg in a bowl and mix well. Dip in the potato slices and arrange on a baking dish. Spoon the remaining mixture over the potatoes. Scatter the grated cheddar cheese on top. Place the baking dish in the air fryer and Bake for 20 minutes. Serve warm and enjoy!

Curried Fruit

Servings: 6
Cooking Time: 20 Minutes
Ingredients:
- 1 cup cubed fresh pineapple
- 1 cup cubed fresh pear (firm, not overly ripe)
- 8 ounces frozen peaches, thawed
- 1 15-ounce can dark, sweet, pitted cherries with juice
- 2 tablespoons brown sugar
- 1 teaspoon curry powder

Directions:
1. Combine all ingredients in large bowl. Stir gently to mix in the sugar and curry.
2. Pour into air fryer baking pan and cook at 360°F for 10minutes.
3. Stir fruit and cook 10 more minutes.
4. Serve hot.

Grits Again

Servings: 2
Cooking Time: 10 Minutes
Ingredients:
- cooked grits
- plain breadcrumbs
- oil for misting or cooking spray
- honey or maple syrup for serving (optional)

Directions:
1. While grits are still warm, spread them into a square or rectangular baking pan, about ½-inch thick. If your grits are thicker than that, scoop some out into another pan.
2. Chill several hours or overnight, until grits are cold and firm.
3. When ready to cook, pour off any water that has collected in pan and cut grits into 2- to 3-inch squares.
4. Dip grits squares in breadcrumbs and place in air fryer basket in single layer, close but not touching.
5. Cook at 390°F for 10 minutes, until heated through and crispy brown on the outside.
6. Serve while hot either plain or with a drizzle of honey or maple syrup.

Burger Bun For One

Servings: 1
Cooking Time: 5 Minutes
Ingredients:
- 2 tablespoons salted butter, melted
- ¼ cup blanched finely ground almond flour
- ¼ teaspoon baking powder
- ⅛ teaspoon apple cider vinegar
- 1 large egg, whisked

Directions:
1. Pour butter into an ungreased 4" ramekin. Add flour, baking powder, and vinegar to ramekin and stir until combined. Add egg and stir until batter is mostly smooth.
2. Place ramekin into air fryer basket. Adjust the temperature to 350°F and set the timer for 5 minutes. When done, the center will be firm and the top slightly browned. Let cool, about 5 minutes, then remove from ramekin and slice in half. Serve.

Turmeric Tofu Cubes

Servings: 2
Cooking Time: 9 Minutes
Ingredients:
- 6 ounces tofu, cubed
- 1 teaspoon avocado oil
- 1 teaspoon apple cider vinegar
- 1 garlic clove, diced
- ¼ teaspoon ground turmeric
- ¼ teaspoon ground paprika
- ½ teaspoon dried cilantro
- ¼ teaspoon lemon zest, grated

Directions:
1. Before cooking, firstly heat your air fryer to 400 degrees F/ 205 degrees C.
2. Mix together apple cider vinegar, ground turmeric, diced garlic, paprika, avocado oil, lime zest, and cilantro in a bowl.
3. Coat the tofu cubes with the oil mixture.
4. Transfer the tofu cubes in the air fryer basket and cook in your air fryer for 9 minutes.
5. During cooking shake the basket from time to time.

Ajillo Mushrooms

Servings: 4
Cooking Time: 30 Minutes
Ingredients:
- 2/3 cup panko bread crumbs
- 1 cup cremini mushrooms
- 1/3 cup all-purpose flour
- 1 egg, beaten
- ½ tsp smoked paprika
- 3 garlic cloves, minced
- Salt and pepper to taste

Directions:
1. Preheat the air fryer to 400°F. Put the flour on a plate. Mix the egg and garlic in a shallow bowl. On a separate plate, combine the panko, smoked paprika, salt, and pepper and mix well. Cut the mushrooms through the stems into quarters. Dip the mushrooms in flour, then the egg, then in the panko mix. Press to coat, then put on a wire rack and set aside. Add the mushrooms to the frying basket in a single layer and spray with cooking oil. Air Fry for 6-8 minutes, flipping them once until crisp. Serve warm.

Radishes And Green Onions Mix

Servings: 4
Cooking Time: 15 Minutes
Ingredients:
- 20 radishes, halved
- 1 tablespoon olive oil
- 3 green onions, chopped
- Black pepper and salt to the taste
- 3 teaspoons black sesame seeds
- 2 tablespoons olive oil

Directions:
1. In a suitable bowl, mix all the recipe ingredients and toss well.
2. Put the radishes in your air fryer basket, Cook at almost 400 degrees F/ 205 degrees C for almost 15 minutes.
3. Serve.

Breadcrumb Crusted Agnolotti

Servings: 6
Cooking Time: 14 Minutes
Ingredients:
- 1 cup flour
- Black pepper and salt
- 4 eggs, beaten
- 2 cups breadcrumbs
- Cooking spray

Directions:
1. Mix flour with black pepper and salt.
2. Dip pasta into the flour, then into the egg, and finally in the breadcrumbs.
3. Spray with oil and arrange in the preheated air fryer in an even layer.
4. Set its temperature to 400 degrees F/ 205 degrees C and cook for 14 minutes, turning once halfway through cooking.
5. Cook until nice and golden.
6. Serve with goat cheese.

Spicy Fries

Servings: 4
Cooking Time: 20 Minutes
Ingredients:
- 2 tsp olive oil
- 2 tsp cayenne pepper
- 1 tsp paprika
- Salt and black pepper

Directions:
1. Place the fries into a bowl and sprinkle with oil, cayenne, paprika, salt, and black pepper. Toss and place them in the fryer. Cook for 7 minutes at 360°F, until golden and crispy. Give it a toss after 7-8 minutes and continue cooking for another 8 minutes. Serve.

Sweet And Sour Tofu

Servings: 2
Cooking Time: 20 Minutes
Ingredients:
- 2 teaspoons apple cider vinegar
- 1 tablespoon sugar
- 1 tablespoon soy sauce
- 3 teaspoons lime juice
- 1 teaspoon ground ginger
- 1 teaspoon garlic powder
- ½ block firm tofu, pressed to remove excess liquid and cut into cubes
- 1 teaspoon cornstarch
- 2 green onions, chopped
- Toasted sesame seeds, for garnish

Directions:
1. In a bowl, thoroughly combine the apple cider vinegar, sugar, soy sauce, lime juice, ground ginger, and garlic powder.
2. Cover the tofu with this mixture and leave to marinate for at least 30 minutes.
3. Preheat the air fryer to 400ºF (204ºC).
4. Transfer the tofu to the air fryer, keeping any excess marinade for the sauce. Air fry for 20 minutes or until crispy.
5. In the meantime, thicken the sauce with the cornstarch over a medium-low heat.
6. Serve the cooked tofu with the sauce, green onions, and sesame seeds.

Fried Cauliflower with Parmesan Lemon Dressing

Servings: 2
Cooking Time: 12 Minutes
Ingredients:
- 4 cups cauliflower florets (about half a large head)
- 1 tablespoon olive oil
- salt and freshly ground black pepper
- 1 teaspoon finely chopped lemon zest
- 1 tablespoon fresh lemon juice (about half a lemon)
- ¼ cup grated Parmigiano-Reggiano cheese
- 4 tablespoons extra virgin olive oil
- ¼ teaspoon salt
- lots of freshly ground black pepper
- 1 tablespoon chopped fresh parsley

Directions:
1. Preheat the air fryer to 400°F.
2. Toss the cauliflower florets with the olive oil, salt and freshly ground black pepper. Air-fry for 12 minutes, shaking the basket a couple of times during the cooking process.
3. While the cauliflower is frying, make the dressing. Combine the lemon zest, lemon juice, Parmigiano-Reggiano cheese and olive oil in a small bowl. Season with salt and lots of freshly ground black pepper. Stir in the parsley.
4. Turn the fried cauliflower out onto a serving platter and drizzle the dressing over the top.

Blistered Tomatoes

Servings: 20
Cooking Time: 15 Minutes
Ingredients:
- 1½ pounds Cherry or grape tomatoes
- Olive oil spray
- 1½ teaspoons Balsamic vinegar
- ¼ teaspoon Table salt
- ¼ teaspoon Ground black pepper

Directions:
1. Put the basket in a drawer-style air fryer, or a baking tray in the lower third of a toaster oven–style air fryer. Place a 6-inch round cake pan in the basket or on the tray for a small batch, a 7-inch round cake pan for a medium batch, or an 8-inch round cake pan for a large one. Heat the air fryer to 400°F with the pan in the basket. When the machine is at temperature, keep heating the pan for 5 minutes more.
2. Place the tomatoes in a large bowl, coat them with the olive oil spray, toss gently, then spritz a couple of times more, tossing after each spritz, until the tomatoes are glistening.
3. Pour the tomatoes into the cake pan and air-fry undisturbed for 10 minutes, or until they split and begin to brown.
4. Use kitchen tongs and a nonstick-safe spatula, or silicone baking mitts, to remove the cake pan from the basket. Toss the hot tomatoes with the vinegar, salt, and pepper. Cool in the pan for a few minutes before serving.

Sweet Potatoes With Zucchini

Servings: 4
Cooking Time: 20 Minutes
Ingredients:
- 2 large-sized sweet potatoes, peeled and quartered
- 1 medium zucchini, sliced
- 1 Serrano pepper, deseeded and thinly sliced
- 1 bell pepper, deseeded and thinly sliced
- 1 to 2 carrots, cut into matchsticks
- ¼ cup olive oil
- 1½ tablespoons maple syrup
- ½ teaspoon porcini powder
- ¼ teaspoon mustard powder
- ½ teaspoon fennel seeds
- 1 tablespoon garlic powder
- ½ teaspoon fine sea salt
- ¼ teaspoon ground black pepper
- Tomato ketchup, for serving

Directions:
1. Put the sweet potatoes, zucchini, peppers, and the carrot into the air fryer basket. Coat with a drizzling of olive oil.
2. Preheat the air fryer to 350ºF (177ºC).
3. Air fry the vegetables for 15 minutes.
4. In the meantime, prepare the sauce by vigorously combining the other ingredients, except for the tomato ketchup, with a whisk.
5. Lightly grease a baking dish.

6. Transfer the cooked vegetables to the baking dish, pour over the sauce and coat the vegetables well.
7. Increase the temperature to 390ºF (199ºC) and air fry the vegetables for an additional 5 minutes.
8. Serve warm with a side of ketchup.

Creamy Cauliflower Puree

Servings: 2
Cooking Time: 8 Minutes
Ingredients:
- 1 ½ cup cauliflower, chopped
- 1 tablespoon butter, melted
- ½ teaspoon salt
- 1 tablespoon fresh parsley, chopped
- ¼ cup heavy cream
- Cooking spray

Directions:
1. Spritz the cooking spray over the inside of the air fryer basket.
2. Place the chopped cauliflower in the air fryer basket.
3. Cook in your air fryer at 400 degrees F/ 205 degrees C for 8 minutes. Stir the cauliflower every 4 minutes.
4. Heat the heavy cream until it is hot. Then pour in a blender, add parsley, butter, salt, and cauliflower.
5. Blend until it is smooth.

Yellow Squash And Zucchinis Dish

Servings: 4
Cooking Time: 45 Minutes
Ingredients:
- 1 yellow squash; halved, deseeded and cut into chunks
- 6 tsp. olive oil
- 1 lb. zucchinis; sliced
- 1/2 lb. carrots; cubed
- 1 tbsp. tarragon; chopped
- Salt and white pepper to the taste

Directions:
1. In your air fryer's basket; mix zucchinis with carrots, squash, salt, pepper and oil; toss well and cook at 400 °F, for 25 minutes. Divide them on plates and serve as a side dish with tarragon sprinkled on top.

Spiced Okra

Servings: 2
Cooking Time: 20 Minutes
Ingredients:
- ½ pound okra, ends trimmed and sliced
- 1 teaspoon olive oil
- ½ teaspoon mango powder
- ½ teaspoon chili powder
- ½ teaspoon ground coriander
- ½ teaspoon ground cumin
- ⅛ teaspoon black pepper
- ¼ teaspoon salt

Directions:
1. At 350 degrees F/ 175 degrees C, preheat your air fryer.
2. Add all the recipe ingredients into the suitable bowl and toss well.

3. Grease its air fryer basket with cooking spray.
4. Transfer okra mixture into the air fryer basket and cook for almost 10 minutes. Shake basket halfway through.
5. Toss okra well and cook for 2 minutes more.
6. Serve and enjoy.

Rosemary New Potatoes

Servings: 4
Cooking Time: 6 Minutes
Ingredients:
- 3 large red potatoes
- ¼ teaspoon ground rosemary
- ¼ teaspoon ground thyme
- ⅛ teaspoon salt
- ⅛ teaspoon ground black pepper
- 2 teaspoons extra-light olive oil

Directions:
1. Preheat air fryer to 330°F.
2. Place potatoes in large bowl and sprinkle with rosemary, thyme, salt, and pepper.
3. Stir with a spoon to distribute seasonings evenly.
4. Add oil to potatoes and stir again to coat well.
5. Cook at 330°F for 4 minutes. Stir and break apart any that have stuck together.
6. Cook an additional 2 minutes or until fork-tender.

Tasty Brussels Sprouts With Guanciale

Servings: 4
Cooking Time: 50 Minutes
Ingredients:
- 3 guanciale slices, halved
- 1 lb Brussels sprouts, halved
- 2 tbsp olive oil
- ¼ tsp salt
- ¼ tsp dried thyme

Directions:
1. Preheat air fryer to 350°F. Air Fry Lay the guanciale in the air fryer, until crispy, 10 minutes. Remove and drain on a paper towel. Give the guanciale a rough chop and Set aside. Coat Brussels sprouts with olive oil in a large bowl. Add salt and thyme, then toss. Place the sprouts in the frying basket. Air Fry for about 12-15 minutes, shake the basket once until the sprouts are golden and tender. Top with guanciale and serve.

Parmesan Zucchini Gratin

Servings: 2
Cooking Time: 15 Minutes
Ingredients:
- 5 ounces parmesan cheese, shredded
- 1 tablespoon coconut flour
- 1 tablespoon dried parsley
- 2 zucchinis
- 1 teaspoon butter, melted

Directions:
1. In a bowl, add the coconut flour and parmesan cheese together.
2. To season, add parsley.

3. Cut the zucchinis lengthwise in half and slice the halves into four slices.
4. Before cooking, heat your air fryer to 400 degrees F/ 205 degrees C.
5. Then coat the zucchinis with the melted butter and dip in the parmesan-flour mixture to thoroughly coat the zucchini slices.
6. Cook in your air fryer for 13 minutes.

Cheesy Loaded Broccoli

Servings: 2
Cooking Time: 10 Minutes
Ingredients:
- 3 cups fresh broccoli florets
- 1 tablespoon coconut oil
- ¼ teaspoon salt
- ½ cup shredded sharp Cheddar cheese
- ¼ cup sour cream
- 4 slices cooked sugar-free bacon, crumbled
- 1 medium scallion, trimmed and sliced on the bias

Directions:
1. Place broccoli into ungreased air fryer basket, drizzle with coconut oil, and sprinkle with salt. Adjust the temperature to 350°F and set the timer for 8 minutes. Shake basket three times during cooking to avoid burned spots.
2. When timer beeps, sprinkle broccoli with Cheddar and set the timer for 2 additional minutes. When done, cheese will be melted and broccoli will be tender.
3. Serve warm in a large serving dish, topped with sour cream, crumbled bacon, and scallion slices.

Broccoli Tots

Servings: 24
Cooking Time: 10 Minutes
Ingredients:
- 2 cups broccoli florets (about ½ pound broccoli crowns)
- 1 egg, beaten
- ⅛ teaspoon onion powder
- ¼ teaspoon salt
- ⅛ teaspoon pepper
- 2 tablespoons grated Parmesan cheese
- ¼ cup panko breadcrumbs
- oil for misting

Directions:
1. Steam broccoli for 2 minutes. Rinse in cold water, drain well, and chop finely.
2. In a large bowl, mix broccoli with all other ingredients except the oil.
3. Scoop out small portions of mixture and shape into 24 tots. Lay them on a cookie sheet or wax paper as you work.
4. Spray tots with oil and place in air fryer basket in single layer.
5. Cook at 390°F for 5 minutes. Shake basket and spray with oil again. Cook 5 minutes longer or until browned and crispy.

Asparagus With Garlic

Servings: 4
Cooking Time: 4 To 5 Minutes, Or 8 To 11 Minutes Depending On Desired Texture
Ingredients:
- 1 pound asparagus, rinsed, ends snapped off where they naturally break (see Tip)
- 2 teaspoons olive oil
- 3 garlic cloves, minced
- 2 tablespoons balsamic vinegar
- ½ teaspoon dried thyme

Directions:
1. In a large bowl, toss the asparagus with the olive oil. Transfer to the air fryer basket.
2. Sprinkle with garlic. Roast for 4 to 5 minutes for crisp-tender or for 8 to 11 minutes for asparagus that is crisp on the outside and tender on the inside.
3. Drizzle with the balsamic vinegar and sprinkle with the thyme leaves. Serve immediately.

Yukon Gold Potato Purée

Servings: 4
Cooking Time: 25 Minutes
Ingredients:
- 1 lb Yukon Gold potatoes, scrubbed and cubed
- 2 tbsp butter, melted
- Salt and pepper to taste
- 1/8 cup whole milk
- ¼ cup cream cheese
- 1 tbsp butter, softened
- ¼ cup chopped dill

Directions:
1. Preheat air fryer at 350ºF. Toss the potatoes and melted butter in a bowl, place them in the frying basket, and Air Fry for 13-15 minutes, tossing once. Transfer them into a bowl. Using a fork, mash the potatoes. Stir in salt, pepper, half of the milk, cream cheese, and 1 tbsp of butter until you reach your desired consistency. Garnish with dill to serve.

Roasted Lemony Broccoli

Servings: 6
Cooking Time: 15 Minutes
Ingredients:
- 2 heads broccoli, cut into florets
- 2 teaspoons extra-virgin olive oil, plus more for coating
- 1 teaspoon salt
- ½ teaspoon black pepper
- 1 clove garlic, minced
- ½ teaspoon lemon juice

Directions:
1. Cover the air fryer basket with aluminum foil and coat with a light brushing of oil.
2. Preheat the air fryer to 375°F (191°C).
3. In a bowl, combine all ingredients, save for the lemon juice, and transfer to the air fryer basket. Roast for 15 minutes.
4. Serve with the lemon juice.

Perfect Broccolini

Servings: 4
Cooking Time: 15 Minutes
Ingredients:
- 1 pound Broccolini
- Olive oil spray
- Coarse sea salt or kosher salt

Directions:
1. Preheat the air fryer to 375°F.
2. Place the broccolini on a cutting board. Generously coat it with olive oil spray, turning the vegetables and rearranging them before spraying a couple of times more, to make sure everything's well coated, even the flowery bits in their heads.
3. When the machine is at temperature, pile the broccolini in the basket, spreading it into as close to one layer as you can. Air-fry for 5 minutes, tossing once to get any covered or touching parts exposed to the air currents, until the leaves begin to get brown and even crisp. Watch carefully and use this visual cue to know the moment to stop the cooking.
4. Transfer the broccolini to a platter. Spread out the pieces and sprinkle them with salt to taste.

Turmeric Cauliflower With Cilantro

Servings: 4
Cooking Time: 8 Minutes
Ingredients:
- 1 pound cauliflower head
- 1 tablespoon ground turmeric
- 1 tablespoon coconut oil
- ½ teaspoon dried cilantro
- ¼ teaspoon salt

Directions:
1. Before cooking, heat your air fryer to 400 degrees F/ 205 degrees C.
2. Cut the cauliflower into 4 steaks. Rub together with salt, dried cilantro, ground turmeric, and the cauliflower steak.
3. Sprinkle the mixture with coconut oil.
4. Transfer the mixture inside the air fryer basket and cook in your air fryer for 4 minutes from each side.

Simple Baked Potatoes With Dill Yogurt

Servings: 4
Cooking Time: 45 Minutes
Ingredients:
- 4 Yukon gold potatoes
- Salt and black pepper
- ½ cup Greek yogurt
- ¼ cup minced dill
- Cooking spray

Directions:
1. Pierce the potatoes with a fork. Lightly coat them with sprays of cooking oil, then season with salt. Preheat air fryer to 400°F. Air Fry the potatoes in the greased frying basket for 30-35 minutes, flipping once halfway through cooking until completely cooked and slightly crispy. A knife will cut into the center of the potato with ease. Remove them to a serving dish. Add toppings of yogurt, dill, salt, and pepper to taste.

Tasty Cauliflower Croquettes

Servings: 4
Cooking Time: 20 Minutes
Ingredients:
- 1 pound cauliflower florets
- 2 eggs
- 1 tablespoon olive oil
- 2 tablespoons scallions, chopped
- 1 garlic clove, minced
- 1 cup Colby cheese, shredded
- ½ cup parmesan cheese, grated
- Salt and black pepper, to taste
- ¼ teaspoon dried dill weed
- 1 teaspoon paprika

Directions:
1. Bring the salted water in a pot and blanch the cauliflower florets until al dente, for about 3 to 4 minutes. Drain well and pulse in a food processor.
2. Add the remaining ingredients; mix to combine well. Shape the cauliflower mixture into bite-sized tots.
3. At 375 degrees F/ 190 degrees C, heat your air fryer in advance.
4. Grease its air fryer basket with cooking spray.
5. Cook the cauliflower croquettes in the preheated air fryer for almost 16 minutes, shaking halfway through the cooking time. Serve with your favorite sauce for dipping. Serve!

Cayenne Chicken Wing Dip

Servings: 4
Cooking Time: 20 Minutes
Ingredients:
- 1 teaspoon cayenne pepper
- Salt to taste
- 2 tablespoon grapeseed oil
- 2 teaspoon chili flakes
- 1 cup heavy cream
- 3 ounces gorgonzola cheese, crumbled
- ½ lemon, juiced
- ½ teaspoon garlic powder

Directions:
1. At 380 degrees F/ 195 degrees C, preheat your air fryer.
2. Coat the chicken with cayenne pepper, salt, and oil.
3. Place in the basket and cook for 20 minutes. In a suitable bowl, mix heavy cream, gorgonzola cheese, lemon juice, and garlic powder.
4. Serve with chicken wings.

Roasted Brown Butter Carrots

Servings: 4
Cooking Time: 20 Minutes
Ingredients:
- 1 tablespoon unsalted butter
- 6 carrots, cut into ½-inch pieces (about 3 cups)

- Salt
- Pepper

Directions:
1. Place a saucepan over high heat. Add the butter. Allow the butter to melt for 2 to 3 minutes.
2. Stirring constantly to ensure it does not scorch, cook for 1 to 2 minutes, until it starts to turn brown. Brown bits will form on the bottom of the pan. Remove the pan from heat.
3. In a large bowl, combine the carrots with the brown butter. Season with salt and pepper to taste.
4. Transfer the carrots to the air fryer. Cook for 6 minutes.
5. Open the air fryer and shake the basket. Cook for an additional 6 minutes.
6. Cool before serving.

Potatoes With Zucchinis

Servings: 4
Cooking Time: 45 Minutes
Ingredients:
- 2 potatoes, peeled and cubed
- 4 carrots, cut into chunks
- 1 head broccoli, cut into florets
- 4 zucchinis, sliced thickly
- Salt and ground black pepper, to taste
- ¼ cup olive oil
- 1 tablespoon dry onion powder

Directions:
1. Preheat the air fryer to 400°F (204°C).
2. In a baking dish, add all the ingredients and combine well.
3. Bake for 45 minutes in the air fryer, ensuring the vegetables are soft and the sides have browned before serving.

Mashed Sweet Potato Tots

Servings: 18
Cooking Time: 12 Minutes
Ingredients:
- 1 cup cooked mashed sweet potatoes
- 1 egg white, beaten
- ⅛ teaspoon ground cinnamon
- 1 dash nutmeg
- 2 tablespoons chopped pecans
- 1½ teaspoons honey
- salt
- ½ cup panko breadcrumbs
- oil for misting or cooking spray

Directions:
1. Preheat air fryer to 390°F.
2. In a large bowl, mix together the potatoes, egg white, cinnamon, nutmeg, pecans, honey, and salt to taste.
3. Place panko crumbs on a sheet of wax paper.
4. For each tot, use about 2 teaspoons of sweet potato mixture. To shape, drop the measure of potato mixture onto panko crumbs and push crumbs up and around potatoes to coat edges. Then turn tot over to coat other side with crumbs.
5. Mist tots with oil or cooking spray and place in air fryer basket in single layer.
6. Cook at 390°F for 12 minutes, until browned and crispy.
7. Repeat steps 5 and 6 to cook remaining tots.

Portobello Pizzas

Servings: 4
Cooking Time: 10 Minutes
Ingredients:
- Olive oil
- 4 large portobello mushroom caps, cleaned and stems removed
- Garlic powder
- 8 tablespoons pizza sauce
- 16 slices turkey pepperoni
- 8 tablespoons mozzarella cheese

Directions:
1. Spray a fryer basket lightly with olive oil.
2. Lightly spray the outside of the mushrooms with olive oil and sprinkle with a little garlic powder, to taste.
3. Turn the mushroom over and lightly spray the sides and top edges of the mushroom with olive oil and sprinkle with garlic powder, to taste.
4. Place the mushrooms in the fryer basket in a single layer with the top side down. Leave room between the mushrooms. You may need to cook them in batches.
5. Air fry for 5 minutes.
6. Spoon 2 tablespoons of pizza sauce on each mushroom. Top each with 4 slices of turkey pepperoni and sprinkle with 2 tablespoons of mozzarella cheese. Press the pepperoni and cheese down into the pizza sauce to help prevent it from flying around inside the air fryer.
7. Air fry until the cheese is melted and lightly browned on top, another 3 to 5 minutes.

Broccoli Au Gratin

Servings: 2
Cooking Time: 25 Minutes
Ingredients:
- 2 cups broccoli florets, chopped
- 6 tbsp grated Gruyère cheese
- 1 tbsp grated Pecorino cheese
- ½ tbsp olive oil
- 1 tbsp flour
- 1/3 cup milk
- ½ tsp ground coriander
- Salt and black pepper
- 2 tbsp panko bread crumbs

Directions:
1. Whisk the olive oil, flour, milk, coriander, salt, and pepper in a bowl. Incorporate broccoli, Gruyere cheese, panko bread crumbs, and Pecorino cheese until well combined. Pour in a greased baking dish.
2. Preheat air fryer to 330°F. Put the baking dish into the frying basket. Bake until the broccoli is crisp-tender and the top is golden, or about 12-15 minutes. Serve warm.

Garlicky Mushrooms With Parsley

Servings: 2
Cooking Time: 12 Minutes
Ingredients:
- 8 ounces mushrooms, sliced
- 1 tablespoon parsley, chopped
- 1 teaspoon soy sauce
- ½ teaspoon garlic powder
- 1 tablespoon olive oil
- Black pepper
- Salt

Directions:
1. Add all the recipe ingredients into the mixing bowl and toss well.
2. Transfer mushrooms in air fryer basket and cook at almost 380 degrees F/ 195 degrees C for almost 10-12 minutes. Shake basket halfway through.
3. Serve and enjoy.

Awesome Chicken Taquitos

Servings: 4
Cooking Time: 12 Minutes
Ingredients:
- 1 cup shredded mozzarella cheese
- ¼ cup salsa
- ¼ cup Greek yogurt
- Salt and black pepper
- 8 flour tortillas

Directions:
1. In a suitable bowl, mix chicken, cheese, salsa, sour cream, salt, and black pepper.
2. Spray 1 side of the tortilla with cooking spray.
3. Lay 2 tablespoon of the chicken mixture at the center of the non-oiled side the tortillas.
4. Roll tightly around the mixture. Arrange taquitos on your air fryer basket.
5. Cook for almost 12 minutes at 380 degrees F/ 195 degrees C.
6. Serve.

Creole Seasoned Okra

Servings: 4
Cooking Time: 25 Minutes
Ingredients:
- 1 teaspoon olive oil, plus more for spraying
- 12 ounces frozen sliced okra
- 1 to 2 teaspoons Creole seasoning

Directions:
1. Spray a fryer basket lightly with olive oil.
2. In a medium bowl, toss the frozen okra with 1 teaspoon of olive oil and the Creole seasoning.
3. Place the okra into the fryer basket. You may need to cook them in batches.
4. Air fry until the okra is browned and crispy, 20 to 25 minutes, making sure to shake the basket and lightly spray with olive oil every 5 minutes.

Spicy Bean Stuffed Potatoes

Servings: 4
Cooking Time: 60 Minutes
Ingredients:
- 1 lb russet potatoes, scrubbed and perforated with a fork
- 1 can diced green chilies, including juice
- 1/3 cup grated Mexican cheese blend
- 1 green bell pepper, diced
- 1 yellow bell pepper, diced
- ¼ cup torn iceberg lettuce
- 2 tsp olive oil
- 2 tbsp sour cream
- ½ tsp chili powder
- 2-3 jalapeños, sliced
- 1 red bell pepper, chopped
- Salt and pepper to taste
- 1/3 cup canned black beans
- 4 grape tomatoes, sliced
- ¼ cup chopped parsley

Directions:
1. Preheat air fryer at 400°F. Brush olive oil over potatoes. Place them in the frying basket and Bake for 45 minutes, turning at 30 minutes mark. Let cool on a cutting board for 10 minutes until cool enough to handle. Slice each potato lengthwise and scoop out all but a ¼" layer of potato to form 4 boats.
2. Mash potato flesh, sour cream, green chilies, cheese, chili powder, jalapeños, green, yellow, and red peppers, salt, and pepper in a bowl until smooth. Fold in black beans. Divide between potato skin boats. Place potato boats in the frying basket and Bake for 2 minutes. Remove them to a serving plate. Top each boat with lettuce, tomatoes, and parsley. Sprinkle tops with salt and serve.

Chapter 10: Desserts And Sweets Recipes

Banana Slices With Cardamom

Servings: 8
Cooking Time: 15 Minutes
Ingredients:
- 4 medium ripe bananas, peeled
- ⅓ cup rice flour, divided
- 2 tablespoons all-purpose flour
- 2 tablespoons corn flour
- 2 tablespoons desiccated coconut
- ½ teaspoon baking powder
- ½ teaspoon ground cardamom
- Pinch of salt
- Water, as required
- ¼ cup sesame seeds

Directions:
1. In a suitable bowl, mix 2 tablespoons of rice flour, all-purpose flour, cornmeal, coconut, baking powder, cardamom and salt.
2. Add the water in the bowl and mix until a thick, smooth dough forms.
3. In another bowl, place the remaining rice flour.
4. In a third bowl, add the sesame seeds.
5. Cut each banana in ½ and then cut each ½ into 2 pieces lengthwise.
6. Dip the banana into the coconut mixture and then top with the remaining rice flour, followed by the sesame seeds.
7. Select the "Air Fry" mode and set the cooking time to 15 minutes.
8. Set the temperature setting to 390 degrees F/ 200 degrees C.
9. Arrange banana slices in air fry basket and place in air fryer.
10. Transfer banana slices to plates to cool slightly.

One-bowl Chocolate Buttermilk Cake

Servings: 6
Cooking Time: 16-20 Minutes
Ingredients:
- ¾ cup All-purpose flour
- ½ cup Granulated white sugar
- 3 tablespoons Unsweetened cocoa powder
- ½ teaspoon Baking soda
- ¼ teaspoon Table salt
- ½ cup Buttermilk
- 2 tablespoons Vegetable oil
- ¾ teaspoon Vanilla extract
- Baking spray (see here)

Directions:
1. Preheat the air fryer to 325°F (or 330°F, if that's the closest setting).
2. Stir the flour, sugar, cocoa powder, baking soda, and salt in a large bowl until well combined. Add the buttermilk, oil, and vanilla. Stir just until a thick, grainy batter forms.
3. Use the baking spray to generously coat the inside of a 6-inch round cake pan for a small batch, a 7-inch round cake pan for a medium batch, or an 8-inch round cake pan for a large batch. Scrape and spread the chocolate batter into this pan, smoothing the batter out to an even layer.
4. Set the pan in the basket and air-fry undisturbed for 16 minutes for a 6-inch layer, 18 minutes for a 7-inch layer, or 20 minutes for an 8-inch layer, or until a toothpick or cake tester inserted into the center of the cake comes out clean. Start checking it at the 14-minute mark to know where you are.
5. Use hot pads or silicone baking mitts to transfer the cake pan to a wire rack. Cool for 5 minutes. To unmold, set a cutting board over the baking pan and invert both the board and the pan. Lift the still-warm pan off the cake layer. Set the wire rack on top of the cake layer and invert all of it with the cutting board so that the cake layer is now right side up on the wire rack. Remove the cutting board and continue cooling the cake for at least 10 minutes or to room temperature, about 30 minutes, before slicing into wedges.

Brownies With White Chocolate

Servings: 6
Cooking Time: 30 Minutes
Ingredients:
- ¼ cup white chocolate chips
- ¼ cup muscovado sugar
- 1 egg
- 2 tbsp white sugar
- 2 tbsp canola oil
- 1 tsp vanilla
- ¼ cup cocoa powder
- 1/3 cup flour

Directions:
1. Preheat air fryer to 340°F. Beat the egg with muscovado sugar and white sugar in a bowl. Mix in the canola oil and vanilla. Next, stir in cocoa powder and flour until just combined. Gently fold in white chocolate chips. Spoon the batter into a lightly pan. Bake until the brownies are set when lightly touched on top, about 20 minutes. Let to cool completely before slicing.

Vanilla Cupcakes With Chocolate Chips

Servings: 2
Cooking Time: 25 Minutes + Cooling Time
Ingredients:
- ½ cup white sugar
- 1 ½ cups flour
- 2 tsp baking powder
- ½ tsp salt
- 2/3 cup sunflower oil
- 1 egg
- 2 tsp maple extract
- ¼ cup vanilla yogurt
- 1 cup chocolate chips

Directions:
1. Preheat air fryer to 350°F. Combine the sugar, flour, baking powder, and salt in a bowl and stir to combine. Whisk the egg in a separate bowl. Pour in the sunflower oil, yogurt, and maple extract, and continue whisking

until light and fluffy. Spoon the wet mixture into the dry ingredients and stir to combine. Gently fold in the chocolate chips with a spatula. Divide the batter between cupcake cups and Bake in the air fryer for 12-15 minutes or until a toothpick comes out dry. Remove the cupcakes let them cool. Serve.

Fried Oreos

Servings: 12
Cooking Time: 6 Minutes Per Batch
Ingredients:
- oil for misting or nonstick spray
- 1 cup complete pancake and waffle mix
- 1 teaspoon vanilla extract
- ½ cup water, plus 2 tablespoons
- 12 Oreos or other chocolate sandwich cookies
- 1 tablespoon confectioners' sugar

Directions:
1. Spray baking pan with oil or nonstick spray and place in basket.
2. Preheat air fryer to 390°F.
3. In a medium bowl, mix together the pancake mix, vanilla, and water.
4. Dip 4 cookies in batter and place in baking pan.
5. Cook for 6minutes, until browned.
6. Repeat steps 4 and 5 for the remaining cookies.
7. Sift sugar over warm cookies.

Lemon Nut Bars

Servings: 10
Cooking Time: 30 Minutes
Ingredients:
- ½ cup coconut oil, softened
- 1 teaspoon baking powder
- 1 teaspoon lemon juice
- 1 cup almond flour
- ½ cup coconut flour
- 3 tablespoons Erythritol
- 1 teaspoon vanilla extract
- 2 eggs, beaten
- 2 oz. hazelnuts, chopped
- 1 oz. macadamia nuts, chopped
- Cooking spray

Directions:
1. Mix the coconut oil, baking powder, lemon juice, almond flour, coconut flour, Erythritol, vanilla extract and eggs well until smooth.
2. Continue to add the hazelnuts and macadamia nuts and stir the mixture until homogenous.
3. Transfer the nut mixture to the cooking basket and use the spatula to flatten it.
4. Cook the mixture at 325 degrees F/ 160 degrees C for 30 minutes.
5. When done, cool the mixture well and cut it into the serving bars.
6. Enjoy.

Vanilla Bars With Sesame Seeds

Servings: 6
Cooking Time: 10 Minutes
Ingredients:
- 1 cup coconut flour
- 2 tablespoons coconut flakes
- 2 eggs, beaten
- 1 teaspoon baking powder
- ¼ cup Erythritol
- 1 teaspoon vanilla extract
- 1 tablespoon butter, softened
- 1 teaspoon sesame seeds
- Cooking spray

Directions:
1. In a suitable bowl, add the coconut flour, coconut flakes, eggs, baking powder, Erythritol, vanilla extract, and sesame seeds, then use a spoon to stir the mixture well until it is homogenous.
2. Roll up the dough into the square and cut into the bars.
3. Cook the coconut bars at 325 degrees F/ 160 degrees C for 10 minutes.
4. When done, serve and enjoy.

Banana And Rice Pudding

Servings: 6
Cooking Time: 20 Minutes
Ingredients:
- 1 cup brown rice
- 3 cups milk
- 2 bananas, peeled and mashed
- ½ cup maple syrup
- 1 teaspoon vanilla extract

Directions:
1. Place all the ingredients in a pan that fits your air fryer; stir well.
2. Put the pan in the fryer and cook at 360°F for 20 minutes.
3. Stir the pudding, divide into cups, refrigerate, and serve cold.

Apple Turnovers

Servings: 4 Servings
Cooking Time: 45 Minutes
Ingredients:
- 2 diced medium Granny Smith apples
- 6 tablespoons of brown sugar
- ¼ cup of powdered sugar
- ½ package pastry (14 ounces) for crust pie
- 4 tablespoons of butter
- 1 teaspoon of cornstarch
- 1 teaspoon of ground cinnamon
- 1 teaspoon of milk
- 2 teaspoons of cold water
- ½ tablespoon of oil

Directions:
1. Put the diced apples, cinnamon, brown sugar, and butter into a non-stick skillet. Cook on medium heat for 5 minutes until it softened.
2. Dissolve the cornstarch in cold water. Pour it into the apples and cook for 1 minute until it thickened. Remove it from the heat and allow to cool.

3. Spread some flour over the work surface, place the dough on it, and roll it out. Cut the rolled dough into rectangles small enough so that 2 can fit in the air fryer at a time. You should make 8 equal rectangles at the end.
4. Put some apple mixture in the center of the rectangles, about ½-inch from each edge. Roll out the other 4 rectangles to make them slightly larger than the filled ones. Put the larger rectangles on the top of the fillings and push the edges down with a fork to stick. Make small cuts in the center of the tops of the pies. Grease the tops with oil.
5. Preheat your air fryer to 385°F. Grease the inside of the air fryer basket with some oil.
6. Place the prepared pies into the preheated air fryer basket. Cook at 385°F for about 8 minutes until golden-brown. Remove them out and cook the other part of the pies.
7. Whisk milk with powdered sugar in a small bowl. Glaze the warm pies with the milk-sugar mixture.
8. Serve warm and enjoy your Apple Turnovers!

Vanilla Muffins With Pecans

Servings: 12
Cooking Time: 15 Minutes
Ingredients:
- 4 eggs
- 1 teaspoon vanilla
- ¼ cup almond milk
- 2 tablespoons butter, melted
- ½ cup swerve
- 1 teaspoon psyllium husk
- 1 tablespoon baking powder
- ½ cup pecans, chopped
- ½ teaspoon ground cinnamon
- 2 teaspoons allspice
- 1 ½ cups almond flour

Directions:
1. At 370 degrees F/ 185 degrees C, preheat your air fryer.
2. Beat eggs, almond milk, vanilla, sweetener, and butter in a suitable bowl using a hand mixer until smooth.
3. Add remaining recipe ingredients and mix until well combined.
4. Pour batter into the silicone muffin molds and place into the air fryer basket in batches.
5. Cook muffins for almost 15 minutes.
6. Serve and enjoy.

Peanut Butter Cup Doughnut Holes

Servings: 24
Cooking Time: 4 Minutes
Ingredients:
- 1½ cups bread flour
- 1 teaspoon active dry yeast
- 1 tablespoon sugar
- ¼ teaspoon salt
- ½ cup warm milk
- ½ teaspoon vanilla extract
- 2 egg yolks
- 2 tablespoons melted butter
- 24 miniature peanut butter cups, plus a few more for garnish
- vegetable oil, in a spray bottle
- Doughnut Topping
- 1 cup chocolate chips
- 2 tablespoons milk

Directions:
1. Combine the flour, yeast, sugar and salt in a bowl. Add the milk, vanilla, egg yolks and butter. Mix well until the dough starts to come together. Transfer the dough to a floured surface and knead by hand for 2 minutes. Shape the dough into a ball and transfer it to a large oiled bowl. Cover the bowl with a towel and let the dough rise in a warm place for 1 to 1½ hours, until the dough has doubled in size.
2. When the dough has risen, punch it down and roll it into a 24-inch long log. Cut the dough into 24 pieces. Push a peanut butter cup into the center of each piece of dough, pinch the dough shut and roll it into a ball. Place the dough balls on a cookie sheet and let them rise in a warm place for 30 minutes.
3. Preheat the air fryer to 400°F.
4. Spray or brush the dough balls lightly with vegetable oil. Air-fry eight at a time, at 400°F for 4 minutes, turning them over halfway through the cooking process.
5. While the doughnuts are air frying, prepare the topping. Place the chocolate chips and milk in a microwave safe bowl. Microwave on high for 1 minute. Stir and microwave for an additional 30 seconds if necessary to get all the chips to melt. Stir until the chips are melted and smooth.
6. Dip the top half of the doughnut holes into the melted chocolate. Place them on a rack to set up for just a few minutes and watch them disappear.

Vanilla Berry Cobbler

Servings: 6
Cooking Time: 10 Minutes
Ingredients:
- 1 egg, lightly beaten
- 1 tablespoon butter, melted
- 2 teaspoons swerve
- ½ teaspoon vanilla
- 1 cup almond flour
- ½ cup raspberries, sliced
- ½ cup strawberries, sliced

Directions:
1. Before cooking, heat your air fryer to 360 degrees F/ 180 degrees C.
2. Combine the sliced raspberries and strawberries in an air fryer baking dish that fits in your air fryer.
3. Pour the sweetener over the berries.
4. In a separate bowl, combine together vanilla, butter, and almond flour.
5. Combine the almond flour mixture with the beaten egg.
6. Top the sliced berries with the almond flour mixture and then use foil to cover the dish.
7. Then transfer the dish inside your air fryer and cook at 360 degrees F/ 180 degrees C for 10 minutes.
8. When cooked, remove from the air fryer and serve.

Struffoli

Servings: X
Cooking Time: 20 Minutes
Ingredients:
- ¼ cup butter, softened
- ⅔ cup sugar
- 5 eggs
- 2 teaspoons vanilla extract
- zest of 1 lemon
- 4 cups all-purpose flour
- 2 teaspoons baking soda
- ¼ teaspoon salt
- 16 ounces honey
- 1 teaspoon ground cinnamon
- zest of 1 orange
- 2 tablespoons water
- nonpareils candy sprinkles

Directions:
1. Cream the butter and sugar together in a bowl until light and fluffy using a hand mixer (or a stand mixer). Add the eggs, vanilla and lemon zest and mix. In a separate bowl, combine the flour, baking soda and salt. Add the dry ingredients to the wet ingredients and mix until you have a soft dough. Shape the dough into a ball, wrap it in plastic and let it rest for 30 minutes.
2. Divide the dough ball into four pieces. Roll each piece into a long rope. Cut each rope into about 25 (½-inch) pieces. Roll each piece into a tight ball. You should have 100 little balls when finished.
3. Preheat the air fryer to 370°F.
4. In batches of about 20, transfer the dough balls to the air fryer basket, leaving a small space in between them. Air-fry the dough balls at 370°F for 3 to 4 minutes, shaking the basket when one minute of cooking time remains.
5. After all the dough balls are air-fried, make the honey topping. Melt the honey in a small saucepan on the stovetop. Add the cinnamon, orange zest, and water. Simmer for one minute. Place the air-fried dough balls in a large bowl and drizzle the honey mixture over top. Gently toss to coat all the dough balls evenly. Transfer the coated struffoli to a platter and sprinkle the nonpareil candy sprinkles over top. You can dress the presentation up by piling the balls into the shape of a wreath or pile them high in a cone shape to resemble a Christmas tree.
6. Struffoli can be made ahead. Store covered tightly.

Brownies

Servings: 8
Cooking Time: 20 Minutes
Ingredients:
- ½ cup all-purpose flour
- 1 cup granulated sugar
- ¼ cup cocoa powder
- ½ teaspoon baking powder
- 6 tablespoons salted butter, melted
- 1 large egg
- ½ cup semisweet chocolate chips

Directions:
1. Preheat the air fryer to 350°F. Generously grease two 6" round cake pans.
2. In a large bowl, combine flour, sugar, cocoa powder, and baking powder.
3. Add butter, egg, and chocolate chips to dry ingredients. Stir until well combined.
4. Divide batter between prepared pans. Place in the air fryer basket and cook 20 minutes until a toothpick inserted into the center comes out clean. Cool 5 minutes before serving.

Vanilla-strawberry Muffins

Servings: 4
Cooking Time: 25 Minutes
Ingredients:
- ¼ cup diced strawberries
- 2 tbsp powdered sugar
- 1 cup flour
- ½ tsp baking soda
- 1/3 cup granulated sugar
- ¼ tsp salt
- 1 tsp vanilla extract
- 1 egg
- 1 tbsp butter, melted
- ½ cup diced strawberries
- 2 tbsp chopped walnuts
- 6 tbsp butter, softened
- 1 ½ cups powdered sugar
- 1/8 tsp peppermint extract

Directions:
1. Preheat air fryer at 375°F. Combine flour, baking soda, granulated sugar, and salt in a bowl. In another bowl, combine the vanilla, egg, walnuts and melted butter. Pour wet ingredients into dry ingredients and toss to combine. Fold in half of the strawberries and spoon mixture into 8 greased silicone cupcake liners.
2. Place cupcakes in the frying basket and Bake for 6-8 minutes. Let cool onto a cooling rack for 10 minutes. Blend the remaining strawberries in a food processor until smooth. Slowly add powdered sugar to softened butter while beating in a bowl. Stir in peppermint extract and puréed strawberries until blended. Spread over cooled cupcakes. Serve sprinkled with powdered sugar

Orange Marmalade

Servings: 4
Cooking Time: 20 Minutes
Ingredients:
- 4 oranges, peeled and chopped
- 3 cups sugar
- 1½ cups water

Directions:
1. In a pan that fits your air fryer, mix the oranges with the sugar and the water; stir.
2. Place the pan in the fryer and cook at 340°F for 20 minutes.
3. Stir well, divide into cups, refrigerate, and serve cold.

Cinnamon Tortilla Crisps

Servings: 4
Cooking Time: 8 Minutes
Ingredients:
- 1 tortilla
- 2 tsp muscovado sugar
- ½ tsp cinnamon

Directions:
1. Preheat air fryer to 350°F. Slice the tortilla into 8 triangles like a pizza. Put the slices on a plate and spray both sides with oil. Sprinkle muscovado sugar and cinnamon on top, then lightly spray the tops with oil. Place in the frying basket in a single layer. Air Fry for 5-6 minutes or until they are light brown. Enjoy warm.

German Streusel-stuffed Baked Apples

Servings: 4
Cooking Time: 40 Minutes
Ingredients:
- 2 large apples
- 3 tbsp flour
- 3 tbsp light brown sugar
- ⅛ tsp ground cinnamon
- 1 tsp vanilla extract
- 1 tsp chopped pecans
- 2 tbsp cold butter
- 2 tbsp salted caramel sauce

Directions:
1. Cut the apples in half through the stem and scoop out the core and seeds. Mix flour, brown sugar, vanilla, pecans and cinnamon in a bowl. Cut in the butter with a fork until it turns into crumbs. Top each apple half with 2 ½ tbsp of the crumble mixture.
2. Preheat air fryer to 325°F. Put the apple halves in the greased frying basket. Cook until soft in the center and the crumble is golden, about 25-30 minutes. Serve warm topped with caramel sauce.

Caramel Apple Crumble

Servings: 6
Cooking Time: 50 Minutes
Ingredients:
- 4 apples, peeled and thinly sliced
- 2 tablespoons sugar
- 1 tablespoon flour
- 1 teaspoon ground cinnamon
- ¼ teaspoon ground allspice
- healthy pinch ground nutmeg
- 10 caramel squares, cut into small pieces
- Crumble Topping:
- ¾ cup rolled oats
- ¼ cup sugar
- ⅓ cup flour
- ¼ teaspoon ground cinnamon
- 6 tablespoons butter, melted

Directions:
1. Preheat the air fryer to 330°F.
2. Combine the apples, sugar, flour, and spices in a large bowl and toss to coat. Add the caramel pieces and mix well. Pour the apple mixture into a 1-quart round baking dish that will fit in your air fryer basket (6-inch diameter).
3. To make the crumble topping, combine the rolled oats, sugar, flour and cinnamon in a small bowl. Add the melted butter and mix well. Top the apples with the crumble mixture. Cover the entire dish with aluminum foil and transfer the dish to the air fryer basket, lowering the dish into the basket using a sling made of aluminum foil (fold a piece of aluminum foil into a strip about 2-inches wide by 24-inches long). Fold the ends of the aluminum foil over the top of the dish before returning the basket to the air fryer.
4. Air-fry at 330°F for 25 minutes. Remove the aluminum foil and continue to air-fry for another 25 minutes. Serve the crumble warm with whipped cream or vanilla ice cream, if desired.

Rich Chocolate Cookie

Servings: 4
Cooking Time: 9 Minutes
Ingredients:
- Nonstick baking spray with flour
- 3 tablespoons softened butter
- ⅓ cup plus 1 tablespoon brown sugar
- 1 egg yolk
- ½ cup flour
- 2 tablespoons ground white chocolate
- ¼ teaspoon baking soda
- ½ teaspoon vanilla
- ¾ cup chocolate chips

Directions:
1. Preheat the air fryer to 350ºF (177ºC).
2. In a medium bowl, beat the butter and brown sugar together until fluffy. Stir in the egg yolk.
3. Add the flour, white chocolate, baking soda, and vanilla, and mix well. Stir in the chocolate chips.
4. Line a baking pan with parchment paper. Spray the parchment paper with nonstick baking spray with flour.
5. Spread the batter into the prepared pan, leaving a ½-inch border on all sides.
6. Bake for about 9 minutes or until the cookie is light brown and just barely set.
7. Remove the pan from the air fryer and let cool for 10 minutes. Remove the cookie from the pan, remove the parchment paper, and let cool on a wire rack.
8. Serve immediately.

Apple-blueberry Hand Pies

Servings: 4
Cooking Time: 7 To 9 Minutes
Ingredients:
- 1 medium Granny Smith apple, peeled and finely chopped
- ½ cup dried blueberries
- 1 tablespoon freshly squeezed orange juice
- 1 tablespoon packed brown sugar
- 2 teaspoons cornstarch
- 4 sheets frozen phyllo dough, thawed
- 8 teaspoons unsalted butter, melted
- 8 teaspoons sugar

- Nonstick cooking spray, for coating the phyllo dough

Directions:
1. In a medium bowl, mix the apple, blueberries, orange juice, brown sugar, and cornstarch.
2. Place 1 sheet of phyllo dough on a work surface with the narrow side facing you. Brush very lightly with 1 teaspoon of butter and sprinkle with 1 teaspoon of sugar. Fold the phyllo sheet in half from left to right.
3. Place one-fourth of the fruit filling at the bottom of the sheet in the center. Fold the left side of the sheet over the filling. Spray lightly with cooking spray. Fold the right side of the sheet over the filling. Brush with 1 teaspoon of butter and sprinkle with 1 teaspoon of sugar.
4. Fold the bottom right corner of the dough up to meet the left side of the pastry sheet to form a triangle. Continue folding the triangles over to enclose the filling, as you would fold a flag. Seal the edge with a bit of water. Spray lightly with cooking spray. Repeat with the remaining 3 sheets of the phyllo, butter, sugar, and cooking spray, making four pies.
5. Place the pies in the air fryer basket. Bake for 7 to 9 minutes, or until golden brown and crisp. Remove the pies and let cool on a wire rack before serving.

Graham Cracker Cheesecake

Servings: 8
Cooking Time: 20 Minutes
Ingredients:
- 1 cup graham cracker crumbs
- 3 tablespoons softened butter
- 1½ (8-ounce / 227-g) packages cream cheese, softened
- ⅓ cup sugar
- 2 eggs
- 1 tablespoon flour
- 1 teaspoon vanilla
- ¼ cup chocolate syrup

Directions:
1. For the crust, combine the graham cracker crumbs and butter in a small bowl and mix well. Press into the bottom of a baking pan and put in the freezer to set.
2. For the filling, combine the cream cheese and sugar in a medium bowl and mix well. Beat in the eggs, one at a time. Add the flour and vanilla.
3. Preheat the air fryer to 450°F (232°C).
4. Remove ⅔ cup of the filling to a small bowl and stir in the chocolate syrup until combined.
5. Pour the vanilla filling into the pan with the crust. Drop the chocolate filling over the vanilla filling by the spoonful. With a clean butter knife, stir the fillings in a zigzag pattern to marbleize them.
6. Bake for 20 minutes or until the cheesecake is just set.
7. Cool on a wire rack for 1 hour, then chill in the refrigerator until the cheesecake is firm.
8. Serve immediately.

Enticing Chocolate Cake

Servings: 6
Cooking Time: 30 Minutes
Ingredients:
- 2 eggs, beaten
- ⅔ cup sour cream
- 1 cup almond flour
- ⅔ cup swerve
- ⅓ cup coconut oil, softened
- ¼ cup cocoa powder
- 2 tablespoons chocolate chips, unsweetened
- 1 ½ teaspoons baking powder
- 1 teaspoon vanilla extract
- ½ teaspoon pure rum extract
- Chocolate Frosting:
- ½ cup butter, softened
- ¼ cup cocoa powder
- 1 cup powdered swerve
- 2 tablespoons milk

Directions:
1. Mix all the recipe ingredients for the chocolate cake with a hand mixer on low speed.
2. Scrape the batter into a cake pan.
3. Air fry at 330 degrees F/ 165 degrees C for 25 to 30 minutes.
4. Then transfer the cake to a wire rack to cool.
5. Meanwhile, whip the butter and cocoa until smooth.
6. Add the powdered swerve. Slowly and gradually, pour in the milk until your frosting reaches desired consistency.
7. Whip until smooth and fluffy; then, frost the cooled cake.
8. Place the frosted cake in your refrigerator for a couple of hours.
9. Serve well chilled.

Strawberry Muffins With Cinnamon

Servings: 12
Cooking Time: 15 Minutes
Ingredients:
- 3 eggs
- 1 teaspoon ground cinnamon
- 2 teaspoons baking powder
- 2 ½ cups almond flour
- ⅔ cup fresh strawberries, diced
- ⅓ cup heavy cream
- 1 teaspoon vanilla
- ½ cup Swerve
- 5 tablespoons butter

Directions:
1. Before cooking, heat your air fryer to 325 degrees F/ 160 degrees C.
2. In a bowl, add the sweetener and butter and use a hand mixer to beat until smooth.
3. Beat in cream, whisked eggs, and vanilla until frothy.
4. Sift the cinnamon, baking powder, salt, and almond flour together in a second bowl.
5. Mix the flour mixture together with the wet ingredients until well incorporated.
6. Then place the strawberries. Fold and press well.
7. Divide the batter into the silicone muffin molds.
8. Cook in batches in your air fryer at 325 degrees F/ 160 degrees C for 15 minutes.
9. Enjoy!

Chocolate Macaroons

Servings: 16
Cooking Time: 8 Minutes
Ingredients:
- 2 Large egg white(s), at room temperature
- ⅛ teaspoon Table salt
- ½ cup Granulated white sugar
- 1½ cups Unsweetened shredded coconut
- 3 tablespoons Unsweetened cocoa powder

Directions:
1. Preheat the air fryer to 375°F.
2. Using an electric mixer at high speed, beat the egg white(s) and salt in a medium or large bowl until stiff peaks can be formed when the turned-off beaters are dipped into the mixture.
3. Still working with the mixer at high speed, beat in the sugar in a slow stream until the meringue is shiny and thick.
4. Scrape down and remove the beaters. Fold in the coconut and cocoa with a rubber spatula until well combined, working carefully to deflate the meringue as little as possible.
5. Scoop up 2 tablespoons of the mixture. Wet your clean hands and roll that little bit of coconut bliss into a ball. Set it aside and continue making more balls: 7 more for a small batch, 15 more for a medium batch, or 23 more for a large one.
6. Line the bottom of the machine's basket or the basket attachment with parchment paper. Set the balls on the parchment with as much air space between them as possible. Air-fry undisturbed for 8 minutes, or until dry, set, and lightly browned.
7. Use a nonstick-safe spatula to transfer the macaroons to a wire rack. Cool for at least 10 minutes before serving. Or cool to room temperature, about 30 minutes, then store in a sealed container at room temperature for up to 3 days.

Apple Chips With Cinnamon

Servings: 4
Cooking Time: 12 Minutes
Ingredients:
- 1 apple, thinly slice using a mandolin slicer
- 1 tablespoon almond butter
- ¼ cup plain yogurt
- 2 teaspoons olive oil
- 1 teaspoon ground cinnamon
- 4 drops liquid stevia

Directions:
1. In a large bowl, toss together oil, cinnamon, and the apple slices.
2. Using cooking spray, spray the air fryer basket.
3. Transfer the apple slices in the air fryer basket.
4. Set the temperature to 375 degrees F/ 190 degrees C and timer for 12 minutes.
5. Turn over the apple slices every 4 minutes.
6. Then mix together the yogurt, sweetener, and the almond butter in a small bowl.
7. When cooked, remove the apple slices from the air fryer.
8. Serve the apple slices with the yogurt dip.

Oreo-coated Peanut Butter Cups

Servings: 8
Cooking Time: 4 Minutes
Ingredients:
- 8 Standard ¾-ounce peanut butter cups, frozen
- ⅓ cup All-purpose flour
- 2 Large egg white(s), beaten until foamy
- 16 Oreos or other creme-filled chocolate sandwich cookies, ground to crumbs in a food processor
- Vegetable oil spray

Directions:
1. Set up and fill three shallow soup plates or small pie plates on your counter: one for the flour, one for the beaten egg white(s), and one for the cookie crumbs.
2. Dip a frozen peanut butter cup in the flour, turning it to coat all sides. Shake off any excess, then set it in the beaten egg white(s). Turn it to coat all sides, then let any excess egg white slip back into the rest. Set the candy bar in the cookie crumbs. Turn to coat on all parts, even the sides. Dip the peanut butter cup back in the egg white(s) as before, then into the cookie crumbs as before, making sure you have a solid, even coating all around the cup. Set aside while you dip and coat the remaining cups.
3. When all the peanut butter cups are dipped and coated, lightly coat them on all sides with the vegetable oil spray. Set them on a plate and freeze while the air fryer heats.
4. Preheat the air fryer to 400°F.
5. Set the dipped cups wider side up in the basket with as much air space between them as possible. Air-fry undisturbed for 4 minutes, or until they feel soft but the coating is set.
6. Turn off the machine and remove the basket from it. Set aside the basket with the fried cups for 10 minutes. Use a nonstick-safe spatula to transfer the fried cups to a wire rack. Cool for at least another 5 minutes before serving.

Fried Pineapple Chunks

Servings: 3
Cooking Time: 10 Minutes
Ingredients:
- 3 tablespoons Cornstarch
- 1 Large egg white, beaten until foamy
- 1 cup Ground vanilla wafer cookies (not low-fat cookies)
- ¼ teaspoon Ground dried ginger
- 18 Fresh 1-inch chunks peeled and cored pineapple

Directions:
1. Preheat the air fryer to 400°F.
2. Put the cornstarch in a medium or large bowl. Put the beaten egg white in a small bowl. Pour the cookie crumbs and ground dried ginger into a large zip-closed plastic bag, shaking it a bit to combine them.
3. Dump the pineapple chunks into the bowl with the cornstarch. Toss and stir until well coated. Use your cleaned fingers or a large fork like a shovel to pick up a few pineapple chunks, shake off any excess cornstarch,

and put them in the bowl with the egg white. Stir gently, then pick them up and let any excess egg white slip back into the rest. Put them in the bag with the crumb mixture. Repeat the cornstarch-then-egg process until all the pineapple chunks are in the bag. Seal the bag and shake gently, turning the bag this way and that, to coat the pieces well.

4. Set the coated pineapple chunks in the basket with as much air space between them as possible. Even a fraction of an inch will work, but they should not touch. Air-fry undisturbed for 10 minutes, or until golden brown and crisp.

5. Gently dump the contents of the basket onto a wire rack. Cool for at least 5 minutes or up to 15 minutes before serving.

Honey-roasted Pears With Ricotta

Servings: 4
Cooking Time: 18 To 23 Minutes
Ingredients:
- 2 large Bosc pears, halved and seeded (see Tip)
- 3 tablespoons honey
- 1 tablespoon unsalted butter
- ½ teaspoon ground cinnamon
- ¼ cup walnuts, chopped
- ¼ cup part skim low-fat ricotta cheese, divided

Directions:
1. In a 6-by-2-inch pan, place the pears cut-side up.
2. In a small microwave-safe bowl, melt the honey, butter, and cinnamon. Brush this mixture over the cut sides of the pears.
3. Pour 3 tablespoons of water around the pears in the pan. Roast the pears for 18 to 23 minutes, or until tender when pierced with a fork and slightly crisp on the edges, basting once with the liquid in the pan.
4. Carefully remove the pears from the pan and place on a serving plate. Drizzle each with some liquid from the pan, sprinkle the walnuts on top, and serve with a spoonful of ricotta cheese.

Moist Cinnamon Muffins

Servings: 20
Cooking Time: 12 Minutes
Ingredients:
- 1 tablespoon cinnamon
- 1 teaspoon baking powder
- 2 scoops vanilla protein: powder
- ½ cup almond flour
- ½ cup coconut oil
- ½ cup pumpkin puree
- ½ cup almond butter

Directions:
1. Before cooking, heat your air fryer to 325 degrees F/ 160 degrees C.
2. Combine together cinnamon, baking powder, vanilla protein: powder, and almond flour in a large bowl.
3. Then mix the dry mixture together with the coconut oil, pumpkin puree, and almond butter until well incorporated.
4. Divide the batter into the silicone muffin molds.
5. Cook in batches in your air fryer for 12 minutes.
6. Serve and enjoy!

Pineapple And Chocolate Cake

Servings: 4
Cooking Time: 35 To 40 Minutes
Ingredients:
- 2 cups flour
- 4 ounces (113 g) butter, melted
- ¼ cup sugar
- ½ pound (227 g) pineapple, chopped
- ½ cup pineapple juice
- 1 ounce (28 g) dark chocolate, grated
- 1 large egg
- 2 tablespoons skimmed milk

Directions:
1. Preheat the air fryer to 370ºF (188ºC).
2. Grease a cake tin with a little oil or butter.
3. In a bowl, combine the butter and flour to create a crumbly consistency.
4. Add the sugar, chopped pineapple, juice, and grated dark chocolate and mix well.
5. In a separate bowl, combine the egg and milk. Add this mixture to the flour mixture and stir well until a soft dough forms.
6. Pour the mixture into the cake tin and transfer to the air fryer.
7. Bake for 35 to 40 minutes.
8. Serve immediately.

Oatmeal Raisin Bars

Servings: 8
Cooking Time: 15 Minutes
Ingredients:
- ⅓ cup all-purpose flour
- ¼ teaspoon kosher salt
- ¼ teaspoon baking powder
- ¼ teaspoon ground cinnamon
- ¼ cup light brown sugar, lightly packed
- ¼ cup granulated sugar
- ½ cup canola oil
- 1 large egg
- 1 teaspoon vanilla extract
- 1⅓ cups quick-cooking oats
- ⅓ cup raisins

Directions:
1. Preheat the air fryer to 360ºF (182ºC).
2. In a large bowl, combine the all-purpose flour, kosher salt, baking powder, ground cinnamon, light brown sugar, granulated sugar, canola oil, egg, vanilla extract, quick-cooking oats, and raisins.
3. Spray a baking pan with nonstick cooking spray, then pour the oat mixture into the pan and press down to evenly distribute. Place the pan in the air fryer and bake for 15 minutes or until golden brown.
4. Remove from the air fryer and allow to cool in the pan on a wire rack for 20 minutes before slicing and serving.

Ricotta Lemon Cake

Servings: 8
Cooking Time: 40 Minutes
Ingredients:
- 1 lb ricotta
- 4 eggs
- 1 lemon juice
- 1 lemon zest
- ¼ cup erythritol

Directions:
1. Preheat the air fryer to 325°F.
2. Spray air fryer baking dish with cooking spray.
3. In a bowl, beat ricotta cheese until smooth.
4. Whisk in the eggs one by one.
5. Whisk in lemon juice and zest.
6. Pour batter into the prepared baking dish and place into the air fryer.
7. Cook for 40 minutes.
8. Allow to cool completely then slice and serve.

Lemon Cookies

Servings: 24
Cooking Time: 5 Minutes
Ingredients:
- ½ teaspoon of salt
- ½ cup of coconut flour
- ½ cup of unsalted butter softened
- ½ teaspoon of liquid vanilla stevia
- ½ cup of swerve granular sweetener
- 1 tablespoon lemon juice
- ¼ teaspoon lemon extract, it is optional
- 2 egg yolks
- For icing
- 3 teaspoons of lemon juice
- ⅔ cup of Swerve confectioner's sweetener

Directions:
1. In a stand mixer bowl, add baking soda, coconut flour, salt and Swerve, mix until well combined.
2. Then add the butter softened to the dry ingredients, mix well.
3. Add all the remaining ingredients but do not add in the yolks yet.
4. Adjust the seasoning of lemon flavor and sweetness to your liking, add more if needed.
5. Add the yolk and combine well.
6. Spread a big piece of plastic wrap on a flat surface, put the batter in the center, roll around the dough and make it into a log form.
7. At 325 degrees F/ 160 degrees C, preheat your air fryer.
8. Cut in ¼ inch cookies, place as many cookies in the air fryer basket in 1 single, do not overcrowd the basket.
9. Air fry for 3-5 minutes, or until the cookies' edges become brown.
10. Once all cookies are air fried, pour the icing over.
11. Serve.

Lemon Creamy Muffins

Servings: 6
Cooking Time: 11 Minutes
Ingredients:
- 1 cup almond flour
- 3 tablespoons Erythritol
- 1 scoop protein: powder
- 1 teaspoon vanilla extract
- 3 tablespoons coconut oil, melted
- 1 egg, beaten
- ½ teaspoon baking powder
- ½ teaspoon instant coffee
- 1 teaspoon lemon juice
- 2 tablespoons heavy cream
- Cooking spray

Directions:
1. After adding the almond flour, Erythritol, protein: powder, vanilla extract, coconut oil, egg, baking powder, instant coffee, lemon juice, and heavy cream in a suitable bowl, use the immersion blender to whisk them until smooth.
2. Spray the muffin molds with cooking spray.
3. Fill half of each muffin mold with muffin batter and arrange them to the cooking basket of your air fryer.
4. Cook them at 360 degrees F/ 180 degrees C for 11 minutes.
5. When done, serve and enjoy.

Chocolate Donuts

Servings:8
Cooking Time: 20 Minutes
Ingredients:
- 1 (8-ounce) can jumbo biscuits
- Cooking oil
- Chocolate sauce, such as Hershey's

Directions:
1. Separate the biscuit dough into 8 biscuits and place them on a flat work surface. Use a small circle cookie cutter or a biscuit cutter to cut a hole in the center of each biscuit. You can also cut the holes using a knife.
2. Spray the air fryer basket with cooking oil.
3. Place 4 donuts in the air fryer. Do not stack. Spray with cooking oil. Cook for 4 minutes.
4. Open the air fryer and flip the donuts. Cook for an additional 4 minutes.
5. Remove the cooked donuts from the air fryer, then repeat steps 3 and 4 for the remaining 4 donuts.
6. Drizzle chocolate sauce over the donuts and enjoy while warm. (For homemade chocolate sauce, see Ingredient tip in Fried Bananas with Chocolate Sauce, here.)

Nutty Fudge Muffins

Servings:10
Cooking Time:10 Minutes
Ingredients:
- 1 package fudge brownie mix
- 1 egg
- 2 teaspoons water
- ¼ cup walnuts, chopped
- 1/3 cup vegetable oil

Directions:
1. Preheat the Air fryer to 300°F and grease 10 muffin tins lightly.
2. Mix brownie mix, egg, oil and water in a bowl.
3. Fold in the walnuts and pour the mixture in the muffin cups.
4. Transfer the muffin tins in the Air fryer basket and cook for about 10 minutes.
5. Dish out and serve immediately.

Simple Donuts

Servings: 4
Cooking Time: 15 Minutes
Ingredients:
- 8 ounces' coconut flour 2 tablespoons stevia
- 1 egg, whisked
- 1-½ tablespoons butter, melted
- 4 ounces' coconut milk
- 1 teaspoon baking powder

Directions:
1. Thoroughly mix up all of the ingredients in a bowl.
2. Form donuts from the mixture.
3. Cook the donuts in your air fryer at 370 degrees F/ 185 degrees C for 15 minutes.
4. When cooked, serve and enjoy.

Simple Almond Muffins With Blueberries

Servings: 2
Cooking Time: 14 Minutes
Ingredients:
- 1 egg
- 1 teaspoon baking powder
- 3 tablespoons butter, melted
- ¾ cup blueberries
- ⅔ cup almond flour
- 2 tablespoons erythritol
- ⅓ cup unsweetened almond milk

Directions:
1. Using cooking spray, spray the silicone muffin molds.
2. In a bowl, combine egg, baking powder, melted butter, blueberries, and almond flour.
3. Add the combined mixture into the muffin molds. Transfer the molds onto the air fryer basket.
4. Cook the muffins in your air fryer at 320 degrees F/ 160 degrees C for 14 minutes.
5. When cooked, remove the muffins onto a wire rack to cool.
6. Now it's time to treat yourself!

Ricotta Lemon Poppy Seed Cake

Servings: 4
Cooking Time: 55 Minutes
Ingredients:
- Unsalted butter, at room temperature
- 1 cup almond flour
- ½ cup sugar
- 3 large eggs
- ¼ cup heavy cream
- ¼ cup full-fat ricotta cheese
- ¼ cup coconut oil, melted
- 2 tablespoons poppy seeds
- 1 teaspoon baking powder
- 1 teaspoon pure lemon extract
- Grated zest and juice of 1 lemon, plus more zest for garnish

Directions:
1. Preheat the air fryer to 325ºF (163ºC).
2. Generously butter a round baking pan. Line the bottom of the pan with parchment paper cut to fit.
3. In a large bowl, combine the almond flour, sugar, eggs, cream, ricotta, coconut oil, poppy seeds, baking powder, lemon extract, lemon zest, and lemon juice. Beat with a hand mixer on medium speed until well blended and fluffy.
4. Pour the batter into the prepared pan. Cover the pan tightly with aluminum foil. Set the pan in the air fryer basket and bake for 45 minutes. Remove the foil and bake for 10 to 15 minutes more until a knife (do not use a toothpick) inserted into the center of the cake comes out clean.
5. Let the cake cool in the pan on a wire rack for 10 minutes. Remove the cake from pan and let it cool on the rack for 15 minutes before slicing.
6. Top with additional lemon zest, slice and serve.

Plum Apple Crumble With Cranberries

Servings: 6-7
Cooking Time: 25 Minutes
Ingredients:
- 2 ½ ounces caster sugar
- ⅓ cup oats
- ⅔ cup flour
- ½ stick butter, chilled
- 1 tablespoon cold water
- 1 tablespoon honey
- ½ teaspoon ground mace
- ¼ pound plums, pitted and chopped
- ¼ pound apples, cored and chopped
- 1 tablespoon lemon juice
- ½ teaspoon vanilla paste
- 1 cup cranberries

Directions:
1. On a flat kitchen surface, plug your air fryer and turn it on.
2. Gently coat your cake pan with cooking oil or spray.
3. Before cooking, heat your air fryer to 390 degrees F/ 200 degrees C for about 4 to 5 minutes.
4. Mix the lemon juice, sugar, honey, mace, apples, and plums in a medium sized bowl.
5. Place the fruits onto the cake pan.
6. In a second medium sized bowl, mix thoroughly the rest of the ingredients and add the fruit mixture on the top. Transfer to the cake pan.
7. Bake the apple crumble in the preheated air fryer for 20 minutes.
8. When cooked, remove from the air fryer and serve warm.

Berry Streusel Cake

Servings: 6
Cooking Time: 60 Minutes
Ingredients:
- 2 tbsp demerara sugar
- 2 tbsp sunflower oil
- ¼ cup almond flour
- 1 cup pastry flour
- ½ cup brown sugar
- 1 tsp baking powder
- 1 tbsp lemon zest
- ¼ tsp salt
- ¾ cup milk
- 2 tbsp olive oil
- 1 tsp vanilla
- 1 cup blueberries
- ½ cup powdered sugar
- 1 tbsp lemon juice
- ⅛ tsp salt

Directions:
1. Mix the demerara sugar, sunflower oil, and almond flour in a bowl and put it in the refrigerator. Whisk the pastry flour, brown sugar, baking powder, lemon zest, and salt in another bowl. Add the milk, olive oil, and vanilla and stir with a rubber spatula until combined. Add the blueberries and stir slowly. Coat the inside of a baking pan with oil and pour the batter into the pan.
2. Preheat air fryer to 310°F. Remove the almond mix from the fridge and spread it over the cake batter. Put the cake in the air fryer and Bake for 45 minutes or until a knife inserted in the center comes out clean and the top is golden. Combine the powdered sugar, lemon juice and salt in a bowl. Once the cake has cooled, slice it into 4 pieces and drizzle each with icing. Serve.

Baked Apple

Servings: 6
Cooking Time: 20 Minutes
Ingredients:
- 3 small Honey Crisp or other baking apples
- 3 tablespoons maple syrup
- 3 tablespoons chopped pecans
- 1 tablespoon firm butter, cut into 6 pieces

Directions:
1. Put ½ cup water in the drawer of the air fryer.
2. Wash apples well and dry them.
3. Split apples in half. Remove core and a little of the flesh to make a cavity for the pecans.
4. Place apple halves in air fryer basket, cut side up.
5. Spoon 1½ teaspoons pecans into each cavity.
6. Spoon ½ tablespoon maple syrup over pecans in each apple.
7. Top each apple with ½ teaspoon butter.
8. Cook at 360°F for 20 minutes, until apples are tender.

Yummy Berry Cheesecake

Servings: 8
Cooking Time: 50 Minutes
Ingredients:
- ½ cup raspberries
- 2 blocks of softened cream cheese, 8 ounces
- 1 teaspoon raspberry or vanilla extract:
- ¼ cup of strawberries
- 2 eggs
- ¼ cup of blackberries
- 1 cup and 2 tablespoons of sugar

Directions:
1. In a big mixing bowl, whip the sugar-alternative confectioner sweetener and cream cheese, mix whip until smooth and creamy.
2. Then add in the raspberry or vanilla extract and eggs, again mix well.
3. In a food processor, pulse the berries and fold into the cream cheese mix with 2 extra tablespoons of sweetener.
4. Take a springform pan and spray the oil generously, pour in the mixture.
5. Put the pan in the air fryer, let it air fryer, and cook for 10 minutes at 300 degrees F/ 150 degrees C.
6. Lower the air fryer's temperature to 400 degrees F/ 205 degrees C and cook for 40 minutes.
7. Take out from the air fryer and cool a bit before chilling in the fridge.
8. Keep in the fridge for 2-4 hours or as long as you have time.
9. Slice and serve.

Cheese Muffins With Cinnamon

Servings: 10
Cooking Time: 16 Minutes
Ingredients:
- 2 eggs
- ½ cup erythritol
- 8 ounces cream cheese
- 1 teaspoon ground cinnamon
- ½ tsp vanilla

Directions:
1. Before cooking, heat your air fryer to 325 degrees F/ 160 degrees C.
2. Mix together vanilla, erythritol, eggs, and cream cheese until smooth.
3. Divide the batter into the silicone muffin molds. Top the muffins with cinnamon.
4. In the air fryer basket, transfer the muffin molds.
5. Cook in your air fryer for 16 minutes.
6. Serve and enjoy!

Grilled Spiced Fruit

Servings: 4
Cooking Time: 3 To 5 Minutes
Ingredients:
- 2 peaches, peeled, pitted, and thickly sliced
- 3 plums, halved and pitted
- 3 nectarines, halved and pitted
- 1 tablespoon honey
- ½ teaspoon ground cinnamon
- ¼ teaspoon ground allspice
- Pinch cayenne pepper

Directions:

1. Thread the fruit, alternating the types, onto 8 bamboo (see Tip, here) or metal skewers that fit into the air fryer.
2. In a small bowl, stir together the honey, cinnamon, allspice, and cayenne. Brush the glaze onto the fruit.
3. Grill the skewers for 3 to 5 minutes, or until lightly browned and caramelized. Cool for 5 minutes and serve.

Banana Bread Cake

Servings: 6
Cooking Time: 18-22 Minutes
Ingredients:
- ¾ cup plus 2 tablespoons All-purpose flour
- ½ teaspoon Baking powder
- ¼ teaspoon Baking soda
- ¼ teaspoon Table salt
- 4 tablespoons (¼ cup/½ stick) Butter, at room temperature
- ½ cup Granulated white sugar
- 2 Small ripe bananas, peeled
- 5 tablespoons Pasteurized egg substitute, such as Egg Beaters
- ¼ cup Buttermilk
- ¾ teaspoon Vanilla extract
- Baking spray (see here)

Directions:
1. Preheat the air fryer to 325°F (or 330°F, if that's the closest setting).
2. Mix the flour, baking powder, baking soda, and salt in a small bowl until well combined.
3. Using an electric hand mixer at medium speed, beat the butter and sugar in a medium bowl until creamy and smooth, about 3 minutes, occasionally scraping down the inside of the bowl.
4. Beat in the bananas until smooth. Then beat in egg substitute or egg, buttermilk, and vanilla until uniform. (The batter may look curdled at this stage. The flour mixture will smooth it out.) Add the flour mixture and beat at low speed until smooth and creamy.
5. Use the baking spray to generously coat the inside of a 6-inch round cake pan for a small batch, a 7-inch round cake pan for a medium batch, or an 8-inch round cake pan for a large batch. Scrape and spread the batter into the pan, smoothing the batter out to an even layer.
6. Set the pan in the basket and air-fry for 18 minutes for a 6-inch layer, 20 minutes for a 7-inch layer, or 22 minutes for an 8-inch layer, or until the cake is well browned and set even if there's a little soft give right at the center. Start checking it at the 16-minute mark to know where you are.
7. Use hot pads or silicone baking mitts to transfer the cake pan to a wire rack. To unmold, set a cutting board over the baking pan and invert both the board and the pan. Lift the still-warm pan off the cake layer. Set the wire rack on top of that layer and invert all of it with the cutting board so that the cake layer is now right side up on the wire rack. Remove the cutting board and continue cooling the cake for at least 10 minutes or to room temperature, about 40 minutes, before slicing into wedges.

Apple Crisp

Servings: 4
Cooking Time: 16 Minutes
Ingredients:
- Filling
- 3 Granny Smith apples, thinly sliced (about 4 cups)
- ¼ teaspoon ground cinnamon
- ⅛ teaspoon salt
- 1½ teaspoons lemon juice
- 2 tablespoons honey
- 1 tablespoon brown sugar
- cooking spray
- Crumb Topping
- 2 tablespoons oats
- 2 tablespoons oat bran
- 2 tablespoons cooked quinoa
- 2 tablespoons chopped walnuts
- 2 tablespoons brown sugar
- 2 teaspoons coconut oil

Directions:
1. Combine all filling ingredients and stir well so that apples are evenly coated.
2. Spray air fryer baking pan with nonstick cooking spray and spoon in the apple mixture.
3. Cook at 360°F for 5minutes. Stir well, scooping up from the bottom to mix apples and sauce.
4. At this point, the apples should be crisp-tender. Continue cooking in 3-minute intervals until apples are as soft as you like.
5. While apples are cooking, combine all topping ingredients in a small bowl. Stir until coconut oil mixes in well and distributes evenly. If your coconut oil is cold, it may be easier to mix in by hand.
6. When apples are cooked to your liking, sprinkle crumb mixture on top. Cook at 360°F for 8 minutes or until crumb topping is golden brown and crispy.

Coffee Cookies

Servings: 12
Cooking Time: 15 Minutes
Ingredients:
- 1 cup almond flour
- 2 eggs, lightly beaten
- 2 teaspoons baking powder
- ½ tablespoon cinnamon
- ¼ cup erythritol
- ¼ cup brewed espresso
- ½ cup ghee, melted

Directions:
1. In a bowl, combine almond flour, the beaten eggs, baking powder, cinnamon, erythritol, brewed espresso, and the melted ghee together.
2. Then shape the mixture into small cookies. Transfer to an oven-safe cookie sheet.
3. Place the sheet onto the air fryer basket.
4. Then cook in your air fryer at 350 degrees F/ 175 degrees C for 15 minutes.
5. When cooked, remove from the air fryer and serve.

Honey Donuts

Servings: 8
Cooking Time: 8 Minutes

Ingredients:
- 1 cup coconut flour
- 4 eggs
- 4 tablespoons coconut oil, melted
- 1 teaspoon baking soda
- ⅔ cup apple cider vinegar:
- 1 teaspoon cinnamon
- 3 tablespoons honey
- a pinch of salt

Directions:
1. Let the air fryer pre-heat to 350 degrees F/ 175 degrees C.
2. Spray oil on a baking tray, spray a generous amount of grease with melted coconut oil.
3. In a suitable bowl, add apple cider vinegar, honey, melted coconut oil, salt mix well, then crack the 4 eggs, and mix it all together.
4. In another bowl, sift the coconut flour, baking soda, and cinnamon so that the dry ingredients will combine well.
5. Add the wet ingredients in a bowl and mix with the dry ingredients until completely combined.
6. Pour the prepared batter into the prepared donut baking pan. And add the batter into cavities.
7. Let it air fry for 10 minutes or 8 minutes at 350 degrees F/ 175 degrees C, or until light golden brown.
8. Serve right away and enjoy.

Recipes Index

A

Air Fried Chicken Tenderloin 78
Air Fried Pork With Fennel 13
Air Fryer Naked Chicken Tenders 73
Ajillo Mushrooms 83
Almond Flour Battered Wings 39
Amazing Blooming Onion 12
Apple Chips With Cinnamon 97
Apple Crisp 102
Apple Turnovers 92
Apple-blueberry Hand Pies 95
Arancini With Marinara 37
Asparagus & Salmon Spring Rolls 60
Asparagus With Garlic 86
Awesome Chicken Taquitos 89

B

Baby Back Ribs 47
Bacon And Broccoli Bread Pudding 27
Bacon Eggs 27
Bacon With Shallot And Greens 45
Bacon-wrapped Scallops 65
Baked Apple 101
Baked Cauliflower With Paprika 22
Baked Eggs With Bacon-tomato Sauce 32
Baked Potato Breakfast Boats 32
Baltimore Crab Cakes 60
Banana And Rice Pudding 92
Banana Bread Cake 102
Banana Slices With Cardamom 91
Barbecued Chicken Thighs 75
Basic Chicken Breasts. 68
Basil Mushroom & Shrimp Spaghetti 65
Basil Turkey With Chili Mayo 71
Beef & Sauerkraut Spring Rolls 52
Beef And Broccoli Stir Fry 46
Beef Steak Sliders 17
Beefy Quesadillas 46
Bell Peppers Cups 39
Berry Streusel Cake 101
Black Bean Corn Dip 20
Blistered Tomatoes 84
Blueberry Scones 28
Breadcrumb Crusted Agnolotti 83
Breakfast Potatoes 32
Breakfast Scramble Casserole 24
Broccoli Au Gratin 88
Broccoli Tots 86
Brownies With White Chocolate 91
Brownies 94
Buffalo Bites 13
Burger Bun For One 83
Buttered Chicken Thighs 77
Buttery Pork Chops 49
Buttery Scallops 30

C

Cajun Salmon 64
Canadian Bacon & Cheese Sandwich 30
Caprese-style Sandwiches 36
Caramel Apple Crumble 95
Carne Asada Tacos 53
Catfish Fillets With Tortilla Chips 62
Cauliflower Steaks Gratin 36
Cayenne Chicken Wing Dip 87
Celery Chicken 69
Cheddar Stuffed Portobellos With Salsa 42
Cheddar Tomatillos With Lettuce 80
Cheddar-ham-corn Muffins 32
Cheese Beef Roll 44
Cheese Muffins With Cinnamon 101
Cheese Turkey Meatloaf 76
Cheese-stuffed Steak Burgers 47
Cheesy Brussel Sprouts 40
Cheesy Chicken Tenders 73
Cheesy Egg Bites 26
Cheesy Loaded Broccoli 86
Cheesy Zucchini Tots 81
Cherry Chipotle Bbq Chicken Wings 18
Chicken Bites With Coconut 19
Chicken Burgers With Blue Cheese Sauce 68
Chicken Pigs In Blankets 70
Chicken Scotch Eggs 26
Chicken Skewers 72
Chicken Tenders With Basil-strawberry Glaze 74
Chicken With 20 Cloves Of Garlic 68
Chili Tofu & Quinoa Bowls 36
Chili-lime Pork Loin 44
Chipotle Pork Meatballs 49
Chocolate Donuts 99
Chocolate Macaroons 97
Chocolate-hazelnut Bear Claws 23
Cinnamon Pear Oat Muffins 24
Cinnamon Tortilla Crisps 95
Classic Cinnamon Rolls 29
Classic Crab Cakes 57
Coconut & Peanut Rice Cereal 29
Cod Nuggets 60
Coffee Cookies 102
Corn Muffins 81
Corn On The Cob 38
Cornflake Chicken Nuggets 70
Cottage And Mayonnaise Stuffed Peppers 38
Crabby Fries 17
Cranberry Turkey Quesadillas 73
Creamy Baked Sausage 33
Creamy Cauliflower Puree 85
Creole Seasoned Okra 89
Crispy Avocados With Pico De Gallo 38

Crispy Deviled Eggs 12
Crispy Italian Chicken Thighs 68
Crispy Parmesan Chicken Breasts 77
Crispy Parmesan Lobster Tails 56
Crusty Catfish With Parmesan Cheese 64
Curly's Cauliflower 14
Curried Fruit 82
Curried Pickle Chips 15
Curried Veggie Samosas 12

D

Dauphinoise (potatoes Au Gratin) 82
Delicious Cheeseburgers 54
Deviled Eggs With Ricotta 16
Dill Chicken Strips 76
Dried Fruit Beignets 27

E

Easy Baked Root Veggies 35
Easy Glazed Carrots 40
Easy Marinated Salmon Fillets 61
Effortless Toffee Zucchini Bread 24
Egg Muffins 29
Egg Roll Pizza Sticks 14
Egg Soufflé With Mushroom And Broccoli 26
Egg White Cups 23
English Scones 29
Enticing Chocolate Cake 96
Enticing Jalapeno Poppers 11

F

Fajita Chicken Strips 69
Fennel Tofu Bites 37
Feta & Shrimp Pita 57
Feta Stuffed Peppers With Broccoli 27
Fish Piccata With Crispy Potatoes 57
Fish Sticks With Tartar Sauce 59
Fish Sticks 66
Fried Bacon Slices 15
Fried Brie With Cherry Tomatoes 19
Fried Cauliflowerwith Parmesan Lemon Dressing 84
Fried Dill Pickle Chips 20
Fried Olives 18
Fried Oreos 92
Fried Pineapple Chunks 97
Fried Potatoes With Bell Peppers 41
Fried Rice With Curried Tofu 42
Fruity Blueberry Muffin Cups 29

G

Garden Fresh Green Beans 40
Garlic Beef With Egg And Bell Pepper 50
Garlic Fillets 50
Garlic Kale Mash 81
Garlic Parmesan Drumsticks 71
Garlic Parmesan Kale Chips 16
Garlic Turkey With Tomato Mix 74
Garlicky Brussel Sprouts With Saffron Aioli 39
Garlicky Brussels Sprouts 80
Garlicky Mushrooms With Parsley 89

Garlic-lemon Scallops 66
Garlic-lemon Steamer Clams 64
German Streusel-stuffed Baked Apples 95
Ginger Salmon Fillet 58
Glazed Chicken Wings 17
Glazed Salmon With Soy Sauce 66
Glazed Tender Pork Chops 44
Goat Cheese Stuffed Turkey Roulade 78
Goat Cheese, Beet, And Kale Frittata 26
Graham Cracker Cheesecake 96
Granola Three Ways 16
Greek Lamb Rack 54
Green Beans Bowls 22
Grilled Cajun Chicken 70
Grilled Spiced Fruit 101
Grits Again 82
Grouper With Miso-honey Sauce 60
Gruyère Asparagus & Chicken Quiche 73

H

Healthy Chicken With Veggies 74
Hearty Greens Chips With Curried Yogurt Sauce 15
Hearty Lemon Salmon 59
Herb Seasoned Turkey Breast 76
Herb-buttermilk Chicken Breast 72
Herbed Omelet 28
Hoisin Turkey Burgers 72
Homemade Ham Cheese Sandwiches 51
Homemade Toad In The Hole 51
Honey Donuts 103
Honey Rosemary Chicken 76
Honey-glazed Salmon 59
Honey-roasted Pears With Ricotta 98

I

Indian Cauliflower Tikka Bites 11
Indian Chicken Tandoori 74
Italian Lamb Chops With Avocado Mayo 49
Italian-style Cheeseburgers With Cheese Slices 54
Italian-style Honey Pork 47

J

Jalapeño Cheese Balls 19
Jerk Chicken Wings 76
Juicy Spiced Rib-eye Steaks 45

L

Lamb Burgers 50
Lemon Cookies 99
Lemon Creamy Muffins 99
Lemon Nut Bars 92
Lemon Shrimp And Zucchinis 61
Lemon-basil On Cod Filet 59
Lemon-roasted Salmon Fillets 58
Lemony Cabbage Slaw 81
Lemony Green Beans 40
Lime Muffins 30
Lollipop Lamb Chops 44
Lorraine Egg Cups 25

M

Mahi-mahi "burrito" Fillets	58
Marinated Beef And Vegetable Stir Fry	51
Mashed Potato Tots	80
Mashed Sweet Potato Tots	88
Meatloaf	51
Mediterranean Granola	25
Moist Cinnamon Muffins	98
Mozzarella Arancini	11
Mozzarella-stuffed Meatloaf	49
Mushroom & Cavolo Nero Egg Muffins	30
Mushroom Bolognese Casserole	38
Mushroom Mozzarella Risotto	81
Mustard Greens Chips With Curried Sauce	17

N

Nutty Chicken Tenders	69
Nutty Fudge Muffins	99
Nutty Shrimp With Amaretto Glaze	65
Nutty Whole Wheat Muffins	31

O

Oat And Chia Porridge	23
Oatmeal Raisin Bars	98
One-bowl Chocolate Buttermilk Cake	91
Open-faced Sandwich	82
Orange Marmalade	94
Orange-glazed Cinnamon Rolls	23
Oreo-coated Peanut Butter Cups	97

P

Pancetta-wrapped Scallops With Pancetta Slices	61
Panko-breaded Pork Chops	48
Paprika Pork Chops	47
Parmesan Cabbage Chips	13
Parmesan Chicken Tenderloins	72
Parmesan Fish Bites	62
Parmesan Tilapia With Parsley	56
Parmesan Zucchini Gratin	85
Party Buffalo Chicken Drumettes	70
Peanut Butter Cup Doughnut Holes	93
Pecan-crusted Tilapia	63
Pecan-crusted Turkey Cutlets	71
Perfect Broccolini	87
Pesto Coated Rack Of Lamb	51
Pineapple And Chocolate Cake	98
Pinto Taquitos	36
Piri-piri Chicken Thighs	68
Pita Chips	14
Plum Apple Crumble With Cranberries	100
Pork Burgers With Cheddar Cheese	52
Pork Kabobs With Pineapple	53
Pork Tenderloins	44
Portobello Pizzas	88
Potato And Broccoli With Tofu Scramble	82
Potato Skins	15
Potatoes With Zucchinis	88
Powerful Jackfruit Fritters	36
Pretzels	25
Provençal Grilled Rib-eye	45
Pumpkin Empanadas	22

Q

Quick & Easy Meatballs	48

R

Radishes And Green Onions Mix	83
Restaurant-style Flounder Cutlets	62
Rib Eye Cheesesteaks With Fried Onions	54
Rib Eye Steak Seasoned With Italian Herb	47
Rice And Meatball Stuffed Bell Peppers	46
Rich Chocolate Cookie	95
Ricotta Lemon Cake	99
Ricotta Lemon Poppy Seed Cake	100
Ricotta Veggie Potpie	35
Ritzy Skirt Steak Fajitas	50
Roasted Brown Butter Carrots	87
Roasted Cauliflower	35
Roasted Chicken And Vegetable Salad	71
Roasted Garlic Ribeye With Mayo	48
Roasted Grape Dip	14
Roasted Lemony Broccoli	86
Roasted Peppers	11
Roasted Red Pepper Dip	11
Roasted Tomato And Cheddar Rolls	31
Roasted Vegetable Lasagna	41
Roasted Vegetable Pita Pizza	38
Rosemary New Potatoes	85

S

Sage & Paprika Turkey Cutlets	75
Sage Pork With Potatoes	45
Salmon Croquettes	66
Salmon	63
Salsa And Cheese Stuffed Mushrooms	13
Salty German-style Shrimp Pancakes	61
Scallops And Spring Veggies	62
Scrambled Eggs With Mushrooms	25
Seedy Bagels	24
Sesame Taj Tofu	81
Sesame-glazed Salmon	56
Shakshuka-style Pepper Cups	22
Shrimp "scampi"	58
Shrimp Sliders With Avocado	64
Shrimp Teriyaki	57
Simple Almond Muffins With Blueberries	100
Simple Baked Potatoes With Dill Yogurt	87
Simple Donuts	100
Simple Scotch Eggs	26
Simple Tomato Cheese Sandwich	23
Smoked Paprika Sweet Potato Fries	39
Snow Crab Legs	65
Southwest Gluten-free Turkey Meatloaf	69
Spanish Garlic Shrimp	61
Spice Meatloaf	48
Spiced Okra	85
Spiced Parsnip Chips	13
Spiced Pork Chops	45
Spiced Shrimp With Zucchini	56
Spicy Bean Stuffed Potatoes	89

Spicy Chickpeas	15
Spicy Fries	83
Spicy Kale Chips	20
Spicy Orange Shrimp	56
Spicy Prawns	62
Spicy Salmon And Fennel Salad	64
Spicy Turkey Meatballs	20
Spinach And Cheese Calzone	41
Spinach And Crab Meat Cups	18
Spinach And Feta Pinwheels	35
Spinach Frittata With Mozzarella	30
Sriracha Pork Strips With Rice	49
Strawberry Muffins With Cinnamon	96
Strawberry Streusel Muffins	28
Struffoli	94
Stuffed Pork Chops	45
Sugar-glazed Walnuts	13
Sweet And Sour Brussel Sprouts	35
Sweet And Sour Glazed Cod	63
Sweet And Sour Tofu	84
Sweet Potatoes With Zucchini	84
Sweet-and-salty Pretzels	12

T

Tacos Norteños	52
Taquito Quesadillas	17
Tasty Brussels Sprouts With Guanciale	85
Tasty Cauliflower Croquettes	87
Tasty Hash Browns With Radish	28
Tasty Pork Chops	53
Tender Steak With Salsa Verde	52
Teriyaki Chicken Bites	70
Teriyaki Salmon	62
Tex-mex Stuffed Sweet Potatoes	41
Thai Burgers	48
Thai Turkey And Zucchini Meatballs	75
The Ultimate Chicken Bulgogi	77

Three-berry Dutch Pancake	31
Tofu & Spinach Lasagna	37
Tomatoes Hash With Cheddar Cheese	22
Tuna And Fruit Kebabs	59
Tuna Platter	80
Tuna-stuffed Tomatoes	63
Turkey Burgers	78
Turkey Sausage With Veggies	75
Turkey Scotch Eggs	77
Turmeric Cauliflower With Cilantro	87
Turmeric Tofu Cubes	83

V

Vanilla Bars With Sesame Seeds	92
Vanilla Berry Cobbler	93
Vanilla Cupcakes With Chocolate Chips	91
Vanilla French Toast Sticks	24
Vanilla Muffins With Pecans	93
Vanilla-strawberry Muffins	94
Vegan Buddha Bowls(2)	39
Vegetarian Eggplant "pizzas"	40
Vegetarian Stuffed Bell Peppers	40
Veggie Cheese Bites	19
Veggie Shrimp Toast	20
Vietnamese Beef Lettuce Wraps	53

Y

Yellow Squash And Zucchinis Dish	85
Yogurt-marinated Chicken Legs	74
Yukon Gold Potato Purée	86
Yummy Berry Cheesecake	101
Yummy Shredded Chicken	78
Yummy Stuffed Chicken Breast	75

Z

Za'atar Chicken Thighs	69
Za'atar Garbanzo Beans	15

Printed in Great Britain
by Amazon